Morte Arthure.

EDITED FROM

ROBERT THORNTON'S MS. (AB. 1440 A.D.)

IN THE LIBRARY OF LINCOLN CATHEDRAL,

BY

GEORGE G. PERRY, M.A.,

PREBENDARY OF LINCOLN AND RECTOR OF WADDINGTON, LATE FELLOW AND TUTOR OF LINCO[LN]
COLLEGE, OXFORD.

LONDON:
PUBLISHED FOR THE EARLY ENGLISH TEXT SOCIETY,
BY TRUBNER & CO., 60, PATERNOSTER ROW.

MDCCCLXV.

PREFACE.

It is confessedly almost impossible to fix on the exact point
of time when the Semi-Saxon dialect, which had replaced the
more formal Anglo-Saxon after the Norman Conquest, passed
into the *Early English.* Those characteristic changes which con-
stitute the *modernization* of a language were proceeding gradually.
Inflections were being lost, distinctive marks of gender and case
neglected, variations of meaning coming to be expressed rather
by combinations of words than by changes in the words themselves, and the result was that about the middle of the
thirteenth century England was speaking a language differing
by a wide interval from that of the country three centuries
before. This *Early English* stage of the language may be con-
sidered to extend from about the beginning of the reign of
Henry III. to the end of that of Edward III., when it was succeeded by the *Middle English.*[1] During the whole of this period
continual modification of the English tongue was going on. The
language of the proclamation to the people of Huntingdonshire
differs greatly from the language of Chaucer, and even from

---

[1] See Dr. Latham on "The English Language," chap. iii.; and "Hallam's Intro
duction to Literature of Europe," chap. i.

that of Piers Plowman and of the poem which is here put
forth. It is probable that the Morte Arthure is somewhat
later in date than Piers Plowman, but that it still falls
within the period marked out for the limits of *Early English.*
In comparing together the writings of this date we are at
once struck by a distinction which seems to separate them
into two classes. In Chaucer we see the tendency towards
foreign words and idioms, and the adoption of the rhyming
metre invented during the decay of the Latin tongue; in Piers
Plowman and the Morte Arthure we trace the prevalence of the
Saxon words and rhythm, the alliterative[1] or accented metre
being preferred to the final cadence.

In the judgment of Warton the latter style was an evident
and palpable barbarism. This critic severely censures the
author of Piers Plowman, and, but that he was unacquainted
with the Morte Arthure, would doubtless have included its
author also in his condemnation—"Instead of availing himself
of the rising and rapid improvements of the English language
Longland prefers and adopts the style of the Anglo-Saxon poets.
Nor did he make these writers the models of his language only:
he likewise imitates their alliterative versification, which con-
sisted in using an aggregate of words beginning with the same
letter. But this imposed constraint of seeking identical initials
and the affectation of obsolete English, by demanding a constant
and necessary departure from the natural and obvious forms of
expression, contributed also to render his manner extremely per-
plexed, and to disgust the readers with obscurities."[2] It is
hoped that the readers of the following poem will not be so

[1] "Alliteration is the general character of all the early Gothic metres."—*Latham.*
[2] Warton's History of English Poetry, i. 266.

readily disgusted ; those very obscurities which were so dis-
tasteful to the polite critic constituting some of the chief re-
commendation of the composition. It is hoped also that the
poem will be welcomed not only on philological and gramma-
tical grounds, but on the ground also of its own intrinsic merit
—for the fire, vigour, and liveliness of its style, and the vast
profusion of descriptive epithets which it pours out before the
reader.

This version of the Morte Arthure is printed from a manuscript in the Library of Lincoln Cathedral, commonly known
as the " Thornton Romances." It is a thick volume containing
several poems of the Arthur type, as well as many pieces in
prose, both English and Latin. The greater part of this
volume was written by Robert Thornton, a native of Oswaldkirk, in Yorkshire, and Archdeacon of Bedford in the Diocese
of Lincoln, about the middle of the fifteenth century. The
date of Archdeacon Thornton and his connection with Lincoln
Cathedral can be ascertained pretty accurately, as among the
archives of the Cathedral there is preserved an instrument or
deed of considerable importance, attested by him as Archdeacon, which bears date 1439.[1]

So valuable is this collection of ancient pieces which has
been preserved by the labour of the Archdeacon, that doubtless
all lovers of antiquity will be willing to concur in the wish
with which the Morte Arthure concludes, " Thornton dictus
sit benedictus." The poem with which we are now concerned
was first published from the Lincoln manuscript by Mr. Halli-

---

[1] This instrument is known by the name of the " *Laudum* of Alnwick," and to this
day every Prebendary of the Church takes oath on his admission to observe it. It is
a decree (*id quod laudatum est*, approved or determined) of Bishop Alnwick, in refer-
ence to certain matters in dispute between the Dean and the Canons.

well in the year 1847. The form which was then adopted was
that of an expensive quarto, and the value of the book was
sought to be further enhanced by a rigid limitation of the issue
to seventy-five copies. These have all, probably, long ago
found their way into the great libraries of the country, and
the poem has become as inaccessible to the general reader
as though it had .never been printed. Under these circumstances the Committee of the Early English Text Society
have judged it desirable that a re-publication of the poem
should be made. The present edition differs from that of Mr.
Halliwell in the printing of two of his lines in one, in the
marking by italic letters all expansions of the manuscript contractions, and the addition of side-notes and a glossary. In
the first of these points the arrangement of the manuscript is
followed, the lines being always written there as here printed.
A comparison of the two methods will also, it is thought, result
in a decided preference, as regards rhythm, of the method here
used. With respect to the expansions of the contractions, it
will be observed that there is no regularity in the spelling
used, a final *e* being sometimes appended to words, sometimes not. Great care has, in fact, been taken to reproduce
exactly the *irregularity* which is one of the most marked
features of the spelling of this manuscript. In no case has a
final *e* been added unless indicated by a strong and decided
mark; while the threefold variation in the writing of words
beginning with *th* has been carefully followed.[1] The form of

---

[1] *The, This, That, Thus, Thou, Thi, These,* etc., are sometimes written in this
manuscript as at present spelled, sometimes with the Y and the final letter put over
it, sometimes with the Y and the other letters following in a line; *e g.* That, Y^t, Yat,
This, Y^s, Yis. In the second of these cases the letters are printed in italic; in the
third in roman type.

the thorn letter (þ) has been adopted in the printing, instead
of the form used in the manuscript (Y), as it has been thought
more agreeable to the date of the composition, and more in
unison with the other publications of the same period printed
by the E.E.T.S. There can be no doubt that the two forms
represent substantially the same sound. The text having un-
dergone several careful collations with the manuscript, it is
hoped that it is as near perfect as may be. In some few points
it will be found to differ from the very accurate edition of Mr.
Halliwell.

As to the poem itself, it is held by Sir F. Madden that this
is the "Gret gest of Arthure" composed by Huchowne, a Scotch
ballad writer of the fourteenth century. This opinion is com-
bated by Mr. Morris in his Preface to "Alliterative Poems,"
who proves that the poem was not originally written in the
Scotch dialect, but in one of the Northumbrian dialects spoken
South of the Tweed. Mr. Morris is also of opinion that the
text of the poem had been considerably altered by a Midland
transcriber before it fell into the hands of Robert Thornton.
Thornton, as a Northumbrian, would probably have preferred the
original reading, but finding the manuscript with its Southern
modifications, he transcribed it as it stood, without attempt at
restoration. In spite, however, of his having yielded to the
changes of Southern transcribers, it is certain that we owe to
Robert Thornton, of Oswaldkirk, a great debt of gratitude for
having made a copy of the poem which has survived to our day.
It is a grand specimen of Early English poetry, exhibiting
some fine traits common to the early poetry of many nations,
and certain special peculiarities of its own which are well worth
careful study.

In almost all early poetry may be noted a simplicity of language united with what may be termed a recklessness of asser-
tion and a contempt of the conditions required for constituting
the probable. Effect is sought to be produced not by the subtle
analysis of thought and feeling, nor by the description of
scenery and natural objects, but by the crowding together of
startling incidents, and the ascription of marvellous powers and
prowess to the favoured hero. Early poetry is, as it were, the
expression of inexperience, of thoughtlessness and light-hearted-
ness, not bearing the marks of a complicated state of society,
where the restless struggle for social superiority absorbs the
energies and gives a grave cast to the reflections. Now this
gay and light-hearted character seems to be eminently characteristic of the Morte Arthure. The ease with which "fifty
thousand of folke are felled at ones" when they stand in the
way of the victory of the knights; the jovial vein in which
Arthur cleaves asunder the giant Colapas, bidding him come
down and "karpe to his feris," for that "he is too high by
half" to do so comfortably in his giant form; the character of
Sir Gawaine, "the gude man of arms," who is so eminent a
favourite with the poet because he was "the gladdest of othire,"

    "And the hendeste in haule undire hevene riche,"
all testify to this.

And united with this light-hearted vein the least glimpse at
the poem will reveal the noble contempt for the probable which
it exhibits. Illustration of this is unnecessary, as the whole
poem illustrates it. The author might indeed plead that he
was not responsible for the "facts;" that he took them from
good authority, even from the grave historian, Geoffrey of
Monmouth, who has duly chronicled, in choice mediæval Latin,

the adventures of Arthur and his wars with "Sir Lucius."
And, truly, few readers of the poem would desire him to have
been possessed of a greater critical acumen, and to have set to
work to discriminate, select, and weigh probabilities. Better is
it to have the original romance in all its richness and raciness,
than any amended or more respectable version of the deeds of
the "rich king." Arthur is here a "kydd conqueror" through-
out; even in his final conflict inflicting poetical justice on the
villain Modred, and dying happily among his people, with the
nation sorrowing at his tomb. But in this poem, not only is a
grand romance given in highly-spirited diction; there are also
passages which show a keen appreciation of the beauties of
nature, and others which breathe a truly touching pathos. Of
the first character especially are the descriptions of the river
banks and woodland copse through which Arthur and his
knights ride when they go to combat the giant,[1] and of the
spot chosen for the midday halt by the party headed by Sir
Florent.[2]

[1] Thane they roode by that ryver, that rynnyd so swythe,
Thare the ryndez overrechez with realle bowghez;
The roo and the rayne-dere reklesse thare rounene,
In ranez and in rosers to ryotte thame selvene.
All the feulez thare fleschez, that flyez with wengez,
Fore thare galede the gowke one grevez fulle lowde.
Of the nyghtgale notez the noisez was swette,
They threpide with the throstills thre-hundreth at ones!
That whate swowynge of watyr, and syngynge of byrdez,
It myghte salve hyme of sore, that sounde was nevere!
—(ll. 920-932.)

[2] And in the myste mornynge one a mede falles,
In swathes sweppene downe fulle of swete floures
Thare unbrydilles theis bolde, and baytes theire horses,
To the grygynge of the daye, that byrdes gane synge;
Whylles the surs of the sonne, that sonde es of Chryste,
That solaces alle synfulle, that syghte has in erthe.
—(ll. 2506-2512.)

Of the latter, Arthur's beautiful lament over Sir Gawaine,[1] and his touching reflections on his dead knights.[2] The writer of this romance was assuredly not wanting in the feeling of true poetry, while his vigorous diction and his extraordinary power of heaping epithets upon epithets prove great skill and proficiency in the difficult style of versification which he had adopted. As specimens of this vigour and life we can, perhaps, adduce no better instances than the account of the banquet given to the Romans,[3] and of the embarcation of Arthur's army.[4]

[1] Dere kosyne o kynde, in kare am I levede !
For nowe my wirchipe es wente, and my were endide !
Here es the hope of my hele, my happynge of armes !
My concelle, my comforthe, that kepide myne herte !
Of alle knyghtes the kynge that undir Criste lifede.
My wele and my wirchipe of alle this werlde riche
Was wonnene thourghe Sir Gawaine, and thourghe his witte one !
　　　　　　　　　　　　—(ll. 3957–3965.)

[2] Here rystys the riche blude of the rownde table,
Rebukkede with a rebawde, and rewthe es the more !
I may helples one hethe house be myne one,
Alles a wafulle wedowe that wanttes hir beryne !
I may werye and wepe, and wrynge myne handys,
For my wytt and my wyrchipe awaye es for ever !
Of alle lordchips I take leve to mye ende !
Here es the Bretones blode broughte owt of lyfe,
And nowe in this journee alle my joye endys !
　　　　　　　　　　　　—(ll 4283–4292.)

[3] Pacockes and plovers in platers of golde,
Grett swannes fulle swythe in sylveryne chargeours,
Tartes of Turky, taste whane thame lykys ;
Gumbaldes graythely, fulle gracious to taste ;
Bernakes and botures in baterde dysches,
Fesauntes enflureschit in flammande silver,
With darielles endordide, and daynteez ynewe.
　　　　　　　　　　　　—(ll. 182–199.)

[4] Coggez and crayers, than crossez thaire mastez,
Wyghtly one the wale thay wye up thaire ankers.
Holly with-owttyne harme thay hale in bottes,
Schipe-mene scharply schotene thaire portez,

One of the most prominent marks of the style of this poem is the "stereotyped" epithet: "the rich king," "the kydd conqueror," "faire stedes," "galyard knights," "cruel words," Sir Cador "the kene," Sir Bedwere "the rich," Sir Gawaine "the good," are constantly recurring. We recognize one of the marked peculiarities of the great father of epic, who wrote of the "swift-footed Achilles," the "glancing-plumed Hector," the "many-murmuring sea," "horse-feeding Argos," and the "long-haired Greeks." The unartificial nature of early poetry allows the constant recurrence of the same ideas. The epithet is rather part of the subject than a predicate, and the main business of the poem being not so much description as narration, there seems a fitness in the hero being constantly kept before our eyes as the possessor of certain attributes, while the great deeds which justify his "style and title" are recorded.

Another noteworthy peculiarity in the poem is the use of the adjective with the demonstrative pronoun without the substantive, *e.g.* "tha steryne," "this sorrowfulle," "that hathelle," "this kene," "that realle." This, which is akin to the Latin use, marks a stage of the language which has long passed away. Of a like character is the idiom common in this poem of putting the objective case of the pronoun before the verb—"ȝif *me* the life happene," "that *him* over land folowes." Observable also is the constant recurrence of the indefinite expressions "when he likes," "when they like," etc. Not only the stereotyped epithet, but the stereotyped phrase also, occurs regularly in

> Launchez lede apone lufe, laechene ther depez,
> Lukkez to the lade-sterne whene the lyghte faillez,
> For drede of the derke nyghte thay drecchede a lyttille,
> And alle the steryne of the streme strekyne at onez.
>
> —ll. 738–755)

certain connections, and sometimes gives a highly ludicrous turn to the narrative by its inappropriateness to the sense.

The strong ecclesiastical tone which pervades the poem will not fail to be noticed by any reader. Not only are the dying knights duly attended by a confessor, shriven and comforted with the last Sacraments, but there is observable in several passages a most zealous care against interfering with the goods of the "spiritualty." When a grant is made of a city it is only "the temporall" which is granted, and the way in which Arthur is made to say

> " I gyffe my protteccione to alle the pope landez,
> It is a foly to offende oure fadyr undire Gode,
> Owther Peter or Paule tha postles of Rome.
> ȝiff we spare the spirituelle, we spede bot the bettire,"

sufficiently speaks for itself.

The Editor desires to express his thanks to Mr. R. Morris for his valuable help in preparing the Glossary.

On the rhythm of the alliterative metre a paper has been kindly communicated by the Rev. W. W. Skeat, M.A., of Christ's College, Cambridge, who has made English metre his especial study. This is here subjoined.

It is only needful further to state that one sheet of the poem having been inadvertently sent to the press before the final collation with the manuscript was made, a list of *corrigenda* (most of them unimportant) has to be supplied.

WADDINGTON RECTORY,
   September, 1865.

ON THE METRE OF THE POEM.

The metre in which the "Morte Arthure" is written may best be understood by comparing it with "Piers Plowman," the accentuation and *swing* of the verse being much better marked in the last-mentioned poem. The principles which govern this peculiar metre may thus be more readily discerned, and, when once understood, may easily be applied to the present poem.

For a similar reason, it will be the simplest method to consider, first of all, a few lines (of "Piers Plowman") where the metre is most strongly marked, and, afterwards, some where it is, apparently, less regular.

It should first, however, be observed that each complete line in an alliterative poem consists generally of two *sections*, which were separated in old manuscripts by a dot, called the *metrical point* or *pause*, and which may conveniently be denoted by a colon (as in the Prayer Book Version of the Psalms), thus :—

> "Schelde us fro schamesdede · and sinfulle werkes;"

or else by printing the lines thus :—

> "Schelde us fro schamesdede,
> And sinfulle werkes."

In reading aloud a pause may conveniently be made between the sections.

The two sections form, however, but one complete line; and, as the metrical point is more necessary when the poem is to be sung or recited than when it is merely to be read, it has not been thought necessary to insert it in this edition, as the reader, when he has once caught the rhythm of the verse, may always be tolerably sure as to where it must occur.

To begin, then ; consider the line—

> "In séttynge and sówynge
> Swónken ful hárde."
> —*Piers Plowman;* ed. Wright, l. 41.

If we use an asterisk to denote a strongly-accented[1] syllable, the figure 1 to denote a *single* unaccented syllable, the figure 2 to mean *two* unaccented syllables immediately succeeding each other, and so on ; we may represent the above line by the scheme,

$$1 \quad * \quad 2 \quad * \quad 1 \quad : \quad * \quad 2 \quad * \quad 1 ;$$

and this may be taken as a convenient type of alliterative lines, from which the scansion of very many others may be readily deduced. Some, however, as will be shewn presently, must be referred to a type somewhat different.

Now, we here observe (1) that each section contains two strong accents ; (2) that, of the strongly-accented syllables, three begin with a common letter, which has been called the *rime-letter;* and (3) of these three, two occur in the first section, and one in the second. Such is the usual and normal arrangement. The *rime-letters* may be either consonants or vowels, and may consist of *single* letters, or of such combinations as *sc, bl, tr,* etc. If vowels, it is sufficient that they *are* so ; they need not be the *same* vowels, and, in practice, are generally *different.*

Again, the last strongly-accented syllable in the line does *not* begin with the rime-letter. This also is the usual and more correct arrangement.

Having once this typical form to refer to, it is easy to enumerate most of the changes which may arise. Let us now take the line,

> " Hire[2] mésse and hire mátyns,
> And mány of hire hoúres."   .
> —*Piers Plowman,* l. 193.

We have here the arrangement

$$1 \quad * \quad 2 \quad * \quad 1 \quad : \quad 1 \quad * \quad 3 \quad * \quad 1$$

---

[1] I use the term *strongly*-accented advisedly, all accents not being equal. Thus, in the line—

> "On the oát-grass and the swórd-grass, and the búlrush in the póol,"

the syllables marked are *strongly*-accented

[2] "Hire is a monosyllable."—*Guest on English Rhythms;* ed. 1838, p. 34.

which shews (1) that an unaccented syllable may be introduced at the beginning of the second section; and (2) that the number of intermediate unaccented syllables may be readily increased to *three*.

Now herein lies the peculiar freedom and elasticity of alliterative verse; we shall soon find by observation that, under certain circumstances, as many as *four* short unaccented syllables (even if they contain among them one that *is* accented *slightly*) may be inserted at pleasure between the emphatic syllables without destroying the rhythm; for it is one addressed to the *ear* only, and not to the *eye*. The chief point which the poet has to take care of is that when he introduces a larger number of unaccented syllables, they should be capable of rapid enunciation, lest the verse seem clogged and unmusical. An example may be seen in the lines,

> " Fáiteden for her fóode,
> Foúghten at the ále."
>
> —*Piers Plowman*, l. 83.

Which may be denoted by

$$* \quad 4 \quad * \quad 1 \quad : \quad * \quad 3 \quad * \quad 1$$

It would take up too much space to explain here the true method of scanning the lines by division into feet; it may suffice to say that the *general effect* of the metre is *dactylic*, supposing the term *dactyl* to be capable of application to an *English* foot, which, to speak strictly, it is not. Indeed, the nomenclature of English prosody is in sore need of alteration. Neither is there space to explain, and to account for, the curious variations which may further be made in the alliterative metre. The view here given is only an approximate one, which will be found useful in practice. A longer passage may exemplify it better—

> " I lóked me on my léft half
> As the lády me taúghte,
> And was wár of a wómman
> Wórthilich y-clóthed,
> Púrfiled with pólure,
> The fýnest upon érthe,
> Y-córouned with a córoun,
> The kýng hath none bétter;
> Fétisliche hyr fíngres
> Were frétted with góld wyr."
>
> —*Piers Plowman*, l. 892.

Analysis:

1	*	4	*	1	:	2	*	2	*	1
2	*	2	*	1	:		*	3	*	1
	*	3	*	1	:	1	*	3	*	1
1	*	4	*	1	:	1	*	2	*	1
	*	3	*	1	:	1	*	2	*	1

One variation, however, found oftenest in the first section, is too important to be passed over. It is that we sometimes find in a section a *third* strongly-accented syllable, thus giving to the line a rather unwieldy length; as in,

> "The móoste mischief on mólde
> Is móuntynne wel fáste."
> —*Piers Plowman*, l. 133.

This third accent is often very awkwardly placed, as in the first line of "Morte Arthure,"

> "Now grétt glórious Gódd · thurgh gráce of hym selvene."

Other noticeable deviations from the strict type may be briefly indicated.

(1) The syllable beginning with the rime-letter is sometimes unemphatic; as in "Morte Arthure," l. 59,

> "In Glamórgan with glée thare gládschip was évere."

(2) Sometimes there are but *two* rime-letters, as in l. 80,

> "So cóme in sódanly, a sénatour of Róme."

(3) Sometimes there is *no* alliteration, as in l. 70 (4) Sometimes there are *four* rime-letters, as l. 32, where all belong to accented syllables,

> "Scáthylle Scóttlande by skýlle : he skýstys as hym lýkys;"

or as in l. 35, where one belongs to an unaccented syllable,

> "Hólaund and Hénawde : they hélde of hym bóthe."

It will now be sufficient, perhaps, to indicate what is probably the correct accentuation of the first fourteen lines, as this will enable the reader to perceive in them a certain vigorous *swing* (well suited for the ballad-reciter), which will suggest the scansion of most other lines, though there is always somewhat of difficulty in it, from the fact that we have now-a-days changed the accentuation of many words, and cannot be quite certain about the final *e*'s.

> "Now grétt glórious Gódd · thurgh gráce of hym sélvene,
> And the précious práyere · of hys prýs móder

Schélde us ffro schámesdede . and sýnfulle wérkes,
And gýffe us gráce to gýe · and góverne us hére
In thys wréchyd wérld . thorowe vért[u]ous lýwynge
That we may káyre till hys coúrte : the kýngdome of hévyne,
Whene oure sáules schall párte : and súndyre ffra the bódy
Ewyre to bélde and to býde · in blýsse wïth hyme sélvene ;
And wýsse me to wérpe owte   some wórde at this týme,
That nothyre vóyde be ne váyne : bot wýrchip tille hyme sélvyne ;
Plésande and prófitabille . to the póple þat theme héres.
þe that liste has to lýth : or lúffes for to hére
Off élders of álde tyme · and of their áwke dédys,
How they were léle in their láwe   and lóvede Gód Almýghty," etc.

The accentuation of the last two lines is a little doubtful. There may
have been an accent on the second *of* in l. 13, owing to its position and
the fact of its beginning with a rime-letter ; while in l. 14 we have the
rather unusual number of six accents, unless "how" was slurred over.

After all, the best way of perceiving the rhythm is to read over
some fifty lines several times till they seem quite familiar, and then to
read them over once more *out loud*, with strong emphasis on the verbs,
substantives, and adjectives, and with a natural and free pronunciation.

Morte Arthure.

Here begynnes Morte Arthure. In nomine Patris et Filii et Spiritus Sancti. Amen pro charite. Amen.

Now grett glorious Godd, thurgh grace of hym selven*e*,
And the *precyous prayere* of hys prys modyr,
Schelde us ffro schamesdede and synfull*e* werkes,

The poet prays for grace,

4 And gyffe us *grace* to gye, and governe us here,
In this wrechyd werld, thorowe vertous lywynge,
That we may kayre til hys courte, the kyngdom*e* of hevyne,
When*e* oure saules schall*e* parte and sundyre ffra the body,

8 Ewyre to belde and to byde in blysse with hym*e* selven*e*;
And wysse me to wērpe owte som*e* worde at this tyme,
That nothyre voyde be ne vayne, bot wyrchip till*e* hym*e* selvyn*e*;

and for power to write something profitable

Plesande *and* profitabill*e* to the pople þat theme heres.

12   Ʒe that liste has to lyth, or luffes for to here,
Off elders of alde tym*e* and of theire awke dedys,

Ye that list to hear of strange deeds of old,

How they were lele in theire lawe, and loved*e* God Almyghty,
Herkynes me heyndly and holdys ʒow styll*e*,

hearken to a tale of the Round Table.

16 And I sall*e* tell*e* ʒow a tale, þat trewe es and nobyll*e*,
Off the ryeall*e* renkys of the rowunde table,
That chefe ware of chevalrye and cheftans nobyll*e*,

These knights were noble, wise, and brave,

Bathe ware in thire werkes and wyse men*e* of armes,

kind, and courte-
ous, and wor-
shipful.

20 Doughty in theire doyngs and dredde ay schame,

Kynde mene and courtays, and couthe of courte thewes.

They slew Lu-
cius, lord of
Rome, and con-
quered his king-
dom.

How they whanne wyth were wyrchippis many,

Sloughe Lucyus þe lÿthyre, that lorde was of Rome,

24 And conqueryd that kyngryke thorowe craftys of armes;

Hear now the
story.

Herkenes now hedyrwarde, and herys this storye.

When King Ar-
thur had won
back all the
realm of Uther,

Qwene that the kynge Arthur by conqueste hade wonne Castelles and kyngdoms, and contreez many,

28 And he had coveicde the coroune of the kyth ryche

Of alle that Uter in erthe aughte in his tyme,

Argyle, Orkney,
and the isles

Orgayle and Orkenay, and alle this owte iles,

Irelande uttirly, as occyane rynnys:

Ireland and Scot-
land,

32 Scathylle Scottlande by skylle he skystys as hym lykys,

Wales, Flanders,
and France,

And Wales of were he wane at hys wille,

had made tribu-
tary Holland and
Hainault, Bur-
gundy and Bra-
bant, Brittany,
Guienne, Goth-
land and Greece.

Bathe fflaundrez and ffraunce fre til hym selvyne;

Holaund and Henawde they helde of hyme bothe,

36 Burgoyne and Brabane, and Bretayne the lesse,

Gyane and Gothelande, and Grece the ryche;

He built Bayonne
and Bordeaux,
Tours and Toul;

Bayone and Burdeux he beldytt fulle faire,

Turoyne and Tholus with toures fulle hye;

was prince of
Poictiers and
Provence, of Va-
lence and Vienne,
of Eruga and
Aniana, of Na-
verne and Nor-
way and Nor-
mandy.
Of Germany, of
Austria, and
many other
lands.
He conquered all
Denmark with
his sword.

40 Off Peyters and of Provynce he was prynce holdyne,

Of Valence and Vyenne, off value so noble;

Of Eruge and Anyone, thos erledoms ryche,

By conqueste fulle cruelle þey knewe hym fore lorde;

44 Of Naverne and Norwaye, and Normaundye eke,

Of Almayne, of Estriche, and oþer ynowe;

Danmarke he dryssede alle by drede of hym selvyne,

Fra Swynne unto Swether-wyke, with his swrede kene!

Then he dubbed
his knights and
gave them lands.

48 Qwenne he thes dedes had done, he doubbyd hys knyghtez,

Dyvysyde dowcherys and delte in dyverse remmes;

Created kings
anointed.

Mad of his cosyns kyngys ennoyntede,

In kyth there they covaitte crounes to bere.

52 Whene he thys rewmes hade redyne and rewlyde the pople,

Then rested the
hero, and held the
Round Table.

Then rystede that ryalle and helde þe Rounde Tabylle;

Suggeourns þat sesone to solace hyme selvene,

In Gretayne þe braddere,[1] as hym beste lykes;

56 Sythyne wente into Wales with his wyes alle,

Sweys into Swaldye with his snelle houndes,

For to hunt at þe hartes in thas hye laundes,

In Glamorgane with glee, thare gladchipe was evere;

60 And thare a citee he sette, be assentte of his lordys,

That Caerlyone was callid, with curious walles,

On the riche revare þat rynnys so faire,

There he myghte semble his sorte to see whenne hym lykyde,

64 Thane aftyre at Carlelele a Cristynmese he haldes,

This ilke kyde conquerour, and helde hym for lorde,

Wyth Dukez and dusperes of dyvers rewmes,

Erles and erchevesqes, and oþer ynowe,

68 Byschopes and bachelers, and banerettes nobille,

Þat bowes to his banere, buske whene hym lykys:

Bot on the Cristynmesdaye, whene they were alle semblyde,

That comlyche conquerour commaundez hym selvyne

72 Þat ylke a lorde sulde lenge, and no lefe take,

To the tende day fully ware takyne to þe ende.

Thus one ryalle araye he helde his rounde table,

With semblant and solace and selcouthe metes;

76 Whas never syche noblay, in no manys tyme,

Mad in mydwynter in þa Weste marchys!

Bot on the newȝere daye, at þe none evyne,

As the bolde at the borde was of brede servyde,

80 So come in sodanly a senatour of Rome,

Wyth sextene knyghtes in a soyte sewande hym one.

He saluȝed the soverayne and the sale aftyr,

Ilke a kynge aftyre kynge,[2] and mad his enclines;

84 Gaynour in hir degre he grette as hym lykyde,

And syne agayne to þe gome he gaffe up his nedys:

"Sir Lucius Iberius, the Emperour of Rome,

---

[1] "The More Bretayne Englond is
As men may rede on Cronyclys."
—*Arthur* (ed. F. J. Furnivall), l. 503.

[2] A tag (†) is appended to these g's, which is taken to indicate a final *e*. Halliwell reads it without the *e*.

After solacing himself in Britain, he goes into Wales,

to hunt the hart with his swift hounds,

and in Glamorgan founds Caerleon upon Usk.

At Caerleon he holds high festival at Christmas-tide with his lords and bishops,

and bids none depart from the feast till ten days are expired.

Never was so noble a feast known.

But on New Year's day, as the knights were feasting,

there came in suddenly a Senator of Rome, attended by sixteen knights, who salutes King Arthur and his knights,

and Guinevre the Queen.

Then, in the name of Sir Lu-

cius Iberius, the
Emperor of
Rome,

Salu; the as sugett, undyre his sele ryche;

88 It es credens, *syr* kyng, wi*th* cruell*e* wordez,

Trow it for no trufles, his targe es to schewe!

Now in this new;ers daye wi*th* notaries sygne,

He summons Ar-
thur to appear at
Rome on Lammas
day,

I make the somouns i*n* sale to sue for þi landys,

92 That on Lam*m*esse daye thare be no lette ffou*n*dene,

þ*at* thou bee redy at Rome wi*th* all*e* thi rounde table,

Appere i*n* his *pr*esens wi*th* thy price knyghtez,

At pryme of the daye, in payne of ;o*u*r lyvys,

96 In þe kydd capytoile before þe kyng selvyn*e*,

Whene he and his senato*ur*s bez sette as them lykes,

to answer why
he occupies his
lands instead of
paying homage
to him,

To ansucre anely why thow ocupyes the laundez,

That awe homage of alde till*e* hym *and* his eld;rs;

100 Why thow has redyn*e* and raymede, *and* raunsound þe pople,

And kylļyde doun*e* his cosyns, kyngys ennoynttyde;

Thare schall*e* thow gyffe rekkynyng*e* for all*e* thy round
table,

and how he dares
to rebel against
him

Why thow arte rebell*e* to Rome, and rentez them*e*
wytholdez!

104 ;iff thow theis som*m*ons wythsytte, he sendes thie thies
wordes,

But if Arthur
will not come,
the Emperor will
invade his land
and take him
captive,

He sall*e* the seke ov*er* þe see wyth sexten*e* kynges,

Bryne Bretayn*e* þe brade, and bryttyn*e* thy knyghtys,

And bryng*e* the bouxsomly as a beste wi*th* brethe whare
hym lykes,

108 That thow ne schall*e* rowte ne ryste undyr the hevene
ryche,

Þofe thow for reddo*ur* of Rome ryne to þe erthe!

and destroy him
wherever he may
fly.

ffor if thow flee into Fraunce or ffreselaund owþ*er*,

þou sall*e* be feched wi*th* force, and oversette for ev*er*!

The Register of
Rome   declares
that Arthur's fa-
ther paid tribute,
which was won
by Julius Cæsar
and his gentle
knights.

112 Thy fadyr mad fewtee, we fynde in oure rollez,

In the regestre of Rome, who so ryghte lukez:

Wi*th*-owttyn*e* more trouflyng the trebute we aske,

That Juli*us* Cesar wan*e* wyth his jentill*e* knyghttes!"

Then did king
Arthur look with
ferocious glance
on the Senator.

116 The kyng*e* blyschit on*e* the beryn*e* with his brode eghn*e*,
þ*at* full*e* brymly for breth brynte as the gledys;

Keste colou*rs* as kyng w*ith* crouell*e* lates,
Luked as a lyon*e*, and on his lypp*e* bytes!

120 The Romaynes for radnesse ruschte to þe erthe,
ffordc ferdnesse of hys face, as they fey were;
Cowchide as kenetez before þe kyng*e* selŭyn*e*,
be-cause of his contenaunce confusedc them*e* semede!

124 Thene cove*r*d up a knyghte, *and* criede ful lowde,[1]
"Kyng*e* coronn*e*de of kynd, curtays and noble,
Misdoo no messengere for menske of þi selvyn*e*,
Sen we are in thy manrede, and m*e*rcy þe besekes;

128 We lenge w*ith* *syr* Lucius, that lordc es of Rome,
That es þe m*e*rvelyousteste man*e* þat on molde lengez;
It es lefull*e* till*e* us his likyng*e* till*e* wyrche;[2]
We come at his commaundment; have us excusede."

132 Then carpys þe conquerou*r* crewell*e* wordez,—
"Haa! cravaunde knyghte! a cowarde þe semez!
Þare some segge in this sale, and he ware sare grevede,
Thow durste noghte full*e* all*e* Lumberdye luke on*e* hym
ones."

136 "Sir," sais þe Senato*ur*, "so Crist mott me helpe,
þe voute of thi vesage has woundyde us all*e*!
Thow arte þe lordlyeste lede þat eve*r* I on*e* lukyde;
By lukyng*e*, w*ith*-owttyn*e* lesse, a lyon*e* the semys!"

140 "Thow has me somond," *quod* þe kyng, "and said what
þe lykes;[3]
Fore sake of thy Sov*e*rayng*e* I suffre the þe more;
Sen I coround in kyth wyth crysum*e* enoyntede,
Was neve*r* creatu*re* to me þat carpede so large!

144 Bot I sall*e* tak concell*e* at kynges enoyntede,
Off dukes *and* duspers and doctou*rs* noble,
Off*e* peres of the p*e*rlement, prelates *and* oþer,
Off þe richeste renkys of þe rounde table;

148 Þus schall*e* I take avisemente of valiant beryns,

---

[1] *hyghe* in text, erased, and *lowde* written in margin.
[2] The text has *shewe* which has been erased, and *wyrohe* written in the margin.
[3] *Likyd* erased and *lykes* written in margin.

Wyrke aftyre the wytte of my wyes knyghttes:
To warpe wordez in waste no wyrchipp it were,
Ne wilfully in þis wrethe to wrekene my selvene.

while the Romans stay a week to refresh themselves. 152 For-þi salle þow lenge here, *and* lugge wyth þise lordes,
This sevenyghte in solace, to suggo*urne* ȝo*ur* horses,
To see whatte lyfe þat wee leede in thees law laundes."
ffor by þe realtee of Rome, þat recheste was ev*er*e,

Sir Cayous is bid to entertain the lords, 156 He comm*and*e s*yr* Cayous, take kepe to thoos lordez,
To styghtylle þa steryne mene as theire statte askys,
That they bee herberde in haste in thoos heghe chambres;
Sythine sittandly in sale servyde ther-aftyr;

and their horses. 160 That they fynd na fawte of fude to thiere horsez,
Nowthire weyn*e* ne wax*e*, ne welthe in þis erthe;

He was not to spare, but to feast them liberally. Spare for no spycerye, bot spende what þe lykys,
That there be largeste one lofte, and no lake foundene;
164 If þou my wyrchip wayte wy be my trouthe,
þou salle have gersoms fulle grett, þat gayne salle þe evere!"

And right richly did they fare. Now er they herberde in hey, *and* in oste holdene,
Hastyly wyth hende mene w*ith*-in thees heghe wallez;

Their chambers were furnished with chimneys. 168 In chambyrs w*ith* chympnes þey chaungen*e* þeire wedez;
And sythyn*e* the chauncelere þeme fetchede w*ith* chevalrye
noble;

The Senator sat at the King's table, and was served like himself, Sone þe senato*ur* was sett, as hym*e* wele semyde,
At þe kyngez ownn*e* borde; twa knyghtes hym s*er*vede,
172 Singulere sothely, as Arthure hym selvyn*e*,
Richely on þe ryghte haunde at the rounde table;

for the Romans are of the most royal blood on earth. Be resoune þat þe Romaynes whare so ryche holdene,
As of þe realeste blode þat reynede in erthe.
176 There come in at þe fyrste course, befor þe kynge selvene,

Boar's-heads there were served upon silver by numerous gaily dressed attendants Barehevedys þat ware bryghte, burnyste w*ith* sylver,
Alle w*ith* taghte mene and towne in togers full*e* ryche,
Of saunke reall*e* in suyte, sexty at ones;

Venison, fatted and wild, with choice bread, 180 fflesch fluriste of fermysone w*ith* frumentee noble
Ther-to wylde to wale, and wynlyche bryddes,[1]

---

[1] *bredes* erased and *bryddes* written in margin.

Pacockes and plovers in platers of golde,

Pygg*es* of porke despyne, *þat* pasturede nev*er*;

184 Sythen*e* herons in hedoyne, hyled full*e* faire;

Grett swannes full*e* swythe in silveryn*e* chargeours,

Tartes of T*u*rky, taste whan*e* þem*e* lykys;

Gumbaldes graythely, full*e* gracious to taste;

188 Scyn*e* bowes of wylde bores w*ith* þ*e* braune lechyde,

Bernakes and boture*s* in baterde dysches,

Þareby braunchers in brede bettyr was nev*er*,

W*ith* brestez of barowes, þ*at* bryghte ware to schewe;

192 Seyn*e* come þer sewes sere, w*ith* solace þ*er-after*,

Ownd of azure all*e* ov*er and* ardant þem semyde,

Of ilke aleche þ*e* lowe laun*s*chide full*e* hye,

Þ*at* all*e* ledes myghte lyke þ*at* lukyde þem*e* apone;

196 Þan*e* cranes *and* curlues craftyly rosted,

Connygez in cretoyne colourede full*e* faire,

ffesauntez enflureschit in flammande silv*er*,

W*ith* darielle*s* endordide, and daynteez ynew*e*;

200 Þan*e* clarett and Creette, clergyally rennen*e*,

With condethes full*e* curio*u*s all*e* of clene silvyre;

Osay and algarde, and oþer ynew*e*,

Rynisch wyn*e* and Rochell*e*, riche*re* was nev*er*;

204 Vernage of Venyce v*er*tuo*u*se and Crete;

In faucetez of fyn*e* golde, fonode whoso lykes;

The kyngez cope-borde was closed in silv*er*,

In grete goblettez overgylte glorious of hewe;

208 There was a cheeff*e* buttlere, a chevalere noble,

Sir Cayou*s* þ*e* curtaise, þ*at* of þ*e* cowpe servede;

Sexty cowpes of suyte offore the kyng selvyn*e*,

Crafty *and* curious corven*e* full*e* faire,

212 In ev*er*-ilk ap*er*ty pyghte w*ith* precyous stones,

That nan*e* enpoysone sulde goo prevely þ*er* undyr*e*,

Bot þ*e* bryght golde for brethe sulde briste alto peces,

Or ells þ*e* venym*e* sulde voyde thurghe vertue of þ*e* stones,

216 And the conquerour hymselven*e*, so clenly arayede

In colo*ur*s of clene golde, cleéde wyth his knyghttys,

Marginal glosses:

peacocks and plovers upon golden plates, sucking pigs, herons in sauce,

huge swans,

tarts and conserves,

hams and brawn in slices, wild geese and ducks, young hawks,

various stews and made dishes ornamented brightly,

Cranes and curlews roasted, rabbits served in sweet sauce, pheasants upon silver, curries made to shine bright, and numerous other dainties. Wine caused to run skilfully in silver conduits.

Rare sorts served in cups of fine gold The King's cupboard was glorious with plate.

The chief butler was Sir Cayous,

who served the wine in goblets decked with precious stones, which hinder the deadly effects of poison.

Arthur was clad in cloth of gold

with his crown on; the doughtiest knight that dwelt on earth.

Drissid with his dyademe one his deesse ryche,

ffore he was demyde þe doughtyeste þat duellyde in erthe.

Then he spake courteous words to those lords.

220 Thane þe conquerour kyndly carpede to þose lordes,

Rehetede þe Romaynes with realle spechc,

"Sirs, be of good cheer, we give you the best our barren country affords, which indeed is but poor."

"Sirs, bez knyghtly of contenaunce, and comfurthes ȝourselvynes,

We knowe noghte in þis countre of curious metez;

224 In thees barayne landez, bredes nons oþer,

ffore-thy wythowttyne feynyng, enforce ȝow þe more

To feede ȝow with syche feble as ȝe be-fore fynde."

"Sir," sais þe Senatour, "so Criste motte me helpe!

"Sir," says the Senator, "Rome itself can show nothing equal to this luxurious feast."

228 There rygnede never syche realtee with-in Rome walles!

There ne es prelatte ne pape, ne prynce in þis erthe,

That ne he myghte be wele payede of þees pryce metes!"

Then they washed and withdrew to the chamber.

Aftyre theyre welthe þey wesche, and went un-to chambyre,

232 þis ilke kydde conquerour with knyghtes ynewe;

Sir Gawaine leads Guinevere.

Sir Gaywayne þe worthye Dame Waynour he hledys;

Sir Owghtreth on þe toþer syde of Turry was lorde.

Spiced drinks were served to all.

Thane spyces unsparyly þay spendyde there-aftyre,

236 Malvesye and muskadelle, þase mervelyous drynkes,

Raykede fulle raythely in rossete cowpes,

Tille alle þe riche on rawe, Romaynes and oþer.

Certain lords were assigned to attend upon the Senator.

Bot the soveraigne sothely, for solauce of hym selvene,

240 Assignyde to þe senatour certaygne lordes,

To lede to his levere, whene he leve askes,

With myrthe and with melodye of mynstralsy noble.

Arthur goes to council in the Giant's tower,

Thane þe conquerour to concelle cayres there aftyre,

244 Wyth lordes of his lygeaunce þat to hymselfe langys;

with his lords, justices, judges, and gentle knights.

To þe geauntes toure jolily he wendes,

Wyth justicez and juggez, and gentille knyghtes.

First speaks Sir Cador of Cornwall.

Sir Cador of Cornewayle to þe kynge carppes,

248 Lughe one hyme luffly with lykande lates;

"I thanke Gode of þat thraa þat us þus thretys!

The letters of Sir Lucius, he says, delight his heart.

ȝow moste be traylede, I trowe, bot ȝife ȝe trett bettyre:

þe lettres of syr Lucius lyghttys myne herte!

252 We hafe as Iosels liffyde many longe daye,
Wyth delyttes in this land *with* lordchipez many,
And forelytenede the loos þat we are layttede :

They had too long lived a life of inglorious peace.

I was abaischite, be oure Lorde, of oure beste bernes,

256 Fore gret dule of deffuse of dedez of armes!
Now wakkenyse þe were! wyrchipide be Cryste!

He rejoices to return again to deeds of arms.

And we salle wynne it agayne be wyghtnesse and strenghe!"
"Sir Cador," *quod* þe kynge, "thy concelle es noble,

The king praises Sir Cador for his bold words,

260 Bot þou arte a *mervailous mane with* thi mery wordez !
ffor thow countez no caas, ne castes no forthire,

spoken from his heart without thought or care.

Bot hurles furthe appone hevede, as thi herte thynkes ;
I moste trette of a trew towchande þise nedes,

264 Talke of thies tythdands þat tenes myne herte ;

He himself is grieved at these tidings.

þou sees þat þe Emperour es angerde a lyttille ;
þat semes be his sandismene þat he es sore grevede ;
His senatour has sommonde me, and said what hym lykyde,

268 Hethely in my halle, wyth heynȝous wordes,

he has been insulted in his own hall by heinous words,

In speche disspysȝede me, *and* sparede me lyttille ;
I myght noghte speke for spytte, so my herte trymblyde !

and insolently summoned to pay tribute to the Emperor of Rome,

He askyde me tyrauntly tribute of Rome,

272 That tenefully tynt was in tyme of myne elders ;
There alyenes, in absence of alle mene of armes,
Coverd it of commons, as cronicles telles ;
I have tide to take tribute of Rome,

of whom he ought rather to demand tribute.

276 Myne ancestres ware emperours, and aughte it þeme selvene,
Belyne *and* Bremyne, *and* Bawdewyne the thyrde,
They ocupyede þe empyre aughte score wynnttyrs,

His ancestors occupied the Empire of Rome eight score winters.

Ilkane ayere aftyre oþer, as awlde mene telles ;

280 Thei coverde þe capitoile, and keste doune þe walles ;
Hyngede of þeire heddys-mene by hundrethes at ones ;
Seyne Constantyne, our kynsmane, conquerid it aftyre,

His kinsman, Constantine, afterwards subdued it—

þat ayere was of Ynglande, and Emperour of Rome,[1]

---

[1] "For the Emperor Constantine
That was the son of Elyne
That was a Bretone of this lond,
Conquered Rome with his hond."
—*Arthur* (ed. F. J. Furnivall), l. 249.

284 He þat conquerid þe Crosse be craftez of armes,

That Criste was on crucifiede, þat kyng es of hevene ;

Thus hafe we evydens to aske þe Emperour þe same,

That þus regnez at Rome, whate ryghte þat he claymes."

288 Than[1] answarde kyng Aungers to Arthure hym selvyne,

"Thow aughte to be overlynge over alle oþer kynges,

ffore wyseste, and worthyeste, and wyghteste of haundes,

The knyghtlyeste of counsaile þat ever corone bare ;

292 I dare saye fore Scottlande, þat we theme schathe lympyde,

Whene the Romaynes regnede, þay raunsounde oure eldyrs,

And rade in theire ryotte, and ravyschett oure wyfes,

With-owttyne resone or ryghte refte us oure gudes ;

296 And I salle make myne avowe devotly to Criste,

And to þe haly vernacle vertuus and noble,

Of this grett velany I salle be venged ones

On þone venemus mene, wyth valiant knyghtes !

300 I salle the forthire of defence fosterde ynewe

ffifty thowsande mene, wyth-in two eldes,

Of my wage for to wende, whare so the lykes,

To fyghte wyth thy ffaa mene, þat us unfaire ledes."

304 Thane the burelyche beryne of Bretayne þe lyttylle

Counsayles syr Arthure, and of hyme besekys

To answere þe alyenes wyth austerene wordes,

To entyce the Emperour to take overe the mounttes.

308 He said, " I make myne avowe verreilly to Cryste,

And to þe haly vernacle, þat voide schalle I nevere,

ffor radnesse of na Romayne þat regnes in erthe ;

Bot ay be redye in araye, and at areste ffoundene,

312 No more dowte the dynte of theire derfe wapyns,

þan þe dewe þat es dannke, whene þat it doune ffalles ;

Ne no more schoune fore þe swape of theire scharpe suerddes,

Then fore þe faireste flour þatt on the folde growes !

316 I salle to batelle the brynge, of brenyede knyghtes

Thyrtty thosaunde be tale, thryftye in armes,

[1] Yan in MS.

Wyth-in a monethe daye in-to whatte marche,
þat þow wylle sothelye assygne, whene thyselfe lykes."

320 "A! A!" sais þe Walsche kynge, "wirchipid be Criste!
Now schalle we wreke fulle wele þe wrethe of oure elders!
In West Walys i-wysse syche woundyrs-þay wroghte,
þat alle for wandrethe may wepe, þat one þat were thynkes.

324 I salle have the avanttwarde wytterly my selvene,
Tylle þat I have renquiste þe Vicounte of Rome,
þat wroghte me at Viterbe a velanye ones,
As I paste in pylgremage by the Pounte Tremble;

328 He was in Tuskayne þat tyme and tuke of oure knyghttes,
Areste theme oonryghttwyslye, and raunsound þame aftyre;
I salle hym surelye ensure, þat saghetylle salle we never,
Are we sadlye assemble by oure selfene ones,

332 And dele dynttys of dethe with oure derfe wapyns!
And I salle wagge to þat were of wyrchipfulle knyghtes,
Of Wyghte and of Walschelande, and of þe Weste marches,
Twa thosande in tale, horsede one stedys,

336 of þe wyghteste wyes in alle ȝone Weste landys!"

    Syre Ewane fytz Uryenee þane egerly fraynez,
        Was cosyne to þe conquerour, corageous hym selfene,
    "Sir, and we wyste ȝour wylle, we walde wirke þer-aftyre;

340 ȝif þis journee sulde halde, or be arouwede[1] forthyre,
To ryde one ȝone Romaynes and ryott theire landez,
We walde schape us there-fore to schippe whene ȝow
        lykys."

    "Cosyne," quod þe conquerour, "kyndly þou asches;
344 ȝife my concelle accorde to conquere ȝone landez,
By the kalendez of Juny we schalle encountre ones,
Wyth fulle creuelle knyghtez, so Cryste mot me helpe!
There-to make I myne avowe devottly to Cryste,

348 And to the holy vernacle vertuous and noble,
I salle at Lammesse take leve, to lenge at my large
In Lorayne or Lumberdye, whethire me leve thynkys;

knights within a month.

Then Arthur exclaims Ah! Ah!
Now shall we have revenge.

He himself would fight at the head of his army till he had revenged himself on the Viscount of Rome for a villainy he once wrought him at Viterbo.

He would take two thousand picked knights.

Then spoke Sir Ewayne and said that they would all follow his command gladly.

Then said Arthur,

"We will be ready by the kalends of June,

and at Lammas will enjoy ourselves in Lorraine or Lombardy.

---

[1] The reading of this word is somewhat doubtful. Halliwell reads aprovede, but there is certainly no trace of a p in the MS.

Merke un-to Meloyne, and myne doune þe wallez,

352 Bathe of Petyrsande, *and* of Pys, and of þe Pounte Trẽble,

In þe Vale of Viterbe vetaile my knyghttes,

Suggourne there sex wokes *and* solace my-selfen*e*;

Send *pr*ekers to þe price toun*e*, and plaunte there my segge,

356 Bot if þay profre me þe pece be processe of tym*e*.''

'' Certys,'' sais *syr* Ewayn*e*, ''and I avowe aftyre,

And I þat hathell*e* may see ev*er* w*ith* myn*e* eghn*e*,

That ocupies thin*e* heritage, the empyere of Rome,

360 I salle auntyre me anes hys egle to touche,

þat born*e* es in his banere of brighte golde ryche,

And raas it from*e* his riche men*e*, and ryste it in sondyre,

Bot he be redily reschowede w*ith* riotou*s* knyghtez ;

364 I salle enforsse ȝowe in þe felde w*ith* fresche men*e* of armes,

ffyfty thosande folke apon*e* faire stedys,

On thi ffoo men*e* to foonde there the faire thynkes,

In ffraunce *or* in ffriselande, feghte when*e* þe lykes !''

368 '' By oure Lorde,'' *quod syr* Launcelott, now lyghttys
myn*e* herte !

I love Gode of þ*is* love þ*is* lordes has avowede !

Nowe may lesse men*e* have leve to say what them*e* lykes,

And hase no lettyng be lawe, bot lystynnys þise wordez ;

372 I sall*e* be at jou*r*nee w*ith* gentill*e* knyghtes,

On a ramby stede full*e* jolyly grethide,

Or any jou*r*nee began*e* to juste w*ith* hym selfen*e*,

Emange all*e* his geauntez genyvers and oþer,

376 Stryke hym styfflye fro his stede, w*ith* strenghe of myn*e*
handys,

ffor all*e* þa steryn*e* in stou*r*, þat in his stale hovys !

Be my retenu arayede, I rekke bot a lyttill*e*

To make rowtte into Rome, w*ith* ryotou*s* knyghtes !

380 With-in a sevenyghte day*e*, w*ith* sex score helmes,

I sall*e* be seen*e* on the see, saile when þe lykes.''

Thane laughes *syr* Lottez, and all*e* on*e* lowde meles,

'' Me likez þat *syr* Luci*us* launges aftyre sorowe ;

384 Now he wylnez þe were, hys wandrethe begynnys,

Marginal glosses:

Sojourn six weeks in the Vale of Viterbo,

and advance skirmishers to Rome unless they offer peace in fitting time." Then S r Ewayne vows vengeance against the Emperor of Rome for occupying Arthur's heritage,

and promises 50,000 men on fair steeds.

Then Lancelot declares his satisfaction at the war.

He is ready to joust with the Emperor himself,

and to carry the war into Rome.

Sir Lotez laughs for joy,

It es owre weredes to wreke the wrethe of oure elders !

I make myne avowe to Gode, and to þe holy vernacle,

And I may se þe Romaynes, þat are so ryche haldene,

388 Arayede in þeire riotes on a rounde felde,

I salle at þe reverence of þe rounde table-.

Ryde thrughte alle þe rowtte, rerewarde *and* oþer,

Redy wayes to make, and renkkes fulle rowme,

392 Rynnande on rede blode, as my stede ruschez !

He þat folowes my fare, and fyrste commes aftyre,

Salle fynde in my fare waye many ffay levyde !"

Thane þe conquerour kyndly comforthes þese knyghtes,

396 Alowes þame gretly theire lordly a-vowes,—

"Alweldande Gode, wyrchip ȝow alle !

And latte me nevere wanntte ȝow, whylls I in werlde regne ;

My menske and my manhede ȝe mayntene in erthe,

400 Myne honour alle owt utterly in oþer kyngys landes ;

My wele and my wyrchipe, of alle þis werlde ryche,

ȝe have knyghtly conqueryde, þat to my coroune langes ;

Hym thare be ferde for no faeos, þat swylke a folke ledes,

404 Bot ever ffresche for to fyghte, in felde whene hym lykes.

I acounte no kynge þat undyr Criste lyffes,

Whilles I see ȝowe alle sounde, I sette be no more."

Qwhene they tristily had tretyd, thay trumppede up aftyre,

408 Descendyd doune with a daunce of dukes and erles ;

Thane þey semblede to sale, and sowpped als swythe,

Alle þis semly sorte, wyth semblante fulle noble.

Thene the roy realle rehetes thes knyghttys,

412 Wyth reverence and ryotte of alle his rounde table,

Tille seven dayes was gone : þe senatour askes

Answere to þe Emperour with austeryne wordez,

Aftyre þe Epiphanye, whene þe purpos was takyne

416 Of peris of þe parlement, prelates and oþer.

The kyng in his concelle, curtaise and noblee,

Utters þe alienes, and ansuers hyme selvene :—

"Gret wele Lucius, thi lorde, and layne noghte þise wordes;

Marginal notes:

and hopes to see the rich Romans in their pomp,

that he may cut his way through them and shed their blood.

Then Arthur praises his knights for upholding his honour.

While they remain true to him he fears no king on earth.
Then the Council broke up.

Music and dancing succeeded,

and they all were feasted in the hall.

After seven days the Senator demands his answer for the Emperor.

Then Arthur bids him greet Lucius

and tell him that
he shall quickly
see him in his
country;

420 Ife þow be lygmane lele, late hyme wiet sone

I salle at Lammese take leve, and loge at my large

In delitte in his laundez, wyth lordes ynewe

Regne in my realtee, and ryste whene me lykes,

that he will hold
his round table
by the river
Rhone,

424 By þe reyvere of Reone halde my rounde table,

ffaunge the fermes in fatthe of alle þa faire rewmes,

ffor alle þe manace of hys myghte, *and* mawgree his eghne !

And merke sythene *over* the mounttez in-to his mayne londez,

and mine down
the walls of
Milan,

428 To Meloyne the mervaylous, and myne doune the walles ;

In Lorrayne ne in Lumberdye lefe schalle I nowthire

Nokyne lede appone liffe, þat þare his lawes ȝemes ;

ravage Tuscany
with his fierce
knights,

And turne in-to Tuschayne, whene me tyme thynkys,

432 Ryde alle þas rowme landes wyth ryotous knyghttes ;

Byde hy[m] make reschewes for menske of hyme selvene,

And mette me fore his manhede in þase mayne landes !

I salle be foundyne in Fraunce, fraiste whene hym lykes,

436 The fyrste daye of feverȝere, in thas faire marches !

Are I be fechyde wyth force, or forfette my landes,

þe floure of his faire folke fulle fay salle be levyde !

I salle hym sekyrly ensure, undyre my seele ryche,

and before seven
winters are gone
besiege Rome,

440 To seege þe cetee of Rome wyth-in sevene wyntyre,

And that so sekerly ensege apone sere halfes,

and many a sen-
ator shall rue his
wrath.

That many a senatour salle syghe for sake of me one !

My sommons er certified, and þow arte fulle servyde

The messenger
may depart as
soon as he
pleases.

444 Of cundit and credense, kayre whene the lykes :

I salle thi journaye engyste, enjoyne theme my selvene,

ffro this place to þe porte, there þou salle passe over ;

He must travel
to Sandwich in
seven days,

Sevene dayes to Sandewyche, sette at the large,

448 Sexty myle on a daye, þe somme es bott lyttille !

Thowe moste spede at the spurs, and spare noghte thi fole,

going by Wat-
ling-street,

Thowe weyndez by Watlyng-strette, and by no waye ells :

stopping at night
wherever he may
chance to be,
tying his horse
to a bush by the
bridle.

Thare thow nyghttes one nyghte, nedez moste þou lenge,

452 Be it foreste or felde, found þou no forthire ;

Bynde thy blonke by a buske with thy brydille evene,

Lugge þi-selfe undyre lynde, as þe leefe thynkes,

There awes none alyenes to ayere apponne nyghttys,

456 With syche a rebawdous rowtte to ryot thy selvene.

Thy lycence es lemete in presence of lordys,

Be now lathe or lette, ryghte as þe thynkes,

For bothe þi lyffe and thi lyme lygges þer-appone,

460 þofe syr Lucius had laide þe lordchipe of Rome ;

ffor be þow foundene a fute with-owte þe flode merkes,

Aftyr þe aughtende day, whene undroune es rungene,

þou salle be hevedede in hye, and with horsse drawene,

464 And seyne heyly be hangede, houndes to gnawene !

The rente ne rede golde, þat un-to Rome langes,

Salle y noghte redily renke, raunsone thyne one !"

"Sir," sais the senatour, "so Crist mot me helpe !

468 Might I with wirchip wynne awaye ones,

I sulde never fore emperour, þat on erthe lenges,

Ofte unto Arthure ayere one syche nedys ;

Bot I am sengilly here, with sex sum of knyghtes ;

472 I be-seke ȝow, syr, that we may sounde passe .

If any unlawefulle lede lette us by þe waye,

With-in thy lycence, lorde, thy loosse es enpeyrede."

"Care noghte," quod the kyng, "thy coundyte es knawene

476 ffro Carlelele to þe coste, there thy cogge lengges ;

þoghe thy cofers ware fulle, cramede with sylver,

Thow myghte be sekyre of my sele sexty myle forthire."

They enclined to þe kynge, and counge þay askede,

480 Cayers owtt of Carelele, catchez one theire horsez ;

Sir Cadore þe curtayes kende theme the wayes,

To Catrike þeme cunvayede, and to Crist þeme be-kennyde.

So þey spede at þe spoures, þey sprangene þeire horses,

484 Hyres þeme hakenayes hastyly þere aftyre ;

So fore reddour þey redene, and risted theme never,

Bot ȝif they luggede undire lynd, whills þeme lyghte failede ;

Bot evere þe senatour for-sothe soghte at þe gayneste,

488 By þe sevende day was gone þe cetee þai rechide ;

Of alle þe glee undire Gode so glade ware þey nevere,

As of þe sounde of þe see and Sandwyche belles !

(marginal notes)

If after the evening of the eighth day he is found in the country, he shall be hanged up for dogs to eat.

Then the Senator declares that if he can only get well away once, he would never again go on such an errand.

He prays that his retinue may be protected on their way.

Then Arthur tells him that if his coffers were crammed full of silver he would be safe with his passport.

Then did the Romans depart with all speed,

and never rested till they had reached Sandwich by the time prescribed.

Never were they as glad of any thing as of the sound of the sea and Sandwich bells.

Wythowttyne more stowuntynge they schippide þeire horsez,

492 Wery to þe wane see þey went alle att ones;

With þe mene of þe walle they weyde up þeire ankyrs,

They crossed the sea to Flanders, And flede at þe fore flude, in Flaundrez þey rowede,

And thorughe Flaundres þey founde, as þeme faire thoghte,[1]

496 Tille Akyne in Almayne, in Arthur landes;

and over Mount St. Gothard into Lombardy, Gosse by þe Mount Goddarde fulle grevous wayes,

And so in-to Lumberddye lykande to schewe;

through Tuscany to Rome. They turne thurghe Tuskayne, with towres fulle heghe,

500 In pris appairelles theme in precious wedez;

The sevondaye in suters þay suggourne þeire horsez,

And sekes þe Seyntez of Rome, be assente of knyghtes;

Then the Senator seeks an audience with the Emperor Lucius. Sythyne prekes to þe pales with portes so ryche,

504 Þare syr Lucius lenges with lordes enowe;

Lowttes to hym lufly, and lettres hym bedes

Of credence enclosyde, with knyghtlyche wordez.

Who asks eagerly for Arthur's answer, and on what ground he resists the power of Rome. Thene the emperour was egree, and enkerly fraynes

508 Þe answere of Arthure; he askes hyme sone

How he arayes þe rewme, and rewlys þe pople;

ȝif he be rebelle to Rome, whate ryghte þat he claymes :

His ambassador ought to have seized his sceptre and sat above him. Arthur, he says, ought himself to have served the Senator. Then answers the Senator, that Arthur is too great to do that for anyone. "Thow sulde his ceptre have sesede, and syttyne aboune,

512 ffor reverence and realtee of Rome þe noble :

By sertes þow was my sandes, and senatour of Rome,

He sulde fore solempnitee hafe servede þe hym selvene."

"That wille he never for no waye of alle þis werlde ryche,

516 Bot who may wynne hym of werre, by wyghtnesse of handes;[2]

Many fey schalle be fyrste appone þe felde levyde,

Are he appere in this place, profre whene þe likes :

I saye the syr Arthure es thyne enmye fore ever,

He claims no less than the Empire of Rome. 520 And ettelles to bee overlynge of þe empyre of Rome,

That alle his ancestres aughte, bot Utere hym-selfe.

---

[1] likyd written first in MS. but erased and thoghte written in margin by same hand.

[2] In the short romance of Arthur, the Senator is still more plain-spoken,
    "His worthiness, Sir Emperor,
    Passes much all youre."—l. 286.

Thy nedes this newe ȝere, I notifiede my-selfene,
   Be-fore þat noble of name *and* neyvesome of kynges;

524 In the moste reale place of þe rounde table,
   I somounde hyme solempnylye, one seeande his knyghtez;
   Sene I was formyde in faythe so ferde was I nevere,
   In alle þe placez ther I passede of pryncez in erthe!

528 I wolde fore-sake alle my suyte of segnoury of Rome,
   Or I efte to þat soveraygne whare sente one suyche nedes!
   He may be chosyne cheftayne, cheefe of alle oþer,
   Bathe be chauncez of armes and chevallrye noble,

532 ffor whyeseste *and* worthyeste, and wyghteste of haundez:
   Of alle the wyes þate I watte in this werlde ryche,
   The knyghtlyeste creatoure in Cristyndome haldene,
   Of kynge or of conquerour, crownede in erthe,

536 Of countenaunce of corage, of crewelle lates,
   The comlyeste of knyghtehode þat undyre Cryste lyffes!
   He maye be spokene in dyspens, despysere of sylvere,
   That no more of golde gyffes þane of grette stones,

540 No more of wyne þane of watyre, that of þe welle rynnys,
   Ne of welthe of þ[i]s werlde bot wyrchipe allone.
   Syche contenaunce was never knowene in no kythe ryche,
   As was with þat counquerour in his courte haldene;

544 I countede at this Crystynmesse, of kyngez enoynttede,
   Hole tene at his table, þat tyme with hyme selfene;
   He wylle werraye i-wysse, be-ware ȝif þe lykes,
   Wage many wyghtemene, and wache thy marches,

548 That they be redye in araye, and at areste foundyne;
   ffor ȝife he reche un-to Rome, he raunsouns it for evere!
   I rede þow dreste the þer-fore, and drawe no lytte langere,
   To sekyre of þi sowdeours, and send to þe mowntes;

552 Be þe quartere of this ȝere, and hym quarte staunde,
   He wylle wyghtlye in a qwhyle one his wayes hye."

"Bee Estyre," sais þe Emperour, "I ettylle my selfene,
   To hostaye in Almayne with armede knyghtez;

556 Sende freklye into Fraunce, þat flour es of rewmes,
   ffande to fette þat freke, and forfette his landez;

He tells the Emperor how he had delivered his message,

and that he was never so frightened since he was born.

Arthur is worthy to be king of men for his wisdom and valour.

He is the most famous knight in Christendom.

To him gold and silver are as nothing,

and wine no more than water.

Ten kings anointed feast at his table.

Good need is there of zealous preparation,

and that soldiers should be dispatched to the mountains forthwith.

"By Easter," says the Emperor, "I undertake to be in Germany with an army, and will send many giants and mighty men to meet him in the mountains.

ffor I salle sette kepers, fulle covaunde *and* noble,

Many geaunte of geene, justers fulle gude,

560 To mete hym in the mountes, *and* martyre hys knyghtes,

Stryke þeme doune in strates, and struye theme fore evere,

A post shall be occupied on Mount St. Goth-ard, with a beacon ready to light,

There salle appone Godarde a garette be rerede,

That schalle be garneschte *and* kepyde w*ith* gude mene of armes,

564 And a bekyne abovene to brynne whene þeme lykys,

Þat nane enmye w*ith* hoste salle entre the mountes ;

and another on Mount St. Ber-nard.

There schalle one mounte Bernarde be beyldede anoþere,

Buschede with banerettes and bachelers noble :

He shall not be suffered to enter Pavia."

568 In at the portes of Pavye schalle no prynce passe,

Thurghe the perelous places, for my pris knyghtes."

Then Lucius sends letters into the East,

Thane *syr* Lucius lordlyche le*tt*res he sendys

Onone in-to þe Oryente, with austeryne knyghtez,

572 Tille Ambyganye and Orcage, and Alysaundyre eke,

To Inde and to Ermonye, as Ewfrates rynnys,

To Asye, and to Affrike, and Ewrope þe large,

To Irritayne and Elamet, and alle þase owte ilez ;

576 To Arraby and Egipt, tille erles and oþer,

That any erthe ocupyes in þase Este marches ;

to demand aid of all the kings and lords Quickly they all came, for fear of his might.

Of Damaske and Damyat, and dukes and erles,

ffor drede of his daungere they dresside þeme sone ;

580 Of Crete and of Capados the honourable kyngys

Come at his commandmente, clenly at ones ;

To Tartary *and* Turky, whene tythynngez es comene,

They turne in by Thebay terauntez fulle hugge,

584 The flour of þe faire folke, of Amazonnes landes ;

All that failed were to forfeit their lands.

Alle thate ffaillez on þe folde be forfette fore evere !

Of Babyloyne and Baldake the burlyche knyghtes,

Bayous w*ith* þeire baronage bydez no langere ,

588 Of Perce and of Pamphile, and Preter Johnne landes,

Iche prynce w*ith* his powere appertlyche graythede ;

The Sowdane of Surrye assemblez his knyghtes,

ffra Nylus to Nazarethe, nommers fulle huge ;

592 To Garyere *and* to Galelé þey gedyre alle at ones ;

The Sowdanes that ware sekyre sowdeours to Rome,

They gadyrede over þe Grekkes see with grevous wapyns,

In theire grete galays, wyth gleterande scheldez ;

From all the East they came sailing across the Greek Sea in their mighty ships armed for war,

596 The kynge of Cyprys one þe see þe Sowdane habydes,

With alle the realles of Roodes, arayede with hyme one :

They sailede with a syde wynde ovre þe salte strandez :

Sodanly þe Sarezenes, as theme selfe lykede,

600 Craftyly at Cornett the kynges are aryesede,

ffra þe ceté of Rome sexti myle large :

and assembled at Civita, sixty miles from Rome.

Be that the Grekes ware graythede, a fulle gret nombyre,

The myghtyeste of Macedone, with mene of þa marches,

There were of Greeks a vast number, and men of Italy, with Saracens from many lands.

604 Pulle and Pruyslande presses with oþer,

The lege-mene of Lettow with legyons ynewe :

Thus they semble in sortes, summes fulle huge,

Sowdanes and Sarezenes owt of sere landes,

608 The Sowdane of Surry and sextene kynges,

At the cetes of Rome assemblede at ones.

Thane yschewes þe Emperour armede at ryghtys,

   Arayede with his Romaynes appone ryche stedys ;

Then goes forth the Emperor with his knights,

612 Sexty geauntes be-fore engenderide with fendez,

With weches and warlaws to wacchene his tentys ;

Ay-ware whare he wendes, wyntrez and ȝeres.

Myghte no blonkes theme bere, thos bustous churlles,

Sixty giants born of fiends, and witches and warlocks precede him.

616 Bot coverde camellez of toures, enclosyde in maylez ;

He ayerez oute with alyenez ostes fulle huge,

Ewyne in-to Almayne, þat Arthure hade wonnyne ;

Rydes in by þe ryvere, and ryottez hyme selvene,

Riding upon camels bearing towers,

620 And ayeres with a huge wylle alle þas hye landez ;

Alle Westwale of werre he wynnys as hym lykes,

Drawes in by Danuby, and dubbez hys knyghtez ;

In the contré of Colome castelles enseggez,

he marches into Germany, and lays it waste.

624 And suggeournez þat sesone wyth Sarazenes ynewe.

At the utas of Hillary, Syr Arthure hym-selvene

   In his kydde councelle commande þe lordes,—

" Kayere to ȝour cuntrez, and semble ȝour knyghtes,

628 And kepys me at Constantyne clenlyche arayede ;

Meanwhile Arthur commands his knights to gather their forces, and to be ready to meet him.

Byddez me at Gareflete apon*e* þa blythe stremes,
Baldly w*ith*-in borde w*ith* ȝowre beste beryns;
I schall*e* menskfully ȝowe mete in thos faire marches."

632 He sendez furthe sodaynly *ser*geantes of armes,

To all*e* hys mariners on rawe, to areste hym schippys;
Wyth-in sexten*e* dayes hys fleet whas assemblede,
At Sandewyche on þe see, saile when*e* hym lykes.

636 In the palcz of ȝorke a *per*lement he haldez,
W*ith* all*e* þe perez of þe rewme, prélates and oþer;
And aftyre þe prechynge in *pre*sence of lordes,
The kyng in his concell*e* carpys þes wordes,—

640 " I am in p*ur*pos to passe p*er*ilou*s* wayes,
To kaire w*ith* my kene men*e*, to conquere ȝone landes,
To owttraye myn*e* enmy, ȝif aventure it schewe,
That ocupyes myn*e* heritage, þe empyre of Rome.

644 I sett ȝow here a sov*er*aynge, ascente ȝif ȝowe lykys,
That es me sybb, my syst*er* sone, Sir Mordrede hym selven*e*,
Salle be my levetenante, w*ith* lordchipez ynewe,
Of all*e* my lele lege-men*e*, þat my landez ȝemes."

648 He ca*r*pes till*e* his cosyne þane, in cou*n*saile hym selven*e*,—
" I make the kepare, s*yr* knyghte, of kyngrykes manye,
Wardayne wyrchipfull*e*, to weilde al my landes,
That I have wonnen*e* of werre, in all*e* þis werlde ryche;

652 I wyll þat Waynou*r*, my weife, in wyrchipe be holden*e*,
That hire waunte noo wele, ne welthe þat hire lykes;
Luke my kydde castells be clenlyche arrayede,

There cho maye suggou*r*ne hire-selfe, wyth semlyche
berynes.

656 ffaunde my fforestez be ffrythede, o frenchepe for ev*er*e,

That nane werreye my wylde, botte Waynou*r* hir selven*e*,
And þat in þe sesone whene grees es assignyde,
That cho take hir solauce in certayne tyms

660 Chauncelere and chambyrleyn*e* chaunge as þe lykes,

Audyto*ur*s and offycers ordayne thy selven*e*,—
Bathe jureez, and juggez, and justicez of landes,
Luke thow justyfye them*e* wele that injurye wyrkes:

664 If me be destaynede to dye at Dryghtyns wylle,

I charge the my sektour, cheffe of alle oþer,

To mynystre my mobles, fore mede of my saule,

To mendynnantez and mysese in myschefe fallene:

668 Take here my testament of tresoure fulle-huge,

As I trayste appone the, be traye thowe me never!

As þow wille answere be-fore the austeryne jugge,

That alle þis werlde wynly wysse as hyme lykes,

672 Luke þat my laste wylle be lelely perfourmede!

Thow has clenly þe cure that to my coroune langez,

Of alle my werdez wele, and my weyffe eke;

Luke þowe kepe the so clere, there be no cause fondene,

676 Whene I to contré come, if Cryste wille it thole,

And thow have grace gudly to governe thy selvene,

I salle coroune þe knyghte kyng with my handez."

Than[1] syr Modrede fulle myldly meles hym selvene,

680 Knelyd to þe conquerour, and carpes þise wordez,—

"I be-seke ȝow, syr, as my sybbe lorde,

þat ȝe wille for charyté cheese ȝow anoþer;

ffor if ȝe putte me in þis plytte, ȝowre pople es dyssavyde;

684 To presente a prynce astate my powere es symple:

Whene oþer of werre wysse are wyrchipide here-aftyre,

Thane may I forsothe be sette bott at lyttille.

To passe in ȝour presance my purpos es takyne,

688 And alle my purveaunce apperte fore my pris knyghtez."

"Thowe arte my nevewe fulle nere, my nurree of olde,

That I have chastyede and chosene, a childe of my chambyre;

ffor the sybredyne of me, fore-sake noghte þis offyce

692 That thow ne wyrk my wille, thow whatte watte it menes."

Nowe he takez hys leve, and lengez no langere,

At lordez, at lege-mene, þat leves hyme byhyndene.

And seyne þat worthilyche wy went un-to chambyre,

696 ffor to comfurthe þe qwene, þat in care lenges;

Waynour waykly wepande hym kyssiz,

Talkez to hym tenderly with teres ynewe,—

"I may wery the wye, that this werre movede,

Marginal notes:

If Arthur dies Mordred is succeed him.

He bids him be faithful to his trust,

and promises to crown him king if he remain so

[1 Yan in MS.]

But Mordred desires to be excused,

and would rather go to the war.

But Arthur bade him, as his nearest of kin, to undertake the office.

Then Arthur takes leave of his Queen.

Guinever laments his departure,

700 That warnes me wyrchippe of my wedde lorde;
Alle my lykynge of lyfe owte of lande wendez,
And I in langour am lefte, leve ȝe for evere!

and would rather
die in his arms.
Schyne myghte I, dere lufe, dye in ȝour armes,

704 Are I þis destanye of dule sulde drye by myne one!"

But Arthur bids
her not to grieve,
"Grefe þe noghte, Gaynour, fore Goddes lufe of hewene,
Ne gruche noghte my ganggynge, it salle to gude turne!
Thy wonrydez and thy wepynge woundez myne herte,

708 I may noghte wit of þis woo, for alle þis werlde ryche;
I have made a kepare, a knyghte of thyne awene,

and tells her that
he has made Mor-
dred, a knight
of her own, his
deputy.
Overlynge of Ynglande undyre thy selvene,
And that es syr Mordrede, þat þow has mekylle praysede,

712 Salle be thy dictour, my dere, to doo whatte the lykes."

Then he kisses
the ladies, and
takes leave of
them.
Thane he takes hys leve at ladys in chambyre,
Kysside them kyndlyche, and to Criste be-teches;

But Guinever
swooned when
he asked for his
sword.
And then cho swounes fulle swythe, whe[n] he hys
    swerde aschede,

716 Twys in a swounyng, swette as cho walde!

The king then
departs hastily
with his knights.
He pressed to his palfray, in presance of lordes,
Prekys of the palez with his prys knyghtes,
Wyth a realle rowte of þe rounde table;

720 Soughte to-warde Sandewyche, cho sees hyme no more!
Thare the grete ware gederyde, wyth galyarde knyghtes,

At Sandwich all
the lords and
their followers
assemble.
Garneschit over þe grene felde and graythelyche arayede;
Dukkes and duzseperes daynttehely rydes,

724 Erlez of Ynglande with archers ynewe:
Schirreves scharply schiftys the comouns,
Rewlys be-fore þe ryche of the rounde table,
Assignez ilke a contree to certayne lordes,

728 In the southe one þe see banke saile whene þeme lykes

Horses, arms,
tents, clothing,
and provisions
are shipped.
Thane bargez theme buskez, and to þe baunke rowes,
Bryngez blonkez one bourde, and burlyche helmes;
Trussez in tristly trappyde stedes,

732 Tentez and othire toylez, and targez fulle ryche,
Cabanes and clathe sokkes, and coferez fulle noble,
Hukes and haknays, and horsez of armez;

Thus they stowe in*e* the stuffe of fulle steryne knyghtez.

736 Qwen*e* alle was schyppede that scholde, they schounte
no lengere,

Bot ventelde theme tyte, as þe tyde rynnez;

Coggez and crayers, þan crossez þaire mastez,

At the commandment of þe kynge, uncoverde at ones.

740 Wyghtly on*e* þe wale thay wy*e* up þaire ankers,

By wytt of þe watyre men*e* of þe wale ythez,

ffrekes on*e* þe forestayne, fakene þei*r*e coblez,

In floynes and fercestez, and Flemesche schyppes,

744 Tytt saillez to þe toppe, and *t*urnez the lufe,

Standez appone stere-bourde, sterynly þay songen*e*,

The pryce schippez of the porte proven*e* theire depnesse,

And fondez wyth fulle saile ower the faw*e* ythez;

748 Holly wi*t*h-owttyne harme þay hale in bottes,

Schipe-men*e* scharply schotene þaire portez,

Launchez lede apon*e* lufe, lacchene þer depez,

Lukkes to þe lade-sterne when*e* þe lyghte faillez;

752 Castez coursez be crafte, when*e* þe clowde rysez,

Wi*t*h þe nedylle and þe stone one þe nyghte tydez;

For drede of þe derke nyghte þay drecchede a lyttille,

And all*e* þe steryne of þe streme strekyne at onez:

756 The kynge was in a gret cogge, wi*t*h knyghtez fulle many,

In a cabane enclosede, clenlyche arayede;

Wi*t*h-in on a ryche bedde rystys a lyttylle,

And wi*t*h þe swoghe of þe see in swefnynge he fell*e*.

760 Hym dremyd of a dragon*e*, dredfulle to beholde,

Come dryfande on*e* þe depe to drenschen*e* hys pople,

Ewen*e* walkande owte of the Weste landez,

Wanderande unworthyly overe the wale ythez;

764 Bothe his hede and hys hals ware halely all*e* ov*er*

Cundyde of azure, enamelde fulle faire:

His sceulders ware schalyde all*e* in clene sylver*e*,

Schreede ov*er* all*e* þe schrympe wi*t*h schrinkande poyntez;

768 Hys wombe and hys wenges of wondyrfulle hewes,

In m*er*vaylo*us* maylys he moun*t*ede full*e* hye;

Margin notes:

Then the ships at the word of command cross their yards,

weigh their anchors,

the well-skilled sailors hoist the sails and steer the vessels.

Then they haul in the boats, shut the ports, heave the lead, look well to the guiding star, and skilfully shape their course by the compass.

After a little delay on account of darkness, they all sail at once.

The king is in a large vessel with many knights,

Reposing himself in his cabin, he falls asleep,

and dreams of a dreadful dragon

His head and neck were blue;

his shoulders covered with silver scales;

his belly and wings of various hues;

Whayme þat he towchede he was tynt for euer!

his feet were black, and out of his mouth there came flame. 772 Hys feete ware floreschede alle in fyne sabylle,
And syche a vennymous flayre flowe fro his lyppez,
That the flode of þe flawez alle one fyre semyde!

Then there came against the dragon a fierce black bear, Thane come of þe oryente, ewyne hyme agaynez,
A blake bustous bere abwene in the clowdes,

776 With yche a pawe as a poste, and paumes fulle huge,

with huge paws and crooked tusks, With pykes fulle perilous, alle plyande þame semyde,
Lothene and lothely, lokkes and oþer,

mis-shapen legs, and foaming lips. Alle with lutterde legges, lokerde unfaire ;

780 Filtyrde unfrely wyth fomaunde lyppez,
The foulleste of fegure that fourmede was ever!

He came capering and mocking, He baltyrde, he bleryde, he braundyschte þer-after ;
To bataile he bounez hym with bustous clowez :

roaring and raging for the strife. 784 He romede, he rarede, that roggede alle þe erthe !
So ruydly he rappyd at to ryot hym selvene !

Then the dragon assailed him, fighting like a falcon with beak and claws. Thane the dragone on dreghe dressede hyme aȝaynez,
And with hys duttez hym drafe one dreghe by þe walkyne :

788 He fares as a fawcone, frekly he strykez ;
Bothe with feete and with fyre he feghttys at ones !
The bere in the bataile þe bygger hym semyde,

The bear butts him with his tusks and causes the blood to flow. And byttes hyme boldlye wyth balefulle tuskez ;
792 Syche buffetez he hym rechez with hys brode klokes,
Hys brest and hys brathelle was blodye alle over !
He rawmpyde so ruydly that alle þe erthe ryfez,
Rynnande one reede blode as rayne of the hevene !

He had killed the dragon but for the fire which he breathes. 796 He hade wereyde the worme by wyghtnesse of strenghte,
Ne ware it fore þe wylde fyre þat he hyme wyth defendez :
Thane wandyrs þe worme awaye to hys heghttez,

Then the dragon flies aloft, and comes swooping down, Comes glydande fro þe clowddez, and cowpez fulle evene ;
800 Towchez hym wyth his talonnez, and terez hys rigge,

tearing a vast rent in the back of the bear, Be-twyx þe taile and the toppe tene fote large !
Thus he brittenyd the bere, and broghte hyme olyfe,

and carrying him off in his claws, lets him drop into the water. Lette hyme falle in the flode, fleete whare hyme lykes :
804 So they bryng þe bolde kyng bynne þe schippe burde,
þat nere he bristez for bale, one bede whare he lyggez.

Thane waknez the wyese kynge, wery fore-travaillede,
Takes hyme two phylozophirs, that folowede hyme ever,
808 In the sevyne scyence the suteleste fondene,
The cony[n]geste of clergye undyre Criste knowene;
He tolde þeme of hys tourmente, þat tyme þat he slepede,
"Drechede with a dragone, and syche a derfe beste,
812 Has mad me fulle wery; ȝe telle me my swefene,
Ore I mone swelte as swythe, as wysse me oure Lorde!"
"Sir," saide þey sone thane, thies sagge philosopherse,
"The dragone þat þow dremyde of, so dredfulle to schewe,
816 That come dryfande over þe deepe, to drynchene thy pople,
Sothely and certayne thy selvene it es,
That thus saillez over þe see with thy sekyre knyghtez:
The colurez þat ware castyne appone his clere wengez,
820 May be thy kyngrykez alle, that thow has ryghte wonnyne;
And the tachesesede taile, with tonges so huge,
Be-takyns þis faire folke, that in thy fleet wendez.
The bere that bryttenede was abowene in þe clowdez,
824 Betakyns the tyrauntez þat tourmentez thy pople;
Or elles with some gyaunt some journee salle happyne,
In syngulere batelle by ȝoure selfe one;
And þow salle hafe þe victorye thurghe helpe of oure Lorde,
828 As þow in thy visione was opynly schewede!
Of this dredfulle dreme ne drede the no more,
Ne kare noghte, syr conquerour, bot comforth thy selvene;
And thise þat saillez over þe see, with thy sekyre knyghtez."
832 With trumppez thene trystly, they trisene upe þaire saillez,
And rowes over the ryche see, this rowtte alle at onez;
The comely coste of Normandye they cachene fulle evene,
And blythely at Barflete theis bolde are arryfede,
836 And fyndys a flete there of frendez ynewe,
The floure and þe faire folke of fyftene rewmez;
ffore kyngez and capytaynez kepyde hyme fayre,
As he at Carelele commaundede at Cristymesse hym selvene.
840 Be they had takene the lande, and tentez upe rerede,
Comez a templere tyte, and towchide to þe kynge—

(marginal notes) Then Arthur awaking was troubled at the dream, and sends for his two philosophers, men very learned in the seven sciences. These wise men tell him that by the dragon is meant himself and his knights. The bear signifies the tyrants who torment his people, or else some giant whom Arthur is destined to overthrow in battle. Arthur is exhorted to be of good courage. They speed on their way, and arrive on the coast of Normandy. At Barflete they find a fleet of friends, the flower of fifteen realms. When they had disembarked and pitched their tents, a Templar

comes to the king,
"Here es a teraunt be-syde that tourmentez thi pople,

and tells him of a ferocious giant who feeds upon men and children,
A grett geaunte of geene, engenderde of fendez;

844 He has fretyne of folke mo thane fyfe hondrethe,

And als fele fawntekyns of freeborne childyre!

This has bene his sustynaunce alle this sevene wynttere,

And ȝut es that sotte noghte sade, so wele hyme it lykez!

848 In þe contree of Constantyne no kynde has he levede,

With-owttyne kydd castelles enclosid wyth walles,

That he ne has clenly distroyede alle the knave childyre,

And theme caryede to þe cragge, and clenly deworyde!

who had that day captured the Duchess of Brittany, and carried her to his den.
852 The duchez of Bretayne to daye has he takyne,[1]

Beside Reynes as scho rade with hire ryche knyghttes;

Ledd hyre to the mountayne, thare þat lede lengez,

To lye by that lady, aye whyls his lyfe lastez.

856 We folowede o ferrome moo thene fyfe hundrethe,

Of beryns, and of burgeys, and bachelers noble,

Bot he coverde the cragge; cho cryede so lowde,

The care of þat creatoure cover salle I never!

She was the flower of all France, and the fairest lady on earth,
860 Scho was flour of alle Fraunce, or of fyfe rewmes,

And one of the fayreste that fourmede was evere,

The gentileste jowelle a-juggede with lordes,

ffro Geene unto Gerone, by Jhesu of hevene!

cousin of Arthur's Queen.
864 Scho was thy wyfes cosyne, knowe it if þe lykez,

Commene of þe rycheste, that regnez in erthe:

As thow arte ryghtwise kynge rewe on thy pople,

Then Sir Arthur bitterly laments her fate,
And fande for to venge theme, that thus are rebuykyde!"

868 "Allas!" said syr Arthure, "so lange have I lyffede,

Hade I wytene of this, wele had me chefede;

Me es noghte fallene faire, bot me es foule happynede,

That thus this faire ladye this fende has dystroyede!

872 I had levere thane alle Fraunce, this fyftene wynter

and wishes he had been there to aid her.
I hade bene be-fore thate freke, a furlange of wayc,

Whene he that ladye had laghte and ledde to þe montez:

I hadde lefte my lyfe arc cho hade harme lymppyde!

---

[1] In the short romance of Arthur this unfortunate lady is described as fair Elaine, cousin to King Hoel.

876 Bot walde þow kene me to þe crage, thare þat kene lengez. *He desires to know where the giant lives,*

I walde cayre to þat coste, and carpe wythe hyme-selvene,

To trete with that tyraunt fore tresone of londes,

And take trewe for a tyme, tille it may tyde bettyre."

880 "Sire, see ȝe ȝone farlande, with ȝone twa-fyrez, *and is directed by the Templar how to find his abode,*

þar filsuez þat fonde, fraist whene the lykes?

Appone the creste of the cragge, by a colde welle,

That enclosez þe clyfe with þe clere strandez,

884 Ther may thow fynde folke fay wyth-owttyne nowmer, *where there are many captives,*

Mo florenez in faythe thane Fraunce es in aftyre;

And more tresour untrewely that traytour has getyne, *and vast treasure stored up.*

Thane in Troye was as I trowe, þat tyme þat it was wonne."

888 Thane romyez the ryche kynge for rewthe of þe pople, *Then Arthur is greatly excited,*

Raykez ryghte to a tente, and restez no lengere!

He welterys, he wristeles, he wryngez hys handez!

Thare was no wy of þis werlde, þat wyste whatt he menede!

892 He calles *syr* Cayous þat of þe cowpe serfede, *and bids Sir Cayous and Sir Bedevere attend him at evening,*

And *syr* Bedvere þe bolde, þat bare hys brande ryche,—

"Luke ȝe aftyre evensange be armyde at-ryghttez,

On blonkez by ȝone buscayle, by ȝone blythe stremez,

896 ffore I wille passe in pilgremage prevely here aftyre,

In the tyme of suppere, whene lordez are servede,

ffor to sekene a saynte be ȝone salte stremes, *pretending that he is going on a pilgrimage.*

In Seynt Mighelle mount, there myraclez are schewede."

900 Aftyre evesange, Sir Arthure hyme-se[l]fene

Wente to hys wardrope, and warpe of hys wedez; *Then Arthur proceeds to dress and arm himself,*

Armede hym in a actone with orfraeez fulle ryche,

Abovene one þat a jeryne of Acres owte over,

904 Abovene þat a jesseraunt of jentylle maylez,

A jupone of Jerodyne jaggede in schredez;

He brayedez one a bacenett burneschte of sylver,

The beste þat was in Basille, wyth bordurs ryche;

908 The creste and þe coronalle, enclosed so faire

Wyth clasppis of clere golde, couched wyth stones;

The vesare, þe aventaile, enarmede so faire,

Voyde with-owttyne vice, with wyndowes of sylver;

912 His gloves gaylyche gilte, and gravene at þe hemmez,
With grayvez and gobelets, glorious of hewe;
He bracez a brade schelde, and his brande aschez,

and mounting a
brown steed, rides
to the spot where
his knights await
him.

Bounede hyme a broune stede, and one þe bente hovys;
916 He sterte tille his sterepe and stridez one lofte,
Streynez hyme stowttly, and sterys hyme faire,
Brochez þe baye stede, and to þe buske rydez,
And there hys knyghtes hyme kepede fulle clenlyche
arayede:

920 Thane they roode by þat ryver, þat rynnyd so swythe,

There was a grove
by the side of the
river full of game
and decked with
flowers.

Þare þe ryndez overrechez with realle bowghez;
The roo and þe rayne-dere reklesse thare rounene,
In ranez and in rosers to ryotte þame selvene;
924 The frithez ware floreschte with flourez fulle many,
Wyth fawcouns and fesantez of ferlyche hewez;
All þe feulez thare fleschez, that flyez with wengez,

Here all birds
abounded,

ffore thare galede þe gowke one grevez fulle lowde,
928 Wyth alkyne gladchipe þay gladdene þeme selvene:

and nightingales
in vast numbers
made sweet mu-
sic.

Of þe nyghtgale notez þe noisez was swette,
They threpide wyth the throstills thre-hundreth at ones!
Þat whate swowynge of watyr, and syngynge of byrdez,
932 It myghte salve hyme of sore, that sounde was nevere!
Thane ferkez this folke, and one fotte lyghttez,

Here they leave
their horses, and
the king bids his
knights to await
his return.

ffestenez theire faire stedez o ferrome by-twene;
And thene the kynge kenely comandyde hys knyghtez
936 ffor to byde with theire blonkez, and bowne no forthyre,—
"ffore I wille soke this seynte by my-selfe one,
And melle with this mayster mane, þat this monte ȝemez;
And seyne salle ȝe offyre, aythyre aftyre oþer,
940 Menskfully at Saynt Mighelle fulle myghty with Criste!"

The king alone
ascends the
mountain,

The kyng coveris þe cragge wyth cloughes fulle hye,
To the creste of the clyffe he clymbez one lofte;
Keste upe hys umbrere, and kenly he lukes,
944 Caughte of þe colde wynde to comforthe hym selvene;
Two fyrez he fyndez fflawmande fulle hye,
The fourtedele a furlange be-twene þis he walkes;

þe waye by þe welle strandez he wandyrde hym one,

948 To wette of þe warlawe, whare þat he lengez;

He ferkez to þe fyrste fyre, and evene there he fyndez

A wery wafulle wedowe, wryngande hire handez,

And gretande on a grave grysely teres,   ˙.

and going to a fire which he sees he finds a woeful widow wringing her hands.

952 Now merkyde one molde, sene myddaye it semede .

He saluʒede þat sorowfulle wıth sittande wordez,

And fraynez aftyre the fende fairely there aftyre :

Thane this wafulle wyfe un-wynly hym gretez,

He asks her concerning the giant.

956 Coverde up on hire kneess, and clappyde hir handez;

Said, "carefulle caremane, thow carpez to lowde !

May ʒone warlawe wyt, he worows us alle !

Weryd worthe þe wyghte ay, that þe thy wytt refede,

960 That mase the to wayfe here in þise wylde lakes !

I warne þe fore wyrchipe, þou wylnez aftyr sorowe !

Whedire buskes þou berne ? unblysside þow semes !

Wenez thow to brittene hyme wıth thy brande ryche ?

She answers with terror, and warns him that he cannot hope to contend with so terrible a monster

964 Ware thow wyghttere thane Wade or Wawayne owthire,

Thow wynnys no wyrchipe, I warne the be-fore !

Thow saynned the unsekyrly to seke to þese mountez,

Siche sex ware to symple to semble wıth hyme one ;

968 ffor and thow see hyme wıth syghte, the servez no herte,

To sayne the sekerly, so semez hym huge !

Thow arte frely and faire, and in thy fyrste flourez,

Bot thow arte fay be my faythe, and þat me for-thynkkys !

972 Ware syche fyfty one a felde, or one a faire erthe,

The freke walde wıth hys fyste felle ʒow at ones !

Loo ! here, the duchez dere, to daye was cho takyne,

Depe dolvene and dede dyked in moldez ;

Fifty such as Arthur he could fell with his fist.

976 He hade morthirede this mylde be myddaye war rongene,

Wıth-owttyne mercy one molde, not watte it ment :

He has forsede hir and fylede, and cho es fay levede ;

He slewe hir un-slely, and slitt hir to þe navylle !

The poor Duchess had been ravished and murdered by him, and the doleful widow, her foster-mother, had buried her.

980 And here have I bawmede hir, and beryede þer aftyr,

ffor bale of þe botelesse, blythe be I never !

Of alle þe frendrez cho hade, þere folowede none aftyre,

and would remain
there till death to
bewail her.

Bot I hir foster modyr of fyftene wynter!

984 To ferke of this farlande, fande salle I never,

Bot here be foundene on felde, tille I be fay levede!"

Thane answers syr Arthure to þat alde wyf;

Then Arthur says
that he comes
from the great
King Arthur on
a mission to
treat with the
giant.

"I am comyne fra the conquerour, curtaise and gentille,

988 As one of þe hathelest of Arthur knyghtez,

Messenger to þis myx, for mendemente of þe pople,

To mele with this maister mane, that here this mounte
ȝemez;

To trete with this tyraunt for tresour of landez,

992 And take trew for a tyme, to bettyr may worthe."

The old wife tells
him that he cares
nothing for laws
or treaties, that
he regards not
gold or treasure;

"ȝa, thire wordis are bot waste," quod this wif thane,

"ffor bothe landez and lythes ffulle lyttille by he settes;

Of rentez ne of rede golde rekkez he never,

996 ffor he wille lenge owt of lawe, as hym-selfe thynkes,

With-owtene licence of lede, as lorde in his awene;

only he has a
famous kyrtle co-
vered with hair,

Bot he has a kyrtille one, kepide for hyme selvene,

That was sponene in Spayne with specyalle byrdez,

1000 And sythyne garncscht in Grece fulle graythly to-gedirs,

That es hydede alle with hare hally al overe,

which is bordered
with the beards
of mighty kings,

And bordyrde with the berdez of burlyche kyngez,

Crispid and kombide, that kempis may knawe

1004 I the kynge by his colour, in kythe there he lengez;

Here the fermez he fangez of fyftene rewmez,

which are sent
to him on each
Easter-eve.

ffor ilke Esterne ewyne, how-ever that it falle;

They send it hyme sothely for saughte of þe pople,

1008 Sekerly at þat sesone with certayne knyghtez,

And he has aschede Arthure alle þis sevene wynter.

He has long
wished for the
beard of Arthur,
and tried to force
the Breton kings
to get it for him.

fforthy hurdez he here, to owttraye hys pople,

Tille þe Bretones kynges have burneschte his lyppys,

1012 And sent his berde to that bolde wyth his beste berynes;

Bot thowe hafe broghte þat berde, bowne the no forthire,

ffor it es butelesse bale, thowe biddez oghte elles;

ffor he has more tresour to take whene hyme lykez,

1016 Than evere aughte Arthure, or any of hys elders;

If he has brought
the beard, he may

If thowe hase broghte þe berde, he bese more blythe

Thane þowe gafe hym Burgoyne, or Bretayne þe more ;

Bot luke nowe for charitee, þow chasty thy lyppes,

1020 That the no wordez eschape, whate so be-tydez ;

Luke þat presante be priste, and presse hym bott lytille,

ffor he es at his sowper, he wille be sone grevyde ;

And þow my concelle doo, þow doffe of thy clothes,

1024 And knele in thy kyrtylle, and calle hym thy lorde ;

He sowppes alle þis sesone with sevene knave childre,

Choppid in a chargour of chalke whytt sylver,

With pekille and powdyre of precious spycez,

1028 And pyment fulle plentevous of Portyngale wynes ;

Thre balefulle birdez his brochez þey turne,

That byddez his bedgatt, his byddynge to wyrche ;

Siche foure scholde be fay with-in foure hourez,

1032 Are his fylth ware filled, that his flesch ȝernes."

"ȝa, I have broghte þe berd," quod he, "the bettyre me
    lykez ;

ffor-thi wille I boune me, and bere it my selvene ;

Bot lefe walde þow lere me whare þat lede lengez,

1036 I salle alowe þe and I liffe, oure Lorde so me helpe !"

"fferke fast to þe fyre," quod cho, "that flawmez so hye ;

Thare fillis þat fende hyme, fraist whene the lykez ;

Bot thow moste seke more southe, syddynges a lyttille,

1040 ffor he wille hafe sent hym-selfe sex myle large."

To þe sowre of þe reke he soghte at þe gayneste,

Sayned hyme sekerly with certayne wordez,

And sydlynges of þe segge the syghte had he rechide,

1044 How un-semly þat sott satt sowpande hym one ;

He lay levand one lange, bugande un-faire,

þe thee of a mans lymme lyfte up by þe haunche ;

His bakke and his bewschers, and his brode lendez,

1048 He bekez by þe bale fyre, and breklesse hyme semede ;

þare ware rostez fulle ruyde, and rewfulle bredez,

Beerynes and bestaile brochede to-geders ;

Cowle-fulle cramede of crysinede childyre,

1052 Sum as brede brochede, and bierdez þame tournede.

[Side notes:]

be sure of a hearty welcome.

But he must approach him with due caution,

and had better doff his clothes and kneel to him.

His supper at this season is composed of seven male children chopped up with pickles and condiments.

Three savage birds act as turn-spits for him.

"Yes," says Arthur, "I have indeed brought this beard ; but show me where I shall find him."

Then she directs him to approach the great fire.

Arthur goes to the fire, and finds the giant lying extended with his back to the fire, picking the thigh of a man.

Roasts of the flesh of children and cattle were spitted together, being prepared for him in various ways

Then Arthur's heart bleeds for the woes inflicted by this wretch.

And þane this comlych kynge, by-cause of his pople,

His herte bledez for bale, one bent ware he standez!

He fastens on his shield and brandishes his bright sword,

Thane he dressede one his schelde, schuntes no lengere,

1056 Braundesche his brighte swerde by þe bryghte hiltez,

Raykez to-warde þe renke reghte with a ruyde wille,

and right boldly addresses the giant.

And hyely hailsez þat hulke with hawtayne wordez,—

" Now, alle-weldand Gode, þat wyrscheppez us alle,

1060 Giff the sorowe and syte, sotte there thow lygges,

He upbraids him with his vile crimes and his unclean meat.

ffor the fulsomeste freke that fourmede was evere!

ffoully thow fedys the, þe fende have thi saule!

Here es cury un-clene, carle, be my trowthe,

1064 Caffe of creatours alle, thow curssede wriche !

For his horrible murders of christian children,

Be-cause that þow killide has þise cresmede childyre,

Thow has marters made, and broghte oute of lyfe,

þat here are brochede one bente, and brittenede with thi handez,

1068 I salle merke þe thy mede, as þou has myche serfed,

he would now take vengeance on him, by the aid of St. Michael, and give his soul to the devil.

Thurghe myghte of Seynt Mighelle, þat þis monte 3emes !

And for this faire ladye, þat þow has fey levyde,

And þus forced one foulde, for fylth of þi-selfene !

1072 Dresse the now, dogge, sone, the develle have þi saule !

ffor þow salle dye this day, thurghe dynt of my handez!''

Then the giant stared with amazement, and gnashed his teeth with fury.

Thane glopnede þe glotone and glorede un-faire ;

He grevede as a grewhounde, with grysly tuskes ;

1076 He gapede, he groned faste, with grucchande latez,

ffor grefe of þe gude kyng, þat hyme with grame gretez !

His fax and his foretoppe was filterede to-geders,

Out of his mouth there came smoke, which covered all his face.

And owte of his face fome ane halfe fote large ;

1080 His frount and his forhevede alle was it over,

As þe felle of a froske, and fraknede it semede,

He was hook-nosed like a hawk, with hair up to his eyes, and beetle brows.

Huke-nebbyde as a hawke, and a hore berde,

And herede to þe hole eyghne with hyngande browes ;

1084 Harske as a hunde-fisch, hardly who so lukez,

His skin was hard as that of a dog-fish ; his ears huge and ugly ; his eyes horrible and burning.

So was þe hyde of þat hulke hally al over !

Erne had he fulle huge, and ugly to schewe,

With eghne fulle horreble, and ardaunt for sothe ;

1088 fflatt mowthede as a fluke, with fleryande lyppys,
　　 And þe flesche in his fortethe fowly as a bere :
　　 His berde was brothy and blake, þat tille his brest rechede,
　　 Grassede as a mereswyne with corkes fulle huge,
1092 And alle falterde þe flesche in his foule lyppys,
　　 Ilke wrethe as a wolfe-hevede, it wraythe owtt at ones !
　　 Bullenekkyde was þat bierne, and brade in the scholders,
　　 Brok-brestede as a brawne, with brustils fulle large,
1096 Ruyd armes as an ake with rusclede sydes,
　　 Lyme and leskes fulle lothyne, leve ȝe for sothe :
　　 Schovelle-fotede was þat schalke, and schaylande hyme
　　　　 semyde,
　　 With schankez unschaply, schowande to-gedyrs ;
1100 Thykke theefe as a thursse, and thikkere in the hanche,
　　 Greesse growene as a galte, fulle grylych he lukez !
　　 Who þe lenghe of þe lede lelly accountes,
　　 ffro þe face to þe fote, was fyfe fadome lange !
1104 Thane stertez he up sturdely one two styffe schankez,
　　 And sone he caughte hyme a clubb alle of clene yryne !
　　 He walde hafe kyllede þe kyng with his kene wapene,
　　 Bot thurghe þe crafte of Cryste ȝit þe carle failede ;
1108 The creest and þe coronalle, þe claspes of sylver,
　　 Clenly with his clubb he crasschede doune at onez !
　　 The kyng castes up his schelde, and covers hym faire,
　　 And with his burlyche brande a box he hyme reches ;
1112 ffulle butt in þe frunt the fromonde he hittez,
　　 That the burnyscht blade to þe brayne rynnez ;
　　 He feyed his fysnamye with his foule hondez,
　　 And frappez faste at hys face fersely þer-aftyr !
1116 The kyng chaungez his fote, eschewes a lyttille,
　　 Ne had he eschapede þat choppe, chevede had evylle ;
　　 He folowes in fersly, and festonesse a dynte
　　 Hye upe one the haunche, with his harde wapyne,
1120 That he hillid the swerde halfe a fote large ;
　　 The hott blode of þe hulke un-to the hilte rynnez,
　　 Ewyne into inmette the gyaunt he hyttez,

Flat-mouthed, with grinning lips, and jaws like a bear. A black beard reached to his breast, with mighty bristles. The flesh of his lips was in uneven folds, each fold, like an outlaw, twisted itself out. He was bull-necked and broad in the shoulders ; breasted like a boar, with huge bristles, his arms like an oak ; his limbs and flanks loathly ; shovel-footed and scaly, with unshapely shanks, of gigantic thickness in his haunches. Fat as a pig, he looks horrible.

In height, full five fathoms.

Up starts this fell giant, and seizing an iron club, aims a blow at Arthur.

The king catches it on his shield, and returns the blow with his sword right upon the forehead. The bright blade pierces to the brain. The giant tears his face with his hands, and strikes fiercely at the king. Arthur draws back,

and then drives his sword into the giant's haunch.

Just to þe genitales, and jaggede þame in sondre!

The monster roars and strikes at random. So mighty is his stroke, that it penetrates a sword's length into the ground. The king nearly swoons at the noise of the blow, but quickly striking him, bursts asunder his groin. His entrails and blood gush out. Then throwing away his club, the giant seizes Arthur in his arms.

1124 Thane he romyede and rarede, and ruydly he strykez
ffulle egerly at Arthur, and one the erthe hittez
A swerde lenghe with-in the swarthe, he swappez at ones,
That nere swounes þe kyng for swoughe of his dynttez!

1128 Bot ʒit the kynge swoperly fulle swythe he byswenkez,
Swappez in with the swerde þat it þe swange brystedd;
Bothe þe guttez and the gorre guschez owte at ones,
Þat alle englaymez þe gresse, one grounde þer he standez!

1132 Thane he castez the clubb, and the kynge hentez,
On þe creeste of þe cragg he caughte hyme in armez,
And enclosez hyme clenly, to crusehene hys rybbez;
So harde haldez he þat hende, that nere his herte brystez!

1136 Þane þe balefulle bierdez bownez to þe erthe,
Knelande and cryande, and clappide þeire handez,—

The baleful birds pray for the success of Arthur.

"Crist comforthe ʒone knyghte, and kepe hym fro sorowe,
And latte never ʒone fende felle hyme olyfe!"

1140 Ʒitt es þe warlow so wyghte, he welters hyme undere,

They have a fearful wrestling match, and fall from the top of the cliff down to the shore.

Wrothely þai wrythyne and wrystille to-gederz,
With welters and walowes over with-in þase buskez,
Tumbellez and turnes faste, and terez þaire wedez,

1144 Untenderly fro þe toppe thai tiltine to-gederz;
Whilome Arthure over, and oþer while undyre,
ffro þe heghe of the hylle un-to the harde roche;
They feyne never are they falle at þe flode merkes;

Arthur stabs the giant,

1148 Bot Arthur with ane anlace egerly smyttez,
And hittez ever in the hulke up to þe hiltez;

who in his death-struggle breaks three of Arthur's ribs.

Þe theefe at þe dede thrawe so throly hyme thryngez,
Þat three rybbys in his syde he thrystez in sundere!

1152 Thenne syr Kayous the kene unto the kynge styrtez,—
Said, "allas! we are lorne, my lorde es confundede,
Over fallene with a fende! us es fulle hapnede!

His knights find him lying exhausted.

We mone be forfetede in faith, and flemyde for ever!"

1156 Þay hafe up hys hawberke þane, and handilez þer-undyre,
His hyde and his haunche eke, one heghte to þe schuldrez;
His flawnke and his feletez, and his faire sydez,

Bothe his bakke and his breste, and his bryghte armez :

1160 Þay ware fayne that they fande no flesche entamede,
And for þat journee made joye, þir gentille knyghttez ;
"Now, certez," saise Sir Bedwere, "it semez, be my
    Lorde !
He sekez seyntez bot seldene, þe sorere he grypes,

1164 That thus clekys this corsaunt owte of þir heghe clyffez,
To carye forthe siche a carle at close hym in silvere ;
Be Myghelle of syche a makke, I hafe myche wondyre
That ever owre soveraygne Lorde suffers hyme in hevene ;

1168 And alle seyntez be syche, þat servez oure Lorde,
I salle never no seynt bee, be my fadyre sawle !"
Thane bourdez þe bolde kyng at Bedvere wordez,—
Þis seynt have I soghte, so helpe me owre Lorde !

1172 ffor-thy brayd owtte þi brande, and broche hyme to þe
    herte ;
Be sekere of this sergeaunt, he has me sore grevede !
I faghte noghte wyth syche a freke þis fyftene wyntyrs,
Bot in the montez of Araby I mett syche anoþer ;

1176 He was þe forcyere be ferre þat had I nere fundene,
Ne had my fortune bene faire, fey had I levede !
Anone stryke of his hevede, and stake it there aftyre,
Gife it to thy sqwyere, fore he es wele horsede ;

1180 Bere it to syr Howelle, þat es in harde bandez,
And byd hyme herte hym wele, his enmy es destruede !
Syne bere it to Bareflete, and brace it in yryne,
And sett it on the barbycane, biernes to schewe ;

1184 My brande and my brode schelde apone þe bent lyggez,
On þe creeste of þe cragge, thare fyrste we encontrede,
And þe clubb þarby, alle of clene irene,
þat many Cristene has kyllyde in Constantyne landez ;

1188 fferke to the far-lande, and fetche me þat wapene,
And late founde tille oure flete, in flode þare it lengez :
If thow wylle any tresour, take whate the lykez ;
Have I the kyrtylle and þe clubb, I coveite noghte elles !"

1192 Now þey caire to þe cragge, þise comlyche knyghtez,

They examine him and find no wound.

Sir Bedever speaks facetiously of this saint whom Arthur had sought.

If all saints are like him no saint would he be.

Arthur bids him stab the monster to the heart, to make sure of him, for only once before had he met with such a terrible foe.

He bids them cut off his head,

and bear it first to Sir Hoel,

then to Barflete, and set it on the barbican.

His sword and shield and the giant's club are to be fetched from the hill.

They may take what treasure they will ; all Arthur desires is the kirtle and the club.

And broghte hyme þe brade schelde, and his bryghte wapene,

The affair was kept a secret till break of day.
The clubb and the cotte alles, Sir Kayous hym selvene, And kayres with conquerour, the kyngez to schewe;

1196 That in coverte the kynge helde closse to hym selvene, Whilles clene day fro þe clowde, clymbyd on lofte.

Be that to courte was comene clamour fulle huge,

Then the people kneel before Arthur, and thank and praise him for slaying the giant.
And be-fore the comlyche kynge they knelyd alle at ones,—

1200 "Welcome, oure liege lorde, to lang has thow duellyde! Governour undyr Gode, graytheste and noble, To whame grace es graunted, and gyffene at his wille! Now thy comly come has comforthede us alle!

1204 Thow has in thy realtee revengyde thy pople! Thurghe helpe of thy hande, thyne enmyse are struyede, That has thy renkes over-ronne, and refte theme theire childyre! What never rewme owte of araye so redyly relevede!"

1208 Thane þe conquerour Cristenly carpez to his pople,
Arthur ascribes all to God.
"Thankes Gode," quod he, "of þis grace, and no gome elles, ffor it was never manes dede, bot myghte of Hymselfene, Or myracle of hys modyre, þat mylde es tille alle!"

He bids his followers distribute the giant's treasure among the clergy and people.
1212 He somond þan þe schippemene scharpely þer-aftyre, To schake furth with þe schyre mene to schifte þe gudez; "Alle þe myche tresour that traytour had wonnene, To commons of the contré, clergye ond oþer,

1216 Luke it be done and delte to my dere pople, That none pleyne of theire parte, o peyne of ȝour lyfez."

He comande hys cosyne, with knyghtlyche wordez,
A church and convent are to be built on the cliff.
To make a kyrke on þe cragg, ther the corse lengez,

1220 And a covent there-in, Criste for to serfe, In mynde of þat martyre, þat in þe monte rystez.

When the giant was slain, Arthur moves from Barflete to Castle Blanc.
Qwen Sir Arthur the kynge had kylled þe gyaunt, Than blythely fro Bareflete he buskes one þe morne,

1224 With his batelle one brede, by þa blythe stremes;

To-warde Castelle Blanke he chesez hym the waye,
Thurghe a faire champayne, undyr schalke hyllis;
The kyng fraystez a-furth over the fresche strandez,
1228 ffoundez with his faire folke over as hym lykez:
ffurthe stepes that steryne, and strekez his tentis
One a strenghe by a strome, in þas straytt landez.
Onone aftyre middaye, in the mene-while,

1232 þare comez two messangeres of tha fere marchez,   Then come two messengers from
ffra þe marschalle of Fraunce, and menskfully hym gretes, the Marshal of France, who acquaint Arthur
Besoghte hyme of sucour, and saide hyme thise wordez,—
"Sir, thi marschalle thi mynistre, thy mercy be-sekez,

1236 Of thy mekille magestee, fore mendement of thy pople,
Of þise marchez-mene, that thus are myskaryede,   with the mischief which the Emperor Lucius is working in France,
And thus merred amange, maugree theire eghne;
I witter þe þe emperour es entirde into Fraunce,

1240 With ostes of enmye, orrible and huge;
Brynnez in Burgoyne thy burghes so ryche,
And brittenes thi baronage, that bieldez thare-in;
He encrochez kenely by craftez of armez,   seizing castles,

1244 Countrese and castelles þat to thy coroun langez;
Confoundez thy commons, clergy and oþer;   confounding the commons,
Bot thow comfurth theme, syr kynge, cover salle they
        never!

He fellez forestez fele, forrayse thi landez,   felling forests,
1248 ffrysthez no fraunchez, bot fraisez the pople;
þus he fellez thi folke, and fangez theire gudez!   taking goods,
ffremedly the Franche tung fey es be-lefede.
He drawes in-to douce Fraunce, as Duchemen tellez,

1252 Dresside with his dragouns, dredfulle to schewe;
Alle to dede they dyghte with dynttys of swerddez,   killing dukes and douze-peers.
Dukez and dusperes, þat dreches thare-ine;
ffor-thy the lordez of the lande, ladys and oþer,

1256 Prayes the for Petyr luffe, þe apostylle of Rome,
Sen thow arte presant in place, þat þow wille profyre make   Therefore they desire Arthur's help.
To þat perilous prynce, be processe of tyme;
He ayers by ȝone hilles, ȝone heghe holtez undyr,

1260 Hufes thare with hale strenghe of haythene kyngez;
Helpe nowe for His lufe, that heghe in hevene sittez,
And talke tristly to theme, that thus us destroyes!"

The kyng biddis syr Boice, "buske the be-lyfe!

1264 Take with the syr Berille, and Bedwere the ryche,
Sir Gawayne and syr Gryme, these galyarde knyghtez,
And graythe yowe to yone grene wode, and gose over
þer nedes;
Saise to syr Lucius, to unlordly he wyrkez,

1268 Thus letherly agaynes law to lede my pople;
I lette hyme or oghte lange, yif me þe lyffe happene,
Or my lyghte salle lawe, þat hyme overe lande folowes;
Comande hym kenely wyth crewelle wordez,

1272 Cayre owte of my kyngryke with his kydd knyghtez;
In caase that he wille noghte, þat cursede wreche,
Come for his curtaisie, and countere me ones!
Thane salle we rekkene fulle rathe, whatt ryghte þat he
claymes,

1276 Thus to ryot þis rewme and raunsone the pople!
Thare salle it derely be delte with dynttez of handez:
The Dryghttene at Domesdaye dele as hyme lykes!"

Now thei graythe theme to goo, theis galyarde knyghttez,

1280 Alle gleterande in golde, appone grete stedes,
To-warde þe grene wode, þat with growndene wapyne,
To grete wele the grett lorde, that wolde be grefede sone;
Thise hende hovez on a hille by þe holte eynes,

1284 Be-helde þe howsyng fulle hye of Hathene kynges;
They herde in theire herbergage hundrethez fulle many,
Hornez of olyfantez fulle helych blawene;
Palaisez proudliche pyghte, þat palyd ware ryche,

1288 Of palle and of purpure, wyth precyous stones;
Pensels and pomelle of ryche prynce armez,
Pighte in þe playne mede, þe pople to schewe:

And thane the Romayns so ryche had arayede their tentez

1292 On rawe by þe ryvere, undyre þe round hillez,
The emperour for honour ewyne in the myddes,

Wyth egles al over ennelled so faire :

And saw hyme and þe Sowdane, and senatours many,

1296 Seke to-warde a sale with sextene kyngez,

Syland softely in, swettly by theme selfene,

To sowpe withe þat soveraygne, fulle selcouthe metez.

Nowe they wende over the watyre, þise wyrchipfulle knyghttez,

1300 Thurghe þe wode to þe wone, there the wyese rystez ;

Reght as þey hade weschene, and went to þe table,

Sir Wawayne þe worthethy un-wynly he spekes,—

"The myghte and þe majestee, that menskes us alle,

1304 That was merked and made thurghe þe myghte of hym-selvene,

Gyffe ʒow sytte in ʒour sette, Sowdane and oþer,

That here are semblede in sale, unfawghte mott ʒe worthe !

And þe fals heretyke, þat emperour hym callez,

1308 That ocupyes in erroure the empyre of Rome,

Sir Arthure herytage, þat honourable kynge,

That alle his auncestres aughte bot Utere hyme one,

That ilke cursynge þat Cayme kaghte for his brothyre,

1312 Cleffe over the cukewalde, with croune ther thow lengez,

ffor the unlordlyeste lede þat I on lukede ever !

My lorde mervailles hym mekylle, mane, be my trouthe,

Why thow morthires his mene, þat no mysse serves,

1316 Commons of þe contré, clergye and oþer,

þat are noghte coupable þer-in, ne knawes noght in armez ;

ffor-thi the comelyche kynge, curtays and noble,

Comandez þe kenely to kaire of his landes,

1320 Ore elles for thy knyghthede encontre hyme ones ;

Sen þow covettes the coroune, latte it be declarede !

I hafe dyschargide me here, chalange whoo lykez,

Be-fore alle thy chevalrye, cheftaynes and oþer :

1324 Schape us an ansuere, and schunte þow no lengere,

þat we may schifte at þe schorte, and schewe to my lorde."

The emperour ansuerde wyth austeryne wordez,

"ʒe are with myne enmy, Sir Arthure hyme selvene !

The Roman Emperor and the Sultan are going to banquet together.

The knights present themselves.

Sir Gawaine delivers the message,

and upbraids with haughty words the Roman Emperor ;

bids him depart, or try a single combat with Arthur.

He challenges all the knights of Rome.

The Emperor replies,

1828 It es none honour to me to owttray hys knyghttez,
þoghe ȝe be irous mene, þat ayres one his nedez;
Bot say to thy soveraygne, I send hyme thes wordez,
Ne ware it for reverence of my ryche table,

1832 þou sulde repent fulle rathe of þi ruyde wordez!
Siche a rebawde as þowe rebuke any lordez,
Wyth theire retenuz arrayede, fulle realle and noble!

Here wille I suggourne, whilles me lefe thynkes,

1336 And sythene seke in by Sayne with solace þer-aftere;
Ensegge all þa cetese be the salte strandez,
And seyne ryde in by Rone, þat rynnes so faire,

And of alle his ryche castelles rusche doune þe wallez;

1340 I salle noghte lefe in Paresche, by processe of tyme,
His parte of a pechelyne, prove whene hyme lykes!"

"Now, certez," sais syr Wawayne, "myche wondyre
have I,
þat syche an alfyne as thow dare speke syche wordez!

1344 I had lever thene alle Fraunce, that hevede es of rewmes,
ffyghte with the faythefully one felde be oure one."

Thane answers syr Gayous fulle gobbede wordes,—
Was eme to þe emperour, and erle hyme selfene,—

1348 "Evere ware þes Bretons braggers of olde!
Loo! how he brawles hyme for hys bryghte wedes,
As he myghte bryttyne us alle with his brande ryche!
Ȝitt he berkes myche boste, ȝone boy þere he standes!"

1352 Thane grevyde syr Gawayne at his grett wordes,

Graythes to-warde þe gome with grucchande herte;
With hys stelyne brande he strykes of hys hevede,
And sterttes owtte to hys stede, and with his stale
wendes!

1356 Thurghe þe wacches þey wente, thes wirchipfulle
knyghtez,
And fyndez in theire fare waye wondyrlyche many;
Over the watyre þey wente by wyghtnesse of horses,
And tuke wynde as þey walde by þe wodde hemes:

1360 Thane folous frekly one fote frekkes ynewe,

And of þe Romayns arrayed appone ryche stedes,

Chasede thurghe a champayne oure chevalrous knyghtez, The Romans give chase.

Tille a cheefe forest, one schalke white horses:

1364 Bot a freke alle in fyne golde, and fretted in salle,

Come forþermaste on a fresone, in flawinande wedes;

A faire floreschte spere in fewtyre he castes,

And folowes faste one owre folke, and freschelye ascryez.

1368 Thane syr Gawayne the gude appone a graye stede, The foremost of the pursuers is slain by Sir Ga-waine.

He gryppes hym a grete spere, and graythely hyme hittez;

Thurghe þe guttez in-to the gorre he gyrdes hyme ewyne,

That the groundene stele glydez to his herte!

1372 The gome and þe grette horse at þe grounde lyggez,

ffulle gryselyche gronande, for grefe of his woundez.

Þane presez a preker ine, fulle proudely arayede,

That beres alle of pourpour, palyde wiþ sylver:

1376 Byggly on a broune stede he profers fulle large; Another knight, a paynim of Persia, by Sir Boys.

He was a Paynyme of Perse þat þus hyme persuede.

Sir Boys un-abaiste alle he buskes hyme a-gaynes,

With a bustous launce he berez hyme thurghe,

1380 Þat þe breme and the brade schelde appone þe bente lyggez!

And he bryngez furthe the blade, and bownez to his felowez.

Thane syr Foltemour of myghte, a man mekylle praysede, Sir Foltemour seeks to avenge Sir Gayous,

Was movede one his manere, and manacede fulle faste;

1384 He graythes to syr Gawayne graythely to wyrche,

ffor grefe of syr Gayous, þat es one grounde levede.

Thane syr Gawayne was glade; agayne hyme he rydez,

Wyth Galuth his gude swerde graythely hyme hyttez;

1388 The knyghte one þe coursere he clevede in sondyre, but Sir Gawaine cleaves him asunder.

Clenlyche fro þe croune his corse he dyvysyde,

And þus he killez þe knyghte wiþ his kydd wapene!

Than a ryche mane of Rome relyede to his byerns,— Then a rich man of Rome suggests a retreat.

1392 "It salle repent us fulle sore and we ryde forthire!

Ȝone are bolde bosturs, þat syche bale wyrkez;

It befelle hym fulle foule, þat þame so fyrste namede."

The rich Romans return,

Thane þe riche Romayns retournes þaire brydilles

1396 To þaire tentis in tene, telles theire lordez

How *syr* Marschalle de Mowne es on þe monte lefede,

ffore-justyde at that *journee*, for his grett japez.

Bot thare chasez on*e* oure men*e* chevallrou*s* knyghtez,

but five thousand horsemen still pursue the knights,

1400 ffyve thosande folke appon*e* faire stedes,

ffaste to a foreste on*e* a fell*e* watyr,

That fillez fro þe falow see fyfty myle large.

and fall upon an ambush of Bretons,

Thare ware Bretons enbuschide, and banarettez noble,

1404 Of þe chevalrye cheefe of þe kyngez chambyre,

Seese them*e* chase oure men*e*, and changen*e* þeire horsez,

And choppe doun*e* cheftaynes, that thoy moste chargyde;

who break out suddenly on them,

Thane þe embuschement of Bretons brake owte at ones,

1408 Brothely at banere, and Bedwyne knyghtez,

Arrestede of þe Romayns, þat by þe fyrthe rydez,

All*e* þe realeste renkes þat to Rome lengez;

Thay iche on þe enmyse and egerly strykkys,

with shouts of "Arthur."

1412 Erles of Inglande, and Arthure ascryes,

Thrughe brenes and bryghte scheldez, brestez they thyrle,

Bretons of the boldeste with theire bryghte swerdez;

Thare was Romayns ov*e*r redyne, and ruydly wondyde,

The Romans are defeated and driven back,

1416 Arrestede as rebawdez, with ryotou*s*.knyghttez!

The Romaynes owte of araye removede at onc*s*,

And rydes awaye in a rowtte, for reddoure it semys!

To þe senato*u*r Petyr a sandes-mane es com*m*yne,

1420 And saide, "*Syr*, sekyrly, ȝour seggez are supprysside!"

but the Senator Peter sends ten thousand men.

Than ten*s* thowsande men*e* he semblede at ones,

And sett sodanly on*e* oure seggez, by þe salte strandez;

Than ware Bretons abaiste, and grevede a lyttille,

1424 Bot ȝit the banerettez bolde, and bachellers noble,

Brekes that battailles wit*h* brestez of stedes;

The Bretons are repulsed, and

Sir Boice and his bolde men*e* myche bale wyrkes!

The Romaynes redyes þan*e*, arrayez þam*e* better,

1428 And al to-ruscheez oure men*e* withe theire ryste horsez,

Arestede of the richeste of þe rounde table,

Ov*e*r-rydez oure rerewarde, and grette rewthe wyrkes!

Thane þe Bretons on þe bente habyddez no lengere,

1432 Bot fleede to þe foreste, and the feelde levede;

Sir Berylle es borne downe and syr Boice takene,

The beste of oure bolde mene unblythely wondyde;

Bot ȝitt oure stale one a strenghe stotais a lyttille,

1436 Alle to-stonayede with þe strokes of þa steryne knyghtez;

Made sorowe fore theire soveraygne, that so þare was nomene,

Be-soughte Gode of socure, sende whene hym lykyde!

Than commez syr Idrus, armede up at alle ryghttez,

1440 Wyth fyve hundrethe mene appone faire stedes,

ffraynez faste at oure folke freschely þare aftyre,

ȝif þer frendez ware ferre, þat one the felde foundide.

Thane sais syr Gawayne, "so me God helpe!

1444 We hafe bene chased to daye, and chullede as hares,

Rebuyked with Romaynes appone þeire ryche stedez,

And we lurkede undyr lee as lowrande wreches!

I luke never one my lorde þe dayes of my lyfe,

1448 And we so lytherly hyme helpe, þat hyme so wele lykede!"

Thane the Bretons brothely brochez theire stedez,

And boldly in batelle appone þe bent rydes;

Alle þe ferse mene be-fore frekly ascryes,

1452 fferkand in þe foreste, to freschene þame selfene;

The Romaynes thane redyly arrayes theme bettyre,

One rawe on a rowm-felde, reghttez theire wapyns,

By þe ryche revare, and rewles þe pople;

1456 And with reddour syr Boice es in areste haldene.

Now thei semblede unsaughte by þe salte strandez;

Gladdly theis sekere mene settys þeire dynttez,

With lufly launcez one lofte they luyschene to-gedyres,

1460 In Lorayne so lordlye on leppande stedes;

Thare ware gomes thurghe girde with grundyne wapynes,

Grisely gayspande with grucchande lotes!

Grete lordes of Greke greffede so hye;

1464 Swyftly with swerdes, they swappene there-aftyre,

Swappez doune fulle sweperlye swelltande knynghtez,

That alle swelltez one swarthe, that they over swyngene,
Se many sweys in swoghe swounande att ones!

Syr Gawayne the gracyous fulle graythelye he wyrkkes,
The gretteste he gretez wyth gryeslye wondes;
Wyth Galuth he gyrdez doune fulle galyarde knyghtez,
ffore greefe of þe grett lorde so grymlye he strykez!

1472 He rydez furthe ryallye and redely there-aftyre,
Thare this realle renke was in areste haldene;
He ryfez ye raunke stele, he ryghttez þeire brenez,
And reste theme the ryche mane, and rade to his strenghes,

1476 The senatour Petur thane persewede hyme aftyre,
Thurghe þe presse of þe peple, wyth his pryce knyghttes;
Appertly fore þe prysonere proves his strenghes,
Wyth prekers the proudeste that to þe presse lengez;

1480 Wrothely one the wrange hande syr Gawayne he strykkes,
Wyth a wapene of were unwynely hyme hittez;
The breny one þe bakhalfe he brystez in sondyre!
Bot ȝit he broghte forthe syr Boyce, for alle þeire bale he biernez!

1484 Thane þe Bretones boldely braggene þeire tromppez,
And fore blysse of syr Boyce was broghte owtte of bandez,
Boldely in batelle they bere doune knyghtes;
With brandes of broune stele they brettened maylez;

1488 þay stekede stedys in stoure with stelene wapynes,
And alle stowede wyth strenghe, þat stode theme agaynes!
Sir Idrus fitz Ewayne þane Arthur ascryeez,
Assemblez one þe senatour wyth sextene knyghttez,

1492 Of þe sekereste mene þat to oure syde lengede;
Sodanly in a soppe they sette in att ones,
ffoynes faste att þe fore breste with flawmande swerdez,
And feghttes faste att þe fronte freschely þare aftyre;

1496 ffelles fele on þe felde appone þe ferrere syde,
ffey on þe faire felde by þa fresche strandez;
Bot syr Idrus fytz Ewayne anters hyme selvene,
And enttens in anly, and egyrly strykez,

1500 Sekez to þe senatour and sesez his brydille,

Sir Gawaine does mighty deeds of valour.
The Senator Peter comes against him,
but in spite of him Sir Gawaine rescues Sir Boice.
Rejoiced at this the British press on more boldly.
Sir Idrus, with sixteen knights, attacks the Senator,

Unsaughtely he saide hym*e* these fittande wordez,—

"ȝelde þe, *syr*, ȝapely, ȝife þou þi lyfe ȝernez,

ffore gyftcz þat þow gyffe may, þou ȝeme now þe selfen*e* ;

and takes him prisoner.

1504 ffore dredlez dreche þow, or droppe any wylez,

Thow sall*e* dy þis daye thorow dyntt of my handez !"

" I ascente," *quod* þe senatour, " so me Criste helpe !

So þat I be safe broghte before the kynge selven*e* ;

The Senator desires ∗ to be brought to the king.

1508 Raunson*e* me resonabillye, as I may ov*er* reche,

Aftyre my rcnttez in Rome may redyly forthire."

Thane answers *syr* Idrus with austeryne wordez,

Sir Idrus answers him roughly.

" Thow salle hafe condycyon*e*, as the kynge lykes,

1512 When*e* thow comes to þe kyth there the *cou*rte haldez ;

In caase his concell*e* bee to kepe the no langere,

To be killyde at his com*m*andment his knyghttez be-fore."

þay ledde hym furth*e* in þe rowte, and lached of*e* his wedes,

1516 Left*e* hym wyth Lyonell*e*, and Lowell*e* hys brothire,

O-lawe in þe laund*e* þane, by þe lythe strandez.

Sir Luci*us* legge-men*e* loste are fore ev*er* !

The senato*ur* Petur es prysoner takyn*e* !

He gives the Senator into the charge of Sir Lionel and Sir Lowell.

1520 Of Perc*e* and of Porte Jaffe full*e* many price knyghtez,

And myche pople wyth all*e*, perischede þam*e* selfen*e* !

ffor presse of þe passage, they plungede at onez !

Thare myghte men*e* see Romaynez rewfully wondyde,

Many of the Romans are slain.

1524 Over-redyn*e* with renkes of the round table !

In þe raik*e* of þe furth*e* they righten*e* theire brenys,

þat ran*e* all*e* on*e* reede blode redylye all*e* over ;

They raughte in þe rerewarde full*e* ryoto*us* knyghtez,

1528 ffor ra*u*msone of rede golde and reall*e* stedys ;

Radly relayes, and restez theire horsez,

In rowtte to þe ryche kynge they rade al at onez.

A knyghte cayrez be-fore, and to þe kynge telles,—

The knights ride back towards the king, and send him the news of their success.

1532 " Sir, here comm*e*z thy messangerez w*it*h myrthez fro
          þe moun*t*ez,

þay hafe ben*e* machede to day*e* w*it*h men*e* of þe marchez,

ffore-maglede[1] in þe marras with mervailo*us* knyghtez !

---

[1] Halliwell reads " fore manglede."

We hafe foughtene in faithe, by ȝone fresche strandez,

They tell him that they have slain fifty thousand men,

1536 With þe frekkeste folke that to þi foo langez;

ffyfty thosaunde one felde of ferse mene of armez,

Wyth-in a furlange of waye, fay ere by-lefede!

We hafe eschewede þis chekke, thurghe chance of oure Lorde,

1540 Of tha chevalrous mene that chargede thy pople!

and taken prisoners the chief Chancellor and the Senator Peter, as well as many paynims.

The cheefe chaunchelere of Rome, a cheftayne fulle noble,

Wille aske þe chartyre of pesse for charitee hym selfene;

And the senatour Petire to presone es takyne.

1544 Of Perse and of Porte Jaffe Paynymmez ynewe

Comez prekande in the presse, with thy prysse knyghttez,

With poverte in thi presone theire paynez to dryȝe;

I be-seke ȝow, sir, say whate ȝowe lykes,

1548 Whethire ȝe suffyre theme saughte, or sone delyverde:

Arthur may demand sixty horse-loads of silver for the Senator,

Ȝe may have fore þe senatour sextie horse chargede

Of silver be Seterdaye, fulle sekyrly payede,

And for þe cheefe chauncelere, þe chevalere noble,

and for the Chancellor, chariots full of gold.

1552 Charottez chokkefulle charegyde with golde;

The remenaunt of þe Romaynez be in areste haldene,

The other prisoners may be kept until their rents are known.

Tille thiere renttez in Rome be rightewissly knawene.

I be-seke ȝow, sir, certyfye ȝone lordez,

1556 Ȝif ȝe wille send þame over þe see, or kepe þame ȝour selfene:

All Arthur's men had escaped, save Sir Ewaine, who was wounded.

Alle ȝour sekyre mene forsothe sounde are by-levyde,

Save syr Ewayne fytz Henry es in þe side wonddede."

The king rejoices.

"Crist be thankyde," quod the kynge, "and hys clere modyre,

1560 That ȝowe comforthede and helpede be crafte of hyme selfene;

The fate of battle, he says, is in the hands of God.

Skilfulle skomfyture he skiftez as hym lykez,

Is none so skathlye may skape, ne skewe fro his handes;

Desteny and doughtynes of dedys of armes,

1564 Alle es demyd and delte at Dryghtynez wille!

He thanks the knight for his tidings, and gives him for reward the city of Tholouse.

I kwne the thanke for thy come, it comfortes us alle!

Sir knyghte," sais þe conquerour, "so me Criste helpe!

I ȝif the for thy thyȝandez Tolouse þe riche,

1568 The tolle and þe tachementez, tavernez and oþer,
The towne and the tenementez with towrez so hye,
That towchez to the temperaltee, whilles my tyme lastez:
Bot say to the senatour I sende hyme þes wordez,

1572 Thare salle no silver hym save, bot Ewayne recovere;
I had lever see hym synke one the salte strandez,
Than the seegge ware seke, þat es so sore woundede;
I salle dissevere that sorte, so me Criste helpe!

1576 And sett theme fulle solytarie, in sere kyngez landez:
Salle he never sownde see his seynowres in Rome,
Ne sitt in þe assemblé, in syghte wyth his feris;
ffor it comes to no kynge þat conquerour es holdene,

1580 To comone with his captifis fore covatys of silver:
It come never of knyghthede, knawe it ȝif hyme lyke,
To carpe of coseri, whene captyfis ere takyne;
It aughte to no presoners to prese no lordez,

1584 Ne come in presens of pryncez, whene partyes are movede:
Comaunde ȝone constable, þe castelle þat ȝemes,
That he be clenlyche kepede, and in close haldene;
He salle have maundement to morne or myddaye be roungene,

1588 To what marche þay salle merke, with mangere to lengene."
Þay convaye this captyfe with clene mene of armez,
And kend hym to þe constable, alles þe kynge byddez;
And seyne to Arthure þey ayre, and egerly hym towchez

1592 The answere of þe emperour, irows of dedez.
Thane syr Arthure one erthe, atheliste of oþere,
At evene at his awene borde avantid his lordez,—
"Me aughte to honour theme in erthe over alle oþer thyngez,

1596 Þat þus in myne absens awnters þeme selfene;
I salle theme luffe whylez I lyffe, so me our Lorde helpe!
And gyfe þeme landys fulle large, whare theme beste lykes;
Thay salle noghte lesse, one þis layke, ȝif me lyfe happene,

1600 Þat þus are lamede for my lufe be þis lythe strandez."

The Senator shall not be ransomed save Sir Ewaine recovers.

The others shall be divided into different countries.

Arthur holds that to accept ransom becomes not a king.

They are to take the Senator to the Constable and bid him keep him safe.

The knights obey, and then return to Arthur to give him the Emperor's message.

Arthur greatly commends his knights for their boldness, and promises them rewards.

In the morning
Sir Cador and his
knights are bid
to take the pri-
soners

Bot in þe clere daweyng, þe dere kynge hyme selfene

Comaundyd syr Cadore with his dere knyghttes,

Sir Cleremus, sir Cleremonde, with clene mene of armez,

1604 Sir Clowdmur, syr Clegis, to convaye theis lordez ;

Sir Boyce and syr Berelle with baners displayede,

Sir Bawdwyne, syr Bryane, and syr Bedwere the ryche,

Sir Raynalde and syr Richere, Rawlaundes childyre,

1608 To ryde with þe Romaynes in rowte wyth theire feres.

to Paris, and to
give them into
the care of the
Provost.

"Prekez now prevalye to Paris the ryche,

Wyth Petir the pryssonere and his price knyghttez ;

Be-teche þam þe proveste, in presens of lordez,

1612 O payne and o perelle þat pendes there too,

That they be weisely wachede and in warde holdene,

Wardede of warantizez with wyrchipfulle knyghttez ;

Wagge hyme wyghte mene, and woonde for no silvyre ;

1616 I haffe warnede þat wy, be ware ȝife hyme lykes !"

Now bownes þe Bretones, als þe kynge byddez,

   Buskez theire batelles, theire baners displayez ;

The British
knights depart
towardsChartres.

To-wardez Chartris they chese, these chevalrous
   knyghttez,

1620 And in the champayne lande fulle faire þay eschewede :

But the Emperor
had dispatched a
chosen band to
intercept them.

ffor þe emperour of myghte had ordande hym selfene

Sir Utolfe and sir Ewandyre, two honourable kyngez,

Erles of þe Orient, with austeryne knyghttez,

1624 Of þe awntrouseste mene þat to his oste lengede,

Sir Sextynour of Lyby and Senatours many,

The kynge of Surrye hym-selfe with Sarazynes ynewe,

The senatour of Sutere wyth sowmes fulle huge,

1628 Whas assyguede to þat courte be sent of his peres,

Traise to-warde Troys þe tresone to wyrke,

To hafe be-trappede with a trayne oure travelande
   knyghttez,

That hade persayfede þat Peter at Parys sulde lenge,

1632 In presonne with þe proveste, his paynez to drye.

ffor-thi they buskede theme bownne with baners displayede,

In the buskayle of his waye, on blonkkes fulle hugge ;

Planttez theme in the pathe with powere arrayede,

1636   To pyke up þe presoners fro oure pryse knyghttez.

Syr Cadore of Cornewalle comaundez his peris,

   Sir Clegis, syr Cleremus, syr Cleremownde þe noble,

" Here es þe close of Clyme with clewes so hye ;

1640   Lokez the contree be clere, the corners are large ;

Discoveres now sekerly skrogges and oþer,

That no skathelle in þe skroggez skorne us here aftyre ;

Loke ȝe skyste it so þat us no skathe lympe,

1644   ffor na skomfitoure in skoulkery is skomfite ever."

Now they hye to þe holte, thes harageous knyghttez,

   To herkene of þe hye mene to helpene theis lordez ;

ffyndez theme helmede hole and horsesyde on stedys,

1648   Hovande one þe hye waye by þe holte hemmes.

With knyghttly contenaunce Sir Clegis hym selfene

Kryes to þe companye, and carpes thees wordez,—

" Es there any kyde knyghte, kaysere or oþer,

1652   Wille kyth for his kynge lufe craftes of armes ?

We are comene fro the kyng of þis lythe ryche,

That knawene es for conquerour, corownde in erthe,

His ryche retenuz here alle of his round table,

1656   To ryde with þat realle in rowtte where hyme lykes ;

We seke justynges of werre, ȝif any wille happyne,

Of þe jolyeste mene a-juggede be lordes ;

If here be any hathelle mane, erle or oþer,

1660   That for þe emperour lufe wille awntere hym-selfene."

And ane erle þane in angerd answeres hym sone,—

" Me angers at Arthure, and att his hathelle bierns,

That thus in his errour ocupyes theis rewmes ;

1664   And owtrayes þe emperour, his erthely lorde !

The araye and þe ryalltez of þe rounde table

Es wyth rankour rehersede in rewmes fulle many ;

Of oure renttez of Rome syche revelle he haldys,

1668   Ne salle ȝife resoune fulle rathe, ȝif us reghte happene, ·

That many salle repente that in his rowtte rydez,
ffor the reklesse roy so rewlez hym-selfone!"

"A !" sais *syr* Clegis þane, " so me Criste helpe !

1672 I knawe be thi carpynge a cowntere þe semes!
Bot be þou auditoure or erle, or emper*our* thi-selfene,
Appone Arthurez by-halve I answere the sone :
The renke so realle, þat rewllez us alle,

1676 The ryot*ous* mene and þe ryche of þe rounde table,
He has araysede his accownte, and redde alle his rollez,

ffor he wylle gyfe a rekenyng that rewe salle aftyre,
That alle þe ryche salle repente þat to Rome langez,

1680 Or þe rereage be requit of rentez þat he claymez !

We crafe of ȝo*ur* curtaisie three coursez of werre,
And claymez of knyghthode, take kepe to ȝour selfene !
Ȝe do bott trayne us to daye wyth trofelande wordez !

1684 Of syche tr*a*vaylande mene trecherye me thynkes !
Sende owte sadly certayne knyghtez,
Or say me sekerly sothe, for sake ȝif ȝowe lykes."

Thane sais þe kynge of Surry, "Alls save me oure Lorde !
1688 Ȝif þow hufe alle þe daye, þou bees noghte delyverede,

Bot thow sekerly ensure with certeyne knyghtez,
þat þi cote and thi breste be knawene w*it*h lordez,
Of armes of ancestrye entyrde w*it*h londez."

1692 "Sir kyng," sais *syr* Clegys, "fulle knyghttly þow
askez :

I trowe it be for cowardys thow carpes thes wordez :
Myne armez are of ancestrye enveryde with lordez,
And has in banere bene borne sene *syr* Brut tyme ;

1696 At the cité of Troye þat tymme was ensegede,
Ofte seene in asawte with certayne knyghttez,
ffro þe Borghte broghte us and alle oure bolde elders,
To Bretayne þe braddere, with-in chippe-burdez."

1700 "Sir," sais *syr* Sextenour, " saye what þe lykez,

And we salle suffyre the, als us beste semes ;
Luke thi troumppez be trussede, and trofulle no lengere,
ffor þoghe þou tarye alle þe daye, the tyddes no bettyr !

1704 ffor there salle never Romayne, þat in my rowt rydez,
Be with rebawdez rebuykyde, whills I in werlde regne!"
Thane syr Clegis to þe kynge a lyttille enclinede,
Kayres to syr Cadore, and knyghtly hym tellez,—

Sir Clegis tells Sir Cador that a vast number of the enemy are drawn up in the wood,

1708 "We have foundene in ȝone firthe, floreschede with leves,
þe flour of þe faireste folke þat to þi foo langez,
ffifty thosandez of folke of ferse mene of armez,
þat faire are fewteride on frounte undyr ȝone fre-bowes;

1712 They are enbuschede one blonkkes, with baners dis-
playede,
In ȝone bechene wode appone the waye sydes;
Thay hafe the furthe forsette alle of þe faire watyre,
That fayfully of force feghte us byhowys;

and suggests a retreat.

1716 ffor thus us schappes to daye, schortly to telle,
Whedyre we schone or schewe, schyst as þe lykes."
"Nay," quod Cadore, "so me Criste helpe!
It ware schame þat we scholde schone for so lytylle!

Sir Cador scorns to retreat.

1720 Sir Lancelott salle never laughe, þat with þe kyng
lengez,
That I sulde lette my waye for lede appone erthe;
I salle be dede and undone ar I here dreche,
ffor drede of any dogge-sone in ȝone dyme schawes!"

Never shall Sir Lancelot laugh at him.

He will die before he turn back for any dog's son of them all.

1724 Syr Cador thane knyghtly comforthes his pople,
And with corage kene he karpes þes wordes,—
"Thynk one þe valyaunt prynce þat vesettez us ever,
With landez and lordscheppez, whare us beste lykes;

Sir Cador exhorts his men, and tells them of the good deeds of Arthur.

1728 That has us ducheres delte, and dubbyde us knyghttez,
Gifene us gersoms and golde, and gardwynes many;
Grewhoundes and grett horse, and alkyne gamnes,
That gaynez tille any gome, that undyre God benez;

1732 Thynke one riche renoune of þe rounde table,
And late it never be refte us fore Romayne in erthe;
ffeyne ȝow noghte feyntly, ne frythes no wapyns,
Bot luke ȝe fyghte faythefully, frekes ȝour-selfone;

1736 I walde be wellyde alle qwyke, and quarterde in sondre,
Bot I wyrke my dede, whils I in wrethe lenge."

Than this doughtty duke dubbyd his knyghttez,
    Joneke and Askanere, Aladuke and oþer,

He dubs some of
them knights.

1740 That ayerez wore of Esexe, and alle þase este marchez;
Howelle and Hardelfe, happy in armez,
Sir Herylle and sir Herygalle, þise harageouse knyghttez:
Than the soverayne assignede certayne lordez,

To certain of
them he gives
the prisoner in
charge.

1744 Sir Wawayne, syr Uryelle, Sir Bedwere þe riche,
Raynallde and Richeere, and Rowlandez childyre,—
"Takez kepe one this prynce with ȝoure price knyghtez,
And ȝife we in þe stour withstondene the better,

1748 Standez here in this stede, and stirrez no forthire;

If he is defeated,
they are to con-
vey him to some
castle, or to Ar-
thur.

And ȝif þe chaunce falle þat we bee over-charggede,
Eschewes to some castelle, and chewyse ȝour-selfene;
Or ryde to þe riche kynge ȝif ȝow roo happyne,

1752 And bidde hym come redily to rescewe hys biernez."

The British pre-
pare for the fight.

And than the Bretons brothely enbrassez þeire scheldez,
Braydez one bacenetez, and buskes theire launcez.
Thus he fittez his folke, and to þe felde rydez,

1756 ffif hundreth one a frounte fewtrede at oncz!
With trompes þay trine, and trappede stedes,
With cornettes and clarions, and clergialle notes;

The fight begins.

Schokkes in with a schakke, and schontez no langere,

1760 There schawes ware scheene undyr þe schire eynez.
And thane the Romaynez rowtte removes a lyttille,
Raykes with a rerewarde þas realle knyghttez;
So raply þay ryde thare, that alle þe rowte ryngez,

1764 Of ryves and raunke stele, and ryche golde maylez;
Thane schotte owtte of þe schawe schiltrounis many,
With scharpe wapynes of ware schotande at ones:

The King of Lebe
leads on the
enemy.

The kynge of Lebe be-fore the wawarde he ledez,

1768 And alle his lele lige mene o laundone ascriez:
Thane this cruelle kynge castis in fewtire,
Kaghte hym a coverde horse, and his course haldez,

He attacks Sir
Beryll and slays
him.

Beris to syr Berille, and brathely hym hittes,

1772 Throwghe golet and gorgere he hurtez hym ewyne!
The gome and þe grette horse at þe grounde liggez,

And gretez graythely to Gode, and gyffes hym þe saule!

Thus es Berelle the bolde broghte owtte of lyve,

1776 And byddez aftyre Beryelle, þat hym beste lykez.

And thane *syr* Cador of Cornewayle es carefulle in herte, Sir Cador is over-whelmed with grief for his loss.

Be-cause of his kynyse mane, þat þus es 'myscaryede;

Umbeclappes the cors, and kyssez hyme ofte,

1780 Gerte kepe hym coverte with his clere knyghttez.

Thane laughes the Lebe kynge, and alle on lowde meles,— The King of Lebe ridicules him.

"ʒone lorde es lyghttede! me lykes the bettyre!

He salle noghte dere us to daye, the devylle have [his] bones!"

1784 "ʒone kynge," said Cador, "karpes fulle large,

Be-cause he killyd þis kene; Criste hafe þi saule!

He salle hafe corne bote, so me Criste helpe! Sir Cador vows vengeance.

Or I kaire of þis coste, we salle encontre ones!

1788 So may þe wynde weile turnne, I quytte hym or ewyne,

Sothely hym selfene, or summe of his ferez!"

Thane *syr* Cador þe kene knyghttly he wyrkez,

Cryez, "A! Cornewale," and castez in fewtere,

1792 Girdez streke thourghe þe stour on a stede ryche! He enacts great deeds of valour.

Many storyne mane he steride by strenghe of hyme one!

Whene his spere was sprongene, he spede hym fulle ʒerne, When his lance is broken he fights with his sword.

Swappede owtte with a swerde, that swykede hym never,

1796 Wroghte wayes fulle wyde, and wounded knyghttez;

Wyrkez his in wayfare fulle werkand sydez,

And hewes of þe hardieste halsez in sondyre,

That alle blendez with blode thare his blanke rynnez!

1800 So many biernez the bolde broughte owt of lyfe,

Tittez tirauntez doune, and temez theire sadilles,

And turnez owte of þe toile, whene hym tyme thynkkez!

Thane the Lebe kynge criez fulle lowde Then the King of Lebe ironically praises his deeds.

1804 One *syr* Cador the kene, with cruelle wordez,

Thowe hase wyrchipe wonne, and wondyde knyghttez!

Thowe wenes fore thi wightenez the werlde es thy nowene!

I salle wayte at thyne honnde, wy, be my trowthe!

1808 I have warnede þe wele, beware ʒif the lykez!"

With cornuse and clariones þeis newe made knyghttez

The new-made knights, with sound of trumpets and spears in rest, rush to the fray.
Lythes un-to þe crye, and castez in fewtire;

fferkes in one a ffrounte one fferaunte stedez,

1812 ffellede at þe fyrste come fyfty att ones!

Schotte thorowe the schiltrouns, and scheverede launcez,

Laid doune in þe lumppe lordly biernez!

Aud thus nobilly oure newe mene notez þeire strenghez.

1816 Bot new notte es onone þat noyes me sore;

The King of Lebe comes against them.
The kynge of Lebe has laughte a stede þat hym lykede,

And comes in lordely in lyonez of silvere,

Umbelappez þe lumpe, and lattes in sondre;

1820 Many lede with his launce þe liffe has he refede!

He makes great havoc among the new men.
Thus he chaces þe childire of þe kyngez chambire,

And killez in þe champanyse chevalrous knyghttez!

With a chasynye spere he choppes doune many!

1824 Thare was syr Alyduke slayne, and Achinour wondyde,

Sir Origge and syr Ermyngalle hewene al to pecez!

And ther was Lewlyne laughte, and Lewlyns brothire,

With lordez of Lebe, and lede to þeire strenghez:

Had not Sir Clegis and Sir Clement come, the new men had gone to nought.
1828 Ne hade syr Clegis comene, and Clemente þe noble,

Oure newe mene hade gone to noghte, and many ma oþer.

Then Sir Cador puts his lance in rest, and strikes the King of Lebe fair on the helmet.
Thane sir Cador the kene castez in fewtire

A cruelle launce and a kene, and to þe kynge rydez,

1832 Hittez hym heghe one the helme with his harde wapene,

That alle the hotte blode of hym to his hande rynnez!

The heathen king falls to the ground mortally wounded.
The hethene harageous kynge appone þe hethe lyggez,

And of his hertly hurte helyde he never!

1836 Thane syr Cador þe kene cryez fulle lowde,—

Sir Cador triumphs over him.
"Thow has corne botte, syr kynge, þare God gyfe þe sorowe,

Thow killyde my cosyne, my kare es the lesse!

Kele the nowe in the claye, and comforthe thi selfene!

1840 Thow skornede us langere with thi skornefulle wordez,

And nowe has þow chevede soo; it es thyne awene skathe!

Holde at þow hente has, it harmez bot lyttille,

ffor hethynge es hame holde, use it who so wille."

1844 The kyng of Surry þane es sorowfulle in herte,
    ffor sake of this soveraygne, þat þus was supprisede ;
    Semblede his Sarazenes, and senatours manye :
    Unsaughtyly þey sette thane appone oure sere knyghttez ;

The King of Syria, full of grief, assembles his Saracens for vengeance.

1848 Sir Cador of Cornewaile he cownterez theme sone,
    With his kydde companye clenlyche arrayede ;
    In the frount of þe fyrthe, as þe waye forthis,
    ffyfty thosande of folke was fellide at ones !

Sir Cador and his men slay fifty thousand of them at once.

1852 Thare was at þe assemblé certayne knyghttez,
    Sore wondede sone appone sere halfes ;
    The sekereste Sarzanez that to þat sorte lengede,
    Be-hynde the sadylles ware sette sex fotte large ;

Certain knights are wounded by Saracens riding behind others.

1856 They scherde in the schiltrone scheldyde knyghttez,
    Schalkes they schotte thrughe schrenkande maylez,
    Thurghe brenys browdene brestez they thirllede,
    Brasers burnyste bristez in sondyre ;

The fight rages furiously.

1860 Blasons blode and blankes they hewene,
    With brandez of browne stele brankkand stedez !
    The Bretones brothely brittenez so many,
    The bente and þe brode felde alle one blode rynnys !

The field runs blood.

1864 Be thane syr Cayous þe kene a capitayne has wonnene,
    Sir Clegis clynges in, and clekes anoþer ;
    The capitayne of Cordewa, undire þe kynge selfene,
    That was keye of þe kythe of alle þat coste ryche,

Sir Clegis takes prisoner the Captain of Cordova.

1868 Utolfe and Ewandre, Joneke had nommene,
    With þe erle of Affryke and oþer grette lordes.
    The kynge of Surry the kene to syr Cador es ȝeldene,
    The Synechalle of Sotere to Segramoure hym selfene.

Sir Cador takes the King of Syria.

1872 When þe chevalryé saw theire cheftanes were nommene,
    To a cheefe foreste they chesene theire wayes,
    And felede theme so feynte, they falle in þe greves,
    In the ferynne of þe fyrthe, fore ferde of oure pople.

The Romans fly into the forest.

1876 Thare myght mene see the ryche ryde in the schawes,
    To rype up the Romaynez ruydlyche wondyde !
    Schowttes aftyre mene, harageous knyghttez,
    Be hunndrethez they hewede doune be þe holte cynys !

Arthur's men slay many of them there.

A few escape to
a castle.

1880   Thus oure chevalrous mene chasez þe pople ;
        To a castelle they eschewede a fewe þat eschappede.
        Thane relyez þe renkez of þe rounde table,
        ffor to ryotte þe wode, þer þe duke restez ;

Arthur's knights
seek for their
companions who
had been slain.
Sir Cador bids
them carry them
to the King.

1884   Ransakes the ryndez alle, raughte up theire feres,
        That in þe fightyng be-fore fay ware by-levyde.
        Sir Cador garte ehare theym, and covere theme faire,
        Kariede theme to the kynge with his beste knyghttez ;

He goes to Paris
with the pri-
soners, and
quickly returns
to Arthur.

1888   And passez un-to Paresche with presoners hym-selfene,
        Betoke theyme the proveste, pryncez and oþer ;
        Tase a sope in the toure, and taryez no langere,
        Bot tournes tytte to þe kynge, and hym wyth tunge telles.

Then he tells him
of the case that
had befallen.

1892   "Syr," sais syr Cador, " a caas es be-fallene ;
            We hafe cownterede to day, in ȝone coste ryche.
        With kyngez and kayseres, krouelle and noble,
        And knyghtes and kene men clenlych arayede !

1896   Thay hade at ȝone foreste forsette us þe wayes,
        At the furthe in þe fyrthe, with ferse mene of armes ;

They had fought
and slain many.

        Thare faughtte we in faythe, and foynede with sperys,
        One felde with thy foo mene, and fellyd theme on lyfe.

1900   The kyng of Lebe es laide, and in þe felde levyde,
        And manye of his lege mene þat þere to hym langede !
        Oþer lordez are laughte of uncouthe ledes ;
        We hafe lede them at lenge, to lyf whilles þe lykez.

Divers of their
best knights were
taken prisoners,

1904   Sir Utere and syr Ewaynedyre, theis honourable knyghttez,
        Be an awntere[1] of armes Joneke has nommene,
        With erlez of þe Oryentte, and austerene knyghttez,
        Of awncestrye þe beste mene þat to þe oste langede ;

the Senator
Barouns, the
King of Syria, the
Seneschall of
Suters.

1908   The senatour Barouns es kaughtè with a knyghtte,
        The capitayne of Cornette, that crewelle es haldene,
        The syneschalle of Suters unsaughte wyth þes oþer,
        The kynge of Surry hym-selfene, and Sarazenes.

But of Arthur's
knights fourteen
were slain.

Sir Beryl was
killed at the first

1912   Bot fay of ours in þe felde a fourtene knyghttez,
            I wille noghte feyne ne forbere, but faythfully tellene
        Sir Berelle es one, a banerette noble,

---

[1] Written in MS. a nawntere.

Was killyde at þe fyrste come with a kynge ryche ; beginning of the fray.
1916 Sir Alidoyke of Towelle, with his tende knyghtez,
Emange þe Turkys was tynte, and in tyme fondene ;
Gude sir Mawrelle of Maunez, and Mawrene his broþer,
Sir Meneduke of Mentoche, with mervailous knyghttez."

1920 Thane the worthy kynge wrythes, and wepede with Then Arthur was grieved,
      his enghne,
Karpes to his cosyne syr Cador theis wordez,—
"Sir Cador, thi corage confundez us alle ! and speaks to his cousin Sir Cador bitter words.
Kowardely thow castez owtte alle my beste knyghttez !
1924 To putte mene in perille, it es no pryce holdene,
Bot þe pertyes ware purvayede, and powere arayede ;
When they ware stade on a strenghe, þou sulde hafe with-stondene,
Bot ʒif thowe wolde alle my steryne stroye for þe nonys !"

1928 "Sir," sair syr Cador, "ʒe knowe wele ʒourselvene ;
ʒe are kynge in this kythe, karpe whatte ʒow lykys ! Sir Cador replies with dignity.
Salle never upbrayde me, þat to þi burde langes,
That I sulde blyne for theire boste, thi byddyng to wyrche ;
1932 Whene any stirttez to stale, stuffe þame þe bettere,
Ore thei wille be stonayede, and stroyede in ʒone strayte
      londez.

I dide my delygens to daye, I doo me one lordez, He had only done his duty,
And in daungere of dede fore dyverse knyghttez,
1936 I hafe no grace to þi gree, bot syche grett wordez ;
ʒif I heven my herte, my hape es no bettyre." but is ill repaid by such hard words.
ʒofe syr Arthure ware angerde, he ansuers faire,
"Thow has doughttily donne, syr duke, with thi handez, Then Arthur retracts.
1940 And has donne thy dever with my dere knyghttez ; He acknowledges Cador had done his devoir.
ffor-thy thow arte demyde, with dukes and erlez,
ffor one of þe doughtyeste þat dubbede was ever ! He was one of the bravest of the brave,
Thare es none ischewe of us, on this erthe sprongene ; and heir apparent to the throne.
1944 Thow arte apparant to be ayere, are one of thi childyre ; Therefore he would never forsake him.
Thow arte my sister sone, for-sake salle I never !"

Thane gerte he in his awene tente a table be sette, Then he makes a noble feast in his own tent for the knights who had been engaged in the fight.
      And tryede in with tromppez travaillede biernez ;
1948 Serfede them solempnely with selkouthe metez,

Swythe semly in syghte with sylverene dischees.

Whene the senatours harde saye þat it so happenede,

But the Senators of Rome tell the Emperor of the defeat of his men.

They saide to þe emperour, "thi seggez are supprsyssede!

1952 Sir Arthure, thyne enmy has owterayede þi lordez,

That rode for þe rescowe of ȝone riche knyghttez !

Thow dosse bot tynnez þi tyme, and turmenttez þi pople;

He had been betrayed by those he trusted most.

Thow arte be-trayede of þi mene, that moste thow on
traystede.

1956 That schalle turne the to tene and torfere for ever."

Then the Emperor is very wroth.

Than the emperour irus was angerde at his herte,

ffor oure valyant biernez siche prowesche had wonnene.

With kynge and with kaysere to consayle they wende,

1960 Soverayngez of Sarazenez, and senatours manye ;

He assembles a council of war.

Thus he semblez fulle sone certayne lordez,

And in the assemble thane he sais them theis wordez,—

He tells them his purpose to go into Saxony,

" My herte sothely es sette, assente ȝif ȝowe lykes,

1964 To seke into Sexone, with my sekyre knyghttez,

To fyghte with my foo mene, if fortune me happene,

ȝif I may fynde the freke with-in the foure halvez ;

and enter into Augusta,

Or entire in-to Awguste awnters to seke,

1968 And byde with my balde mene with-in þe burghe ryche;

to riot and revel till the arrival of Sir Leo and the Lords of Lombardy.

Riste us and revelle, and ryotte oure selfene,

Lende þare in delyttc in lordechippez ynewe,

To syr Leo be comene with alle his lele knyghtez,

1972 With lordez of Lumberdye, to lette hyme the wayes."

King Arthur, getting intelligence of this, withdraws his men secretly by the woods;

Bot owre wycse kyng es warre to wayttene his renkes,
    And wyesly by þe woddez voydez his oste ;

Gerte felschene his fyrez, flawmande fulle heghe,

1976 Trussene fulle traystely, and treunt there aftyre.

takes the shortest road into Saxony;

Seþene into Sessoyne, he soughte at the gayneste,

And at the surs of þe sonne disseverez his knyghttez :

fforsette theme the cite appone sere halfez,

suddenly attacks the city with seven bands.

1980 So-daynly on iche halfe, with sevene grett stales.

Anely in the vale a vawewarde enbusches ;

Sir Valiant makes a vow to vanquish the Viscount of Rome.

Sir Valyant of Vyleris, with valyant knyghttez,

Be-fore þe kyngez visage made siche avowez,

1984 To venquyse by victorie the vescownte of Rome!
ffor-thi the kynge chargez hym, what chaunce so be-falle,
Cheftayne of the cheekke, with chevalrous knyghttez,
And sythyne meles with mouthe, þat he moste traystez:

The King gives him command of the vanguard;

1988 Demenys the medylwarde menskfully hyme selfene,
ffittes his fote-mene, alles hym faire thynkkes;
On frounte in the fore breste, the flour of his knyghtez,
His archers on aythere halfe he ordaynede þer-aftyre

he himself directs the centre.

He arranges the archers on either flank,

1992 To schake in a sheltrone, to schotte whene þame lykez;
He arrayed in þe rerewarde fulle rialle knyghtez,
With renkkes renownd of þe rounde table,
Sir Raynalde, sir Richere, that rade was never,

Places renowned knights for a rearguard.

1996 The riche Duke of Rowne wyt ryders ynewe;
Sir Cayous, sir Clegis, and clene mene of armes,
The kyng castes to kepe þe þaa clere strandes.
Sir Lott and syr Launcelott, þise lordly knyghttez,

2000 Salle lenge on his lefte hande, wyth legyones ynewe,
To meve in þe morne, while ȝif þe myste happynne;
Sir Cador of Cornewaile, and his kene knyghtez,
To kepe at þe Karfuke, to close in ther opere:

Sir Lott and Sir Lancelot command a band on the left band, which is to move in the mist of early morning.

Sir Cador and his men are to keep guard over the passes.

2004 He plantez in siche placez pryncez and erlez,
That no powere sulde passe þe no prevé wayes.

Bot the emperour onone, with honourable knyghtez
and erlez, enteres the vale, awnters to seke,

The Emperor and his knights quickly enter the vale in search of adventures.

2008 And fyndez sir Arthure with hostez arayede;
And at his in-come, to ekkene his sorowe,
Oure burlyche bolde kynge appone the bente howes,
With his bataile one brede, and baners displayede.

He finds Arthur's host drawn up in battle array,

2012 He hade þe ceté for-sett appone sere halfes,
Bothe the clewez and þe clyfez with clene mene of armez!
The mosse and þe marrasse, the mounttez so hye,
With gret multytude of mene, to marre hym in þe wayes.

and all the positions occupied.

2016 Whene syr Lucius sees, he sais to his lordez,
"This traytour has truaunt[1] this tresone to wyrche!
He has the ceté forsett appone sere halfez,

Then Sir Lucius declares with

[1] Or treunt.

wrath that there is no way else but to fight, for fly he may not.

Alle þe clewez and the cleyffez with clene mene of armez !

2020 Here es no waye i-wys, ne no wytt elles,

Bot feghte with oure foo-mene, for flee may we never !

Thane this ryche mane rathe arayes his byernez,

He arrays his rich Romans.
Rowlede his Romaynez, and realle knyghtez ;

The Viscount is in the van.
2024 Buschez in the avawmewarde the vescounte of Rome,

ffro Viterbe to Venyse, theis valyante knyghtez :

Hoists his standard, the golden dragon enamelled with eagles.
Dresses up dredfully the dragone of golde,

With egles al-over, enamelede of sable ;

2028 Drawene dreghely the wyne, and drynkyne thereaftyre,

They drink and make merry.
Dukkez and dusseperez, dubbede knyghtez,

ffor dauncesynge of Duche-mene, and dynnynge of pypez,

Alle dynned fore dyne that in þe dale hovede.

2032 And thane syr Lucius on lowde said lordlyche wordez,

Sir Lucius exhorts them to think on the great renown of Rome — how it had conquered all Christendom,
"Thynke one the myche renownne of ȝour ryche fadyrs ;

And the riatours of Rome, þat regnede with lordez ;

And the renkez over rane alle that regnede in erthe,

2036 Encrochede alle Cristyndome be craftes of armes ;

In everiche a viage the victorie was haldene ;

and all the land of the Saracens, from Jaffa to the gates of Paradise.
In sette alle þe Sarazenes within sevene wyntter,

The parte ffro the Porte Jaffe to Paradyse ȝatez !

2040 Thoghe a rewme be rebelle, we rekke it bot lyttille !

Without doubt they will quickly reduce these rebels.
It es resone and righte the renke be restreynede !

Do dresse we tharefore, and byde we no langere,

ffore dredlesse with-owttyne dowtte, the daye schalle be ourez !"

2044 Whene þeise wordez was saide, the Walsche kynge hym selfene

Was warre of this wyderwyne, þat werrayede his knyghttez :

Arthur calls upon the Viscount of Valence, and threatens him with vengeance.
Brothely in the vale with voyce he ascryez, —

"Viscownte of Valewnce, envyous of dedys,

2048 The vassalage of Viterbe to daye schalle be revengede !

Unvenquiste for þis place voyde schalle I never !"

The Viscount boldly prepares for the fray.
Thane the vyscownte valiante, with a voyse noble,

Avoycdyde the avawewarde, enverounde his horse ;

2052 He drissede in a derfe schelde, endenttyd with sable,
With a dragone engowschede, dredfulle to schewe,
Devorande a dolphyne with dolefulle lates,

His device is a
dragon devour-
ing a dolphin.

In seyne that oure soveraygne sulde be distroyede,

2056 And alle done of dawez with dynttez of swreddez;
ffor thare es noghte bot dede thare the dragone es raissede!
Thane the comlyche kynge castez in fewtyre,
With a crewelle launce cowpez fulle evene

Sir Valiant lays
his lance in rest,
and pierces him
through the short
ribs.

2060 Abowne þe spayre a spanne, emange þe schortte rybbys,
That the splent and the spleene on the spere lengez!
The blode sprente owtte and sprede as þe horse spryngez,
And he sproulez fulle spakely, bot spekes he no more!

2064 And thus has syr Valyant haldene his avowez,

And thus did he
redeem his word.

And venqwyste þe viscownte, thate victor was haldene!
Thane syr Ewayne syr Fytz Uriene fulle enkerlye rydez

Sir Ewaine makes
a bold attempt to
reach the Em-
peror.

Onone to the emperour his egle to towche;

2068 Thrughe his brode bataile he buskes be-lyfe,
Braydez owt his brande with a blyth chere,
Roverssede it redelye, and awaye rydys;
fferkez in with the fewle in his faire handez,

2072 And ffittez in freely one ffrounte with his feris.
Now buskez syr Lanncelot, and braydez fulle evene
To syr Lucius the lorde, and lothelye hyme hyttez;

Sir Lancelot slays
the Lord Lucius.

Thurghe pawnce and platez he percede the maylez,

2076 That the prowde penselle in his pawnche lengez!
The hede hayledе owtt be-hynde ane halfe fote large,
Thurghe hawberke and hanche, with þe harde wapyne!
The stede and the steryne mane strykes to þe grownde,

2080 Strake downe a standerde, and to his stale wendez!
"Me lykez wele," sais syr Loth, "jone lordez are dely-

Sir Lott rejoices
that his turn is
now come.

verede!
The lott lengez nowe on me, with leve of my lorde:
To day salle my name be laide, and my life aftyre,

2084 Bot some leppe fro the lyfe, that one jone lawnde hovez!"
Thane strekez the steryne, and streynys his brydylle,
Strykez in-to the stowre on a stede ryche,

He slays a giant,
Enjoynede with a geaunt, and jaggede hym thorowe!
2088 Jolyly this gentille for-justede anoþer,
Wroghte wayes fulle wyde, werrayande knyghtez,
And wondes alle wathely, that in þe waye stondez!
ffyghttez with alle the ffrappe a furlange of waye,

and many war-riors beside. 2092 ffelled fele appone felde with his faire wapene,
Venquiste and has the victorie of valyaunt knyghtez,
And alle enverounde the vale, and voyde whene hym
likede!

The British bow-men discharge their arrows. Thane bowmene of Bretayne brothely ther-aftyre
2096 Bekerde with bregaundez of ferre in tha laundez,
With flonez fleterede þay flitt fulle fresoly þer frekez,
ffichene with fetheris thurghe þe fyne maylez:
Sithe flyttynge es foule that so the flesche derys,
2100 That flowe o ferrome in flawnkkes of stedez;

The Dutchmen throw darts. Dartes the Duche-mene daltene aȝaynes,
With derfe dynttez of dede, dagges thurghe scheldez;
Qwarelles qwayntly swappez thorowe knyghtez
2104 With iryne so wekyrly, that wynche they never.

Many are slain by the sharp arrows. So they schérenkene fore schotte of þe scharppe arowes,
That all the scheltrone schonte, and schoderide at ones!
Thane riche stedes rependez, and rasches one armes;
2108 The hale howndrethe one hye appone heyghe lygges,
Bot ȝitte þe hathelieste on hy, haythene and oþer;

But the giants make a terrible charge, All hoursches over hede harmes to wyrke.
And alle theis geauntez be-fore, engenderide with fendez,
2112 Joynez on sir Jenitalle, and gentille knyghtez,

and with their iron clubs destroy many cavaliers on white steeds. With clubbez of clene stele clenkkede in helmes,
Graschede doune crestez, and craschede braynez;
Kyllede cousers and coverde stedes,
2116 Choppode thurghe chevalers one chalke-whytte stedez.
Was never stele ne stede myghte stande them aȝaynez,

Nothing can stand against them until Ar-thur comes. Bot stonays and strykez doune, that in þe stale hovys.
Tille þe conquerour come with his kene knyghttez,
2120 With crowelle contenaunce he cryede fulle lowde,—

He despises them, "I wende no Bretouns walde bee basschede for so lyttille,

And fore bare-legyde boyes, þat one the bente hovys!"

He clekys owtte Collbrande fulle clenlyche burneschte,

2124 Graythes hyme to Golapas, þat grevyde moste;

Kuttes hyme evene by þe knees clenly in sondyre.

"Come downe," quod the kynge, "and karpe to thy ferys!

Thowe arte to hye by þe halfe, I hete þe in trouthe!

2128 Thowe salle be handsomere hye, with þe helpe of my
Lorde!"

With þat stelene brande he strake ofe his hede.

Sterynly in þat stoure he strykes anoþer.

Thus he settez on sevene with his sekyre knyghttez:

2132 Whylles sexty ware servede soo, ne sessede they never!

And thus at the joyenyge the geauntez are dystroyede,

And at þat journey for-justede with gentille lordez.

Than the Romaynes, and the renkkes of þe rounde table,

2136 Rewles them in arraye, rerewarde ande oþer,

With wyghte wapynez of werre, thay wroghtene one
helmes,

Rittez with rennke stele fulle ryalle maylez;

Bot they fut theme fayre, thes frekk byernez,

2140 ffewters in freely one fferaunte stedes,

ffoynes fulle felly with flyschande speris,

ffretene of orfrayes feste appone scheldez.

So fele fay es in fyghte appone þe felde levyde,

2144 That iche a furthe in the firthe of rede blode rynnys!

By that swyftely one swarthe þe swett es bylevede,

Swerdez swangene in two, sweltand knyghtez

Lyes wyde opyne welterande one walopande stedez;

2148 Wondes of wale mene werkande sydys,

ffacez fetteled unfaire in filterede lakes,

Alle craysed for-trodyne with trappede stedez,

The faireste fygured folde that fygurede was ever,

2152 Alles ferre alles a furlange, a thosande at ones!

Be than the Romaynez ware rebuykyde a lyttille,

With-drawes theyme drerely, and dreches no lengare;

Oure prynce with his powere persewes theyme aftyre,

Marginal notes:

and plucking out Colbrand, quickly cuts the giant Golapas in two at the knees;

telling him "he was too high by half." Then he strikes off his head.

He and his knights slay sixty giants.

The Romans rally and make a fierce resistance.

Many men are slain. Rivers of blood run into the sea.

The Romans begin to retreat, and Arthur presses on them.

2156 Prekez on*e* þe proudeste wi*th* his price knyghttez.

Sir Kayou*s*, sir Clegis, with clene men*e* of armez,

Enconters them*e* at þe clyffe wi*th* clene men*e* of armez;

Sir Cayous and
his men slay five
hundred. ffyghttes faste in þe fyrth, frythes no wapen*e*,

2160 ffelled at þe firste come fyfe hundrethe at ones!

And when they fande theym foresett with oure fers
        knyghtez,

ffewe men*e* agayne fele, mot fyche them*e* bettyre;

ffeghttez wi*th* all*e* þe frappe, foynes wi*th* speres,

2164 And faughte with the frekkeste þat to Fraunce langez.

He kills a king, Bot sir Kayou*s* þe kene castis in fewtyre,

Chasez on*e* a cou*r*sere, and to a kyng*e* rydys;

With a launce of Lettowe he thirllez his sydez,

2168 That the lyv*er* and þe lunggez on þe launce lengez.

The schafte scodyrde and schott in the schire byerne,

And soughte thorowowte þe schelde, and in þe schalke
        rystez.

but is sorely
wounded by a
coward knight
from behind. Bot Kayou*s* at the income was kepyd un-fayre

2172 With a cowarde knyghte of þe kythe ryche;

At the turnyng*e* that tyme the traytou*r*s hym hitte

In thorowe the felettes, and in þe flawnke aftyre,

That the boustous launce þe bewelles attamede,

2176 þat braste at þe brawlyng, and brake in þe myddys.

Sir Kayou*s* knewe wele, be þat kyde wounde,

That he was dede of þe dynte, and don*e* owte of lyfe.

He feels that he
has received a
mortal wound,
but strikes down
the coward. Than he raykes on*e* arraye and one rawe rydez,

2180 One this ryall*e* his dede to revenge;

"Kepe the, cowarde," and calles hym sone,

Cleves hym wyth his clere brande clenliche in sondire!

"Hadde thow wele delte thy dynt with thi handes,

2184 I hade forgeffen*e* þe my dede, be Crist now of hewyn*e*!"

He makes his
way to Arthur,
and tells him that
he is dying. He weyndes to þe wyese kyng*e*, and wynly hym gretes,

"I am wathely woundide, waresche mon*e* I nev*er*!

Wirke nowe thi wirchipe, as þe worlde askes,

2188 And brynge me to beryell*e*, byd I no more!

He bids him
greet for him the Grete wele my ladye þe qwene, ȝife þe werlde happyne,

And alle þe burliche birdes þat to hir boure lengez ;

And my worthily weife, þat wrethide me never,

2192 Bid hire fore hir wyrchipe wirke for my saulle !"

The kyngez confessour come, with Criste in his handes,

ffor to comforthe the knyghte, kende hym þe wordes ;

The knyghte coueride on his knees with a kaunt herte,

2196 And caughte his Creatoure þat comfurthes us alle !

Thane remmes þe riche kynge fore rewthe at his herte,

Rydes in-to rowte his dede to revenge ;

Presede in-to þe plumpe, and with a prynce metes,

2200 That was ayere of Egipt in thos este marches ;

Cleves hym with Collbrande clenlyche in sondyre !

He broches evene thorowe þe byerne, and þe sadille bristes,

And at þe bake of þe blonke þe bewelles entamede !

2204 Manly in his malycoly he metes anoþer,

The medille of þat myghtty, þat hym myche grevede ;

He merkes thurghe the maylez the myddes in sondyre,

That the myddys of þe mane on þe mounte fallez,

2208 þe toþer halfe of þe haunche on þe horse levyde.

Of þat hurte, alls I hope, heles he never !

He schotte thorowe þe schiltrouns with his scharpe wapene,

Schalkez he schrede thurghe, and schrenkede maylez ;

2212 Baneres he bare downne, bryttenede scheldes,

Brothely with browne stele his brethe he þare wrekes :

Wrothely he wryththis by wyghtnesse of strenghe,

Woundes þese whydyrewyns, werrayede knyghttes,

2216 Threppede thorowe þe thykkys thryttene sythis,

Thryngez throly in the thrange, and chis evene aftyre !

Thane sir Gawayne the gude, with wyrchipfulle knyghttez,

Wendez in the avawewarde be tha wodde hemmys ;

2220 Was warre of syr Lucius, one launde there he hovys,

With lordez and ligge mene, that to hyme-selfe lengede.

Thane the emperour enkerly askes hym sonne,

" What wille thow, Gawayne, wyrke with thi wapyne ?

2224 I watte be thi waveryng, thow willnez aftyre sorowe ;

I salle be wrokyne on thi wrethe, for alle thi grete
    wordez?"

But Lucius with
his long sword
wounds Sir
Lionel,

He laughte owtte a lange swerde, and luyschede one ffuste,
And *syr* Lyonelle in the launde lordely hym strykes,

2228 Hittes hym on þe hede, þat þe helme bristis;
Hurttes his herne-pane an haunde-brede large!
Thus he layes one þe lumppe, and lordlye þeme served,
Wondide worthily wirchipfulle knyghttez!

and makes the
blood flow from
Sir Florent.

2232 ffighttez with Florent that beste es of swerdez,
Tille þe fomande blode tille his fyste rynnes!
Thane þe Romayns relevyde, þat are ware rebuykkyde,
And alle to-rattys oure mene with theire riste horsses;

The Romans, ex-
cited by his
bravery, got the
better of Arthur's
men.

2236 ffore they see þaire cheftayne be chauffede so sore,
They chasse and choppe doune oure chevalrous knyghttes!
Sir Bedwere was borne thurghe, and his breste thyrllede,

Sir Bedwere is
slain.

With a burlyche braunde, brode at þe hiltes;

2240 The ryalle raunke stele to his hertte rynnys,
And he rusches to þe erthe, rewthe es the more!

Then Arthur
comes to the
rescue.

Thane þe conquerour tuke kepe, and come with his
    strenghes
To reschewe þe ryche mene of þe rounde table,

2244 To owttraye þe emperour, ʒif auntire it schewe,
Ewyne to þe egle, and Arthure askryes.
The emperour thane egerly at Arthure he strykez,

The Emperor
strikes Arthur on
the visor, and
wounds his face.

Awkwarde on þe umbrere, and egerly hym hittez!

2248 The nakyde swerde at þe nese noyes hym sare,
The blode of bolde kynge over þe breste rynnys,
Beblede at þe brode schelde and þe bryghte mayles!
Oure bolde kynge bowes þe blonke be þe bryghte brydylle,

Arthur gives him
a buffet that cuts
through his head
and breast.

2252 With his burlyche brande a buffette hym reches,
Thourghe þe brene and þe breste with his bryghte wapyne,
O-slante doune fro þe slote he slyttes at ones!

Sir Lucius dies,
and the Romans
fly.

Thus endys þe emperour of Arthure hondes,

2256 And all his austeryne oste þare-of ware affrayede!
Now they ferke to þe fyrthe, a fewe þat are levede,
ffor ferdnesse of oure folke, by þe fresche strandez!

The floure of oure ferse mene one fferant stedez
2260 ffolowes frekly on þe frekes, thate ffrayede was never.

Arthur's men pursue.

Thane þe kyde conquerour cryes fulle lowde,—
"Cosyne of Cornewaile, take kepe to þi-selfene,
That no captayne be kepyde for none silver,

The King bids them give no quarter.

2264 Or syr Kayous dede be cruelly vengede!"
"Nay," sais syr Cador, "so me Criste helpe!
Thare ne es kaysere ne kynge, þat undire Criste rygnnes,
þat I ne schalle kille colde dede be crafte of my handez!"

Sir Cador declares that he will spare neither king nor kaisar.

2268 Thare myghte mene see chiftaynes, on chalke whitte stedez,
Choppe doune in the chaas chevalryc noble;
Romaynes þe rycheste and ryalle kyngez,
Braste with ranke stele theire rybbys in sondyre!

A fearful carnage follows.

2272 Grayves fore-brustene thurghe burneste helmes,
With brandez for-brittenede one brede in þe laundez;
They hewede doune haythene mene with hiltede swerdez,
Be hole hundrethez on hye, by þe holte eynyes!

Heathen men are slain by hundreds.

2276 Thare myghte no silver theym save, ne socoure theire lyves,
Sowdane ne Sarazene,—ne senatour of Rome!
Thane relevis þe renkes of the rounde table
Be þe riche revare, that rynnys so faire;

2280 Lugegez thaym luflye by þa lyghte strandez,
Alle on lawe in þe lawnde, that lordlyche byernes:
Thay kaire to þe karyage, and tuke whate them likes,
Kamelles and sekadrisses, and cofirs fulle riche,

Arthur's men plunder the rich camp of the Romans.

2284 Hekes and hakkenays, and horses of armes,
Howsynge and herbergage of heythene kyngez;
They drewe owt of dromondaries dyverse lordes,
Moyllez mylke whitte, and mervaillous bestez,

Horses, camels, dromedaries, milk-white mules, elephants, and many marvellous beasts are captured.

2288 Elfaydes, and Arrabys, and olyfauntez noble,
þer are of þe Oryent, with honourable kynges.
Bot syr Arthure onone ayeres þer-aftyre
Ewyne to the Emperour, with honourable kyngis;
2292 Laughte hym upe fulle lovelyly with lordliche knyghttez,
And ledde hyme to þe layere, thare the kyng lygges.

Thane harawdez heghely, at hoste of the lordes,

Hunttes upe the haythemene, that on heghte lygges,

The bodies of the
Emperor and
chief men of
Rome are em-
balmed and
wrapped in lead, 2296 The Sowdane of Surry, and certayne kynges,

Sexty of þe cheefe senatours of Rome.

Thane they bussches and bawmede þaire honourliche
    kynges,

Sewed theme in sendelle sexti faulde aftire,

2300 Lappede them in lede, lesse that they schulde

Chawnge or chawffe, ȝif þay myghte escheffe ;

enclosed in
chests, and sent
to Rome with
their banners
displayed over
them. Closed in kystys clene un-to Rome,

With theire baners abowne, theire bagis there-undyre,

2304 In whate countre þay kaire that knyghttes myghte knawe

Iche kynge be his colours, in kyth whare lengede.

Onone one the secounde daye, sone by þe morne,

Twa senatours ther come, and certayne knyghttez,

2308 Hodles fro þe hethe, over þe holte eynes,

Two Senators
come barefoot
and kneel before
the conqueror. Barefote over þe bente, with brondes so ryche,

Bowes to þe bolde kynge, and biddis hym þe hiltes,

Whethire he wille hang theym or hedde, or halde theyme
    on lyfe :

2312 Knelyde be-fore þe conquerour in kyrtilles allone ;

With carefulle contenaunce þay karpide þese wordes,—

"Twa senatours we are, thi subgettez of Rome,

That has savede oure lyfe by þeise salte strandys ;

2316 Hyd us in þe heghe wode, thurghe þe helpynge of Criste !

Besekes the of socoure, as soveraygne and lorde !

Grante us lyffe and lyme with liberalle herte,

ffor his luffe that the lente this lordchipe in erthe !"

The King grants
them their lives
on condition of
their carrying a
message for him
to Rome. 2320 "I graunte," quod gude kynge, "thurghe grace of my-
    selfene,

I giffe ȝowe lyffe and lyme, and leve for to passe,

So ȝe doo my message menskefully at Rome,

That ilke charge þat I ȝow ȝiffe here be-fore my cheefe
    knyghttez."

2324 "Ȝis," sais the senatours, "that salle we ensure,

Sekerly be oure trowhes thi sayenges to fullfille ;

We salle lett for no lede þat lyffes in erthe,

ffore pape ne for potestate, ne prynce so noble,

2328 That ne salle lelely in lande thi letteres pronounce,

ffor duke ne fore dussepere, to dye in þe payne!"

Thane the banerettez of Bretayne broghte þeme to tentes;

There barbours ware bownne, with basyns one lofte, **The British lords bring barbers and**

2332 With warme watire i-wys they wette theme fulle sone; **basons and baths for them, in order**

They schovene this schalkes scharpely ther-aftyre, **to prove their submission.**

To rekkene theis Romaynes recreaunt and ȝoldene;

ffor-thy schove they theme to schewe, for skomfitte of Rome.

2336 They coupylde þe kystys on kamelles be-lyve, **They fastened the coffins two and two on camels.**

On asses and arrabyes, theis honourable kynges;

The emperoure for honoure, alle by hym one, **The Emperor's body, for honour,**

Evene appone ane olyfaunte, hys egle owtt overe; **was by itself on an elephant.**

2340 Be-kende theme the captyfis the kynge dide hym-selfene,

And alle byfore his kene mene karpede thees wordes,—

"Here are the kystis," quod the kyng, "kaire over þe mownttez; **Arthur charges them to say that they have brought the arrears of tribute due from him to Rome**

Mette fulle monee þat ȝe have mekylle ȝernede,

2344 The taxe and þe trebutte of tene schore wyntteres,

That was tenefully tynte in tyme of oure elders:

Saye to the senatoure, þe ceté þat ȝemes,

That I sende hyme þe somme, assaye how hyme likes!

2348 Bott byde theme nevere be so bolde, whylles my blode regnes, **This is the only tribute they will ever get from him.**

Efte for to brawllee þeme for my brode landez,

Ne to aske trybut ne taxe be nakyne tytle,

Bot syche tresoure as this, whilles my tyme lastez."

2352 Nowe they raike to Rome the redyeste wayes, **They hasten to Rome and summon the people to the Capitol.**

Knylles in the capatoylle, and comowns assembles,

Soverayngez and senatours, tho ceté þat ȝemes;

Be-kende theme the caryage, kystis and oþer,

2356 Alls þe conquerour comaunde with cruelle wordes. . **Perform Arthur's message as he directed.**

"We hafe trystily trayvellede þis tribute to feche,

The taxe and þe trewage of fowre score wynteris,

They have brought the tax dues from England and Ireland, and all the west.

Of Iglande, of Irelande and alle þir owtt illes,

2360 That Arthure in the occedente ocupyes att ones:

He byddis ȝow nevere be so bolde, whills his blode regnes

To brawle ȝowe fore Bretayne ne his brode landes,

Ne aske hyme trebute ne taxe be nonkyns title,

2364 Bot syche tresoure as this, whills his tyme lastis.

They declare that they have suffered defeat and great loss,

We haffe foughttene in ffrance, and us es foule happenede,

And alle oure myche faire folke faye are by-levede!

Eschappide there ne chevallrye, ne cheftaynes noþer,

2368 Bott choppede downne in the chasse, syche chawnce es be-fallene!

We rede ȝo store ȝowe of stone, and stuffene ȝour walles:

and bid the Romans beware.

ȝow wakkens wandrethe and werre; be-ware, ȝif ȝow lykes!"

This great battle between Arthur and the Romans was fought in the calends of May.

In the kalendez of Maye this caas es be-fallene:

2372 The roy ryalle renownde, with his rownde table,

One the coste of Constantyne by þe clere strandez,

It was a blow from which the Romans could not recover.

Has þe Romaynes ryche rebuykede for ever!

Whene he hade foughttene in Fraunce, and the felde wonnene,

2376 And fersely his foomene fellde owtte of lyfe,

After the defeat Arthur buries his knights.

He bydes for þe beryenge of his bolde knyghtez, .

That in batelle with brandez ware broughte owte of lyfe.

Sir Bedwere at Bayonne;
Sir Cayous at Camelot;

He beryes at Bayone syr Bedwere þe ryche;

2380 The cors of Kayone þe kene at Came es belevefede,

Koveride with a crystalle clenly alle over;

His fadyre conqueride þat kyth knyghtly with hondes:

In Burgundy, Berade, and Baldwin, and Bedwar;
Sir Cador at Camelot.
In the August after Arthur enters into Germany,

Seyne in Burgoyne he bade to bery mo knyghttez,

2384 Sir Berade and Bawdwyne, sir Bedwar þe ryche,

And syr Cador at Came, as his kynde askes.

Thane syr Arthure onone, in þe Auguste-þer-aftyre,

Enteres to Almayne wyth ostez arrayed;

2388 Lengez at Lusscheburghe, to lechene hys knyghttez,

With his lele ligge-mene, as lorde in his awene :

And one *Chri*spofre daye a concelle he haldez,

Withe kynges and kaysers, clerkkes and oþer,

2392 Comandez them kenely to caste alle þeire wittys,

How he may *con*quere by crafe the kythe þat he claymes.

Bot the co*n*querour kene, curtais and noble,

Karpes in the concelle theys knyghtly wordez,—

2396 "Here es a knyghte in theis klevys, enclesside with hilles,

That I have cowayte to knawe, be-cause of his wordez,

That es Lorayne þe lele, I kepe noghte to layne ;

The lordchipe es lovely, as ledes me telles :

2400 I wille that Ducherye devyse, and dele as me lykes,

And seyne dresse wyth þe duke, if destyny suffre :

The renke rebelle has bene un-to my rownde table,

Redy aye with Romaynes, and ryotte my landes !

2404 We salle rekkene fulle rathe, if resone so happene,

Who has ryghte to þat rente, by ryche Gode of hevene !

Thane wille I by Lumbardye lykande to schawe,

Sett lawe in þe lande, þat laste salle ever.

2408 The tyrauntez of T*er*kayne tempeste a littylle,

Talke with þe temperalle, whilles my tyme lastez ;

I gyffe my protteccione to alle þe pope landez,

My ryche penselle of pes my pople to schewe :

2412 It es a foly to offende oure fadyr undire Gode,

Owþer Peter or Paule, þa postles of Rome.

Ʒiff we spare the spir*i*tuelle, we spede bot the bettire ;

Whilles we have for to speke, spille salle it nev*er* !" [1]

2416 Now they spede at þe spurres, wi*th*-owttyne speche more,

To þe Marche of Meyes, theis manliche knyghtez,

That es Lorrayne alofede, as London*e* es here ;

Pety of þat seynʒowre, that sov*er*aynge es holdene.

2420 The kyng ferkes furthe on a faire stede,

and encamps at Luxemburg.

He holds a council on Christmas-day to devise how he may conquer all the territory that he claims.

He makes a speech in the council, saying that he much desires the possessions of the Duke of Lorraine,

who has been long a rank rebel to his Round Table.

He will soon show him who is the rightful owner of those lands !

Afterwards he will go to Lombardy and then visit the tyrants of Turkey,

but he will give protection to all the lands of the Pope, for it is folly to offend our Father under God.

If we spare the goods of the spiritualty we shall speed the better.

Arthur straightway leads his knights to lay siege to Metz.

---

[1] This passage may be taken as tolerably conclusive evidence that the poem was composed by an ecclesiastic.

With ferreraunde ferawnte, and oþer foure knyghtez;

Abowte the cete þa sevene, thay soughte at þe nextte,

They seek a place to fix the engines.

To seke theme a sekyre place to sett withe engeynes;

2424 Thane they beneyde in burghe bowes of vyse,

The citizens shoot at them with arrows and bolts.

Bekyrs at þe bolde kynge with boustouse lates,

All-blawsters at Arthure egerly schottes,

ffor to hurte hyme or his horse with þat hard wapene :

The king, with-out his shield, remains close to the walls within range of the arrows.

2428 The kynge schonte for no schotte, ne no schelde askys,

Bot schewes hym scharpely in his schene wedys;

Lenges alle at laysere, and lokes one the wallys,

Whare þey ware laweste the ledes to assaille.

Sir Ferrere re-monstrates with him for exposing himself to such danger.

2432 "Sir," said syr fferere, "a ffoly thowe wirkkes,

Thus nakede in thy noblaye to neghe to þe walles,

Sengely in thy surcotte, this ceté to reche,

And schewe þe with-in, there to schende us alle.

2436 Hye us hastylye heynne, or we mone fulle happone,

ffor hitt they the or thy horse, it harmes for ever !"

Arthur scorns him, and tells him

"Ife thowe be ferde," quod the kyng, "I rede thow ryde uttere,

Lesse þat þey rywe the with theire rownd wapyne !

2440 Thow arte bot a fawntkyne, ne ferly me thynkkys !

that he would be afraid of a fly that lighted on him.

Þou wille be flayede for a flye þat one thy flesche lyghttes !

I ame nothynge agaste, so me Gode helpe !

As for him, he fears not such poor creatures as these.

Þof siche gadlynges be grevede, it greves me bot lyttille !

2444 Thay wyne no wirchipe of me, bot wastys theire takle !

They salle wante or I weende, I wagene myne hevede !

Never knave will be allowed to kill a crowned king.

Salle never harlotte have happe, thorowe helpe of my Lorde,

To kylle a crownde kynge with krysome enoynttede !"

Then come the gallant troops of Arthur.

2448 Thane come þe herbarjours, harageous knyghtez,

The hale batelles one hye harrawnte ther-aftyre;

And oure forreours ferse, appone fele halfes,

First the light forayers on nim-ble steeds;

Come flyeande be-fore one ferawnt stedes;

2452 fferkande in arraye theire ryalle knyghttez,

then the renown-ed champions of the Round Table;

The renkez renownde of þe rownnd table :

Alle þe frekke mene of Fraunce folowede thare aftyre,

ffaire fittyde one frownte, and one the felde hovys.

2456 Thane the schalkes scharpelye scheftys theire horsez,

To schewene them semly in theire scheene wedes ;

Buskes in batayle with baners displayede,

With brode scheldes enbrassede, and burlyche helmys,

2460 With pennons and penselles of ylke prynce armes,

Appayrellde with perrye and pretious stones :

The lawnces with loraynes, and lemande scheldes,

Lyghtenande as þe levenynge, and lemand al over.

2464 Thane the price mene prekes, and proves þeire horsez,

Satilles to þe ceté, appone sere halfes ;

Enserches the subbarbes sadly thare-aftyre,

Discoveris of schotte-mene, and skyrmys a lyttille ;

2468 Skayres þaire skottefers, and theire skowtte waches,

Brittenes theire barrers with theire bryghte wapyns ;

Bett downe a barbycane, and þe brygge wynnys,

Ne hade the garnysone bene gude at þe grete ʒates,

2472 Thay hade wonne that wone be theire awene strenghe !

Thane with-drawes oure mene, and drisses theme bettyre,

ffor dred of þe drawe-brigge dasschede in sondre ;

Hyes to þe harbergage, thare the kynge hovys

2476 With his battelle one heghe, horsyde on stedys ;

Thane was þe prynce purvayede, and þeire places nomene,

Pyghte pavyllyons of palle, and plattes in seegge.

Thane lenge they lordly, as þeme leefe thoghte,

2480 Waches in ylke warde, as to þe werre falles,

Settes up sodaynly certayne engynes ;

One Sonondaye be þe soone has a fleche ʒoldene.

The kynge calles one Florente, þat flour was of knyghttez,—

2484 "The Fraunche-mene enfeblesches, ne farly me thynkkys!

They are un-fondyde folke in þa faire marches,

ffor theme wantes þe flesche and fude that theme lykes.

Here are fforestez faire appone fele halves,

2488 And thedyre feemene are flede with freliche bestes !

Thow salle foonde to þe felle, and forraye the mountes ;

Sir fforawnt and *syr* Florydas salle folowe thi brydylle;

Us moste with some fresche mette refresche our pople,

2492 That are feedde in þe fyrthe with þe froyte of þe erthe.

Sir Gawaine himself, the worshipful warden, shall accompany them,

Thare salle weende to þis viage sir Gawayne hym-selfene,

Wardayne fulle wyrchipfulle, and so hym wele semes :

Sir Wecharde, *syr* Waltyre, theis wyrchipfulle knyghtes,

and many other knights of name.

2496 With alle wyseste mene of þe Weste marches :

Sir Clegis, *syr* Clarybalde, *syr* Clarymownde þe noble,

The capytayne oo wardyfe clenlyche arrayede.

Goo now, warne alle þe wache, Gawayne and oþer,

2500 And weendes furthe on ȝour waye withowttyne moo

wordes."

These fresh men of arms start in their journey through woods and over hills.

Now ferkes to þe fyrthe thees frosche mene of armes,

To þe felle so fewe, theis fresclyche byernes,

Thorowe hopes and hymlande hillys and oþer,

2504 Holtis and hare woddes with heslyne schawes,

Thorowe marasse and mosse and montes so heghe ;

And in the myste mornynge one a mede falles,

They fall upon a field of grass newly mown,

Mawene and un-made, maynoyrede bott lyttylle,

2508 In swathes sweppene downe fulle of swete floures :

where they bait their horses,

Thare unbrydilles theis bolde, and baytes þeire horses,

To þe grygynge of þe daye, that byrdes gane synge ;

while the birds sweetly sing.

Whylles the surs of þe sonne, þat sonde es of Cryste,

2512 That solaces alle synfulle, þat syghte has in erthe.

Thane weendes owtt the wardayne, *syr* Gawayne hym-

selfene,

Sir Gawaine goes forth by himself to seek adventures.

Alles he þat weysse was and wyghte, wondyrs to seke ;

Thane was he warre of a wye wondyre wele armyde,

He sees a knight well armed,

2516 Baytand one a wattire banke by þe wodde eynis,

Buskede in brenyes bryghte to be-halde,

Enbrassede a brode schelde on a blonke ryche,

With birenne ony borne, bot a boye one

and a page carrying his spear.

2520 Hoves by hym on a blonke, and his spere holdes ;

He bare sessenande in golde thre grayhondes of sable,

On his shield his coat of arms was displayed.

With chapes a cheynes of chalke whytte sylver,

A charbocle in þe cheefe, chawngawnde of hewes,

2524 And a cheefe anterous, chalange who lykes

Sir Gawayne glystes on the gome with a glade wille!
A grete spere fro his grome he grypes in hondes,
Gyrdes ewene overe the streme one a stede ryche

Sir Gawaine beholds him with great joy, and goes across the stream towards him.

2528 To þat steryne in stour, one strenghe þare he hovys!
Egerly one Inglisce Arthure he askryes,
The toþer irouslye answers hyme sone
On a launde of Lorrayne with a lowde stevene,

He shouts his cry, "Arthur of England."

The other shouts "Lorraine."

2532 That ledes myghte lystene þe lenghe of a myle!
"Whedyr prykkes thow, pilour, þat profers so large?
Here pykes thowe no praye, profire whene þe lykes!
Bot thow in þis perelle put of the bettire,

Then does the strange knight declare that Gawaine shall be his prisoner.

2536 Thow salle be my presonere, for alle thy prowde lates!"
"Sir," sais syr Gawayne, "so me Gode helpe!
Siche glaverande gomes greves me bot lyttille!
Bot if thowe graythe thy gere, the wille grefe happene,

Sir Gawaine treats his great words with contempt.

2540 Or thowe goo of þis greve, for alle thy grete wordes!"
Thane þeire launces they lachene, thes lordlyche byernez,
Laggene with longe speres one lyarde stedes;
Cowpene at awntere be brastes of armes,

Then they lay their spears in rest, and meet.

2544 Tille bothe þe crowelle speres broustene att ones!
Thorowe scheldys þey schotte, and scherde thorowe males,
Bothe schere thorowe schoulders a schaftmonde large!
Thus worthylye þes wyes wondede ere bothene;

Both the spears strike fair, and wound the knights.

2548 Or they wreke þeme of wrethe a-waye wille þey never!
Than they raughte in the reyne and a-gayne rydes,
Redely theis rathe mene rusches owtte swordez,
Hittes one hellmes fulle hertelyche dynttys,

Then they rein in their horses and return to the fight with swords.

2552 Hewes appone hawberkes with fulle harde wapyns!
ffulle stowttly þey stryke thire steryne knyghttes,
Stokes at þe stomake with stelyne poynttes,
ffeghttene and floresche withe flawmande swerdez,

Fearful blows are exchanged.

2556 Tille þe flawes of fyre flawmes one theire helmes.
Thane syr Gawayne was grevede, and grythgide fulle sore;
With Galuthe his gude swerde grymlye he strykes!
Clefe þe knyghttes schelde clenliche in sondre!

Sir Gawaine waxes wroth, and strikes grimly with his sword Galuth.

<table>
<tr><td>He cleaves the knight's shield asunder, and lays open his side.</td><td>2560</td><td>Who lukes to þe lefte syde, whene his horse launches,
With þe lyghte of þe sonne men myghte see his lyvere!
Thane granes þe gome fore greefe of his wondys,</td></tr>
</table>

He cleaves the knight's shield asunder, and lays open his side.

2560 Who lukes to þe lefte syde, whene his horse launches,
With þe lyghte of þe sonne men myghte see his lyvere!
Thane granes þe gome fore greefe of his wondys,

The knight strikes fiercely at Sir Gawaine.

And gyrdis at *syr* Gawayne, as he by glentis;
2564 And awkewarde egerly sore he hym smyttes;
An alet enamelde he oches in sondire,
Bristes þe rerebrace with the bronde ryche,
Kerves of at þe coutere with þe clene egge,
2568 Anetis þe avawmbrace vrayllede with silver!

He cuts through his armour and draws blood,

Thorowe a dowble vesture of velvett ryche,
With þe venymous swerde a vayne has he towchede!
That voydes so violently þat alle his witte changede!

which flows over all his dress.

2572 The vesere, the aventaile, his vesturis ryche,
With the valyant blode was verrede alle over!
Thane this tyrante tite turnes þe brydille,
Talkes un-tendirly, and sais, "þow arte towchede!

Then the knight jeers at him, and says the blood shall never be staunched.

2576 Us bus have a blode bande, or thi ble change,
ffor alle þe barbours of Bretayne salle noghte thy blode
    stawnche!
ffor he þat es blemeste with þis brade brande, blyne
    schalle he never."

Sir Gawaine despises his words,

"ȝa," *quod syr* Gawayne, "thow greves me bot lyttille!
2580 Thowe wenys to glopyne me with thy gret wordez!
Thow trowes with thy talkynge þat my harte talmes!
Thow betydes torfere or thowe hyene turne,

but would know what can stop the bleeding.

Bot thow telle me tytte, and tarye no lengere,
2584 What may staunche this blode þat thus faste rynnes."
"ȝife I say þe sothely, and sekire þe my trowthe,

The knight will tell him if Gawaine will allow him to have shrift and prepare himself for his end.

No surggone in Salarne salle save þe bettyre;
With-thy þat thowe suffre me, for sake of thy Cryste,
2588 To schewe schortly my schrifte, and schape for myne
    · ende."

Gawaine readily grants this.

"ȝis," *quod syr* Gawayne, "so me God helpe!
I gyfe þe grace and graunt, thofe þou hafe grefe servede!
2592 With-thy thowe say me sothe what thowe here sekes,
Thus sengilly and sulayne alle þi-selfe one;

And whate laye thow leves one, layne noghte þe sothe,
And whate legyaunce, and whaie þow arte lorde."

2596 "My name es *syr* Priamus; a prince es my fadyre,
Praysede in his *per*tyes with provede kynges;
In Rome thare he regnes he es riche halden*e*;
He has bene rebell*e* to Rome, and redon*e* theire landes,
2600 Werreyand weisely wyntters and ȝeres,
Be witt and be wyssdome, and be wyghte strenghe,
And be wyrchipfull*e* werre his awen*e* has he wonn*e*.
He es of Alexandire blode, ov*er*lynge of kynges,
2604 The uncle of his ayele, *syr* Ector of Troye;
And here es the kynreden*e* that I of come,
And Judas and Josue, þise gentill*e* knyghtes:
I ame apparaunt his ayere, and eldeste of oþ*er*;
2608 Of Alexandere and Aufrike, and all*e* þa owte landes,
I am in possessione, and plenerly sessede.
In all*e* þe price cetees that to þe porte langes,
I sall*e* hafe trewly the tresou*r* and the londes,
2612 And bothe trebute and taxe whill*es* my tyme la̋stes;
I was so hawtayne of herte, whill*es* I at home lengede,
I helde nane my hippe heghte undire heven*e* ryche;
ffor-thy was I sente hedire with seven*e* score knyghttez,
2616 To asaye of this werre, be sente of my fadire;
And I am for Cyr*us* witryo schamely supprisede,
And be awtire of armes owtrayede for ev*er*e!
Now hafe I taulde the þe kyne that I ofe come,
2620 Wille thow for knyghthede kene me thy name?"
"Be Criste," *quod syr* Gawayne, "knyghte wys I nev*er*!
With þe kydde conquerou*r* a knafe of his chambyre:
Has wroghte in his wardrope wyntters and ȝeres,
2624 One his long*e* armour that hym beste lykid;
I poyne all*e* his pavelyoun*s* þat to hym-selfe pendes,
Dyghttes his dowblettez for dukes and erles,
Aketoun*s* aven*a*unt for Arthure hym selfen*e*,
2628 That he usede in werre alle this aughte wyntt*er*!
He made me ȝomane at ȝole, and gafe me gret gyftes,

The stranger
knight tells him
that his name is
Sir Priamus, son
of a prince,

who rebelled
against Rome,
and gained a
kingdom

He is of the blood
of Alexander and
Hector of Troy;

related also to
Judas and
Joshua;

heir of Africa.

When at home he
was so proud and
overbearing,

that he was sent
by his father to
this war with a
band of knights.

He desires to
know Sir Ga-
waine's name.

Sir Gawaine an-
swers deceitfully
that he is only a
knave of Arthur's
chamber,

who had given
him a horse and
harness as a re-
ward for service.

And c. pound and a horse, and harnayse fulle ryche;

Gife I happe to my hele that hende for to serve,

2632   I be holpene in haste, I hotte the for-sothe!"

"If his knaves
be such, what
can his knights
be?" exclaims Sir
Priamus.
Alexander and
Hector will be
nothing to him.

"Giffe his knafes be syche, his knyghttez are noble!

There es no kynge undire Criste may kempe with hym one!

He wille be Alexander ayre, þat alle þe erthe lowttede,

2636   Abillere þane ever was syr Ector of Troye."

"Now fore the krisome þat þou kaghte that day þou
     was crystenede,

Then Sir Gawaine
tells him the
truth.

Whethire thowe be knyghte or knaffe, knawe now þe
     sothe :

My name es syr Gawayne, I graunt þe forsothe,

He is Sir Ga-
waine, cousin to
the Conqueror,
the richest knight
of all the Round
Table.

2640   Cosyne to the conquerour, he knawes it hyme selfene;

Kydd in his kalander a knyghte of his chambyre,

And rollede the richeste of alle þe rounde table!

I ame þe dussepere and duke he dubbede with his hondes,

2644   Deynttely on a daye be-fore his dere knyghtes;

Gruche noghte, gude syr, þofe me this grace happene;

It es þe gifte of Gode, the gree es hys awene!"

Then Sir Priamus
says this is better
to him than any
earthly posses-
sions.

"Petire!" sais Priamus, "now payes me bettire

2648   Thane I of Provynce warre prynce, and of Paresche ryche!

ffore me ware lever prevely be prykkyd to þe harte,

Than ever any prikkere had siche a pryse wonnyne!

In recompense,
he warns Ga-
waine that the
Duke of Lorraine
with his knights
is lying in the
wood near.

Bot here es herberde at handes, in zone huge holtes,

2652   Halle bataile one heyghe, take hede ʒif the lyke!

The duke of Lorrayne the derfe, with his dere knyghtes,

The doughtyest of Dolfmede, and Duchemene many,

The lordes of Lumbardye that leders are haldene,

2656   The garnysone of Godarde gaylyche arrayede,

The wyese of þe Westvale, wirchipfulle biernez,

Of Sessoyne and Surylande Sarazenes enewe ;

A mighty host
well armed.

They are nowmerde fulle neghe, and namede in rollez

2660   Sexty thowsande and tene for-sothe of sekyre mene of
     armez ;

Bot ʒif thow hye fro þis hethe, it harmes us bothe,

And bot my hurtes be sone holpene, hole be I never!

Tak heede to þ*is* hausemen*e*, þat he no horn*e* blawe,

2664 Arc thowe heyly in haste beese hewen*e* al to peces ;

ffor they are my retenuz to rydc whare I wyll*e*,

Es non*e* redyare renkes regnande in erthe ;

Be thow raghte w*ith* þat rowtt, thow rȳdes no foi þer,

2668 Ne thow bees nev*er* rawnsonede for reches in erthe !"

Ṣir Gawayn*e* wente or þe wathe come, whare hym beste lykede,

With this wortheliche wye, that wondyd was sore ;

Merkes to þe mountayne there ouie men*e* lenges,

2672 Baytaynde theire blonkes þer on þe brode mede ;

Lordes lenande lowe on*e* lemand*e* scheldes,

With lowde laghttirs on*e* loft*e* for lykyng*e* of byrdez,

Of larkez, of lynkwhyttcz, þat lufflyche songen*e*,

'676 And some was sleghte on*e* slepe w*ith* slaughte of þe pople,

That sange in þe seson*e* in the schen*ne* schawes,

So lawe in þe lawndcz so lykand*e* notes.

Thane *syr* Whycher whas warre þaire wardayne was wondyde,

2680 And went to hym wepand, and wryngande his handes ,

Sir Wychere, *syr* Walchere, theis weise men*e* of armes,

Had wondyre of *syr* Gawayne, and wente hym*e* agayns :

Mctt hym in the mydwaye, and m*er*vaile them*e* toghte

2684 How he maisterede þat man*e*, so myghtty of strenghes !

Be all*e* þe welthe of þe werlde, so woo was þeme nev*er* !

"ffor all*e* our wirchippe i-wysse awayc cs in crthc !"

"Greve ȝow noghte," *quod* Gawayne, "for Godis luffe of heven*e* ;

2688 ffoie this es bot gosesemere, and gyffen*e* on*e* erles ;

þoffc my schouldire be schrede, and my schelde thyrllede,

And the wielde of myn*e* arme werkkes a littill*e*,

This prissoner*e* *syr* Pr*i*am*us*, that has p*er*ilo*u*s wondes,

2692 Sais þat he has salvez sall*e* soften*e* us botchen*e*."

Thane stirttes to his sterape sterynfull*e* knyghttez,

And he lordely lȝghttes and laghte of his bryḍill*e*,

And lete his builyche blonke baite on þe flores ;

He bids him beware lest they should discover and destroy him.

Sir Gawaine goes with the wounded knight to Arthur's men.

They are reposing themselves in different ways,

listening to the songs of the birds.

Sir Whycher perceives that Sir Gawaine is wounded,

and wonders how he could have conquered this mighty knight.

Sir Gawaine makes light of his wounds.

His prisoner, Sir Priamus, has salves that will heal them.

They assist him to dismount.

2696 Braydes of his bacenette and his ryche wedis,

He bends from
exhaustion and
loss of blood

Bownnes to his brode schelde and bowes to þe erthe,

In alle the bodye of that bolde es no blode leved !

Than preses to syr Priamous precious knyghtes,

2700 Avyssely of his horse hentis hym in armes;

His helme and his hawberke thay takene of aftyre,

Sir Priamus is
lifted from his
horse.

And hastily for his hurtte alle his herte chawngyd ;

Thay laide hyme downe in the lawndez, and laghte of
his wedes,

2704 And he levede hym one lange, or how hym beste lykede ;

They find at his
girdle a gold box
filled with the
flower of Para-
dise.

A ffoyle of fyne golde they fande at his gyrdille,

þat es fulle of þe flour of þe foure welle,

þat flowes owte of Paradice whene þe flode ryses,

2708 That myche froyt of fallez, þat feede schalle us alle ;

Be it frette on his flesche, þare synnes are entamede,

The freke schalle be fische halle with-in fowre howres.

With this the
knights are
healed.

They uncovere þat cors with fulle clene hondes ;

2712 With clere watire a knyghte clensis theire wondes,

Keled theyme kyndly, and comforthed þer hertes.

And whene þe carffes ware clene, þay clede them aȝayne ;

Barelle ferrers they brochede, and broghte theme the wyne,

Then wine and
provisions are
brought to them.

2716 Bothe brede and brawne, and bredis fulle ryche ;

Whene þay hade etene anone they armede after.

Thane tha awntrende men as armes askryes,

With a claryoune clere, thire knyghtez to-gedyre,

The scouts bring
news of the army
encamped in the
wood.

2720 Callys to concelle, and of this case tellys :—

" ȝondyr es a companye of clene mene of armes,

The keneste in contek þat undir Criste lenges ;

In ȝone okene wode an oste are arrayede,

2724 Undir takande mene of þiese owte londes ;

As sais us syr Priamous, so helpe seynt Peter !"

Sir Gawaine is for
attacking them,

"Go, mene, quod Gawayne, "and grape in ȝoure hertez,

Who salle graythe to ȝone greve to ȝone gret lordes ;

2728 ȝif we gettlesse goo home, the kyng wille be grevede,

but refers to Sir
Florent, the
leader of the
party.

And say we are gadlynges, agaste for a lyttille :

We are with syr Florente, as to-daye falles,

That es floure of ffraunce, for he fleede nev*er*;
2732 He was chosen*e* and chargegide in chambire of þe kynge,
Chiftayne of þ*is* journee w*ith* chevalryc noble;
Whethire he fyghte or he flee, we sall*e* folowe aftyre,
ffore all*e* þe fere of ȝone folke forsake sall*e* I nev*er*!"

2736 "ffadyre," sais *syr* Florent, "full*e* faire ȝe it telle!
Bot I ame bot a fawntkyn*e*, unfraystede in armes,
ȝif any foly be-fall*e*, þe fawte sall*e* be owrs,
And freindly 'o Fraunce be flemede for ev*er*!

2740 Woundes noghte ȝo*ur* wirchipe, my witte es bot symple;
ȝe arc owre wardaync i-wysse, wyrke as ȝowe lykes;
ȝe arc at the ferreste noghte passande fyve hundrethe,
And þ*at* es fully to fewe to feghte with them*e* all*e*,

2744 ffore harlottez and hausemene sall*e* helpe bott littill*e*;
They will*e* hye theym*e* hyene for all*e* þe*i*re gret wordes!
I rede ȝe wyrke aftyre witte, as wyesse men of armes,
And warpes wylily a-waye, as wirchipfull*e* knyghtes."

2748 "I grawnte," *quod syr* Gawayne, "so me Gode helpe!
Bot here are galyarde gomes þ*at* of þe gre servis,
The kreuelleste knyghttes of þe kynges chambyre,
That kane carpe with the copp*e* knyghtly wordes;

2752 We sall*e* prove to daye who sall*e* the prys wyne."
N owe ferriours fers un-to þe fyrthe rydez,
And foun*g*ez a faire felde, and on fotte lyghttez;
Prekes aftyre þe pray, as pryce men*e* of armes.

2756 fflorent and Floridas, with fyve score knyghttez,
ffolowede in þe foreste, and on þe way fowndys,
fflyngande a faste trott, and on þe folke dryffes.
Than felewes fast to our folke wele a fyve hundreth

2760 Of freke men*e* to þe fyrthe, appon*e* fresche horses;
One *syr* Feraunt be-fore, apon*e* a fayre stede,
(Was fosterde in Famacoste, the fende was his fadyre)
He flenges to *syr* Florent, and prystly he kryes,—

2764 "Why flees thow, falls knyghte? þe fende hafe þ*i* saule!"
Thane *syr* fflorent was fayne, and in fewter castys;
One fawnell*e* of ffryselande to fferaunt he rydys,

6

And raghte in þe reyne on þe stede ryche,

2768 And rydes to-warde the rowte, restes he no lengere!

who with his
lance in rest
pierces him
through the face
and brain.
ffulle butt in þe frounte he flysches hyme evene,

And alle dysfegoures his face with his felle wapene!

Thurghe his bryghte bacenette his brayne has he towchede,

2772 And brustene his neke-bone, þat all his breste stoppede!

Thane his cosyne askryede, and cryede fulle lowde,

His cousin vows
vengeance for his
death,
"Thowe has killede colde dede þe kynge of alle knyghttes!

He has bene fraistede on felde in fyftene rewmes;

2776 He fonde never no freke myghte foghte with hym one!

Thow schalle dye for his dede with my derfe wapene,

And all þe doughtty for dule þat in ȝone dale hoves!"

but Sir Floridas
quickly disposes
of him.
"ffy," sais syr fforidas, "thow ffleryande wryche!

2780 Thow wenes for to flay us, ffloke-mowthede schrewe!"

Bot ffloridas with a swerde, as he by glenttys,

Alle þe flesche of þe flanke he flappes in sondyre,

That alle the filthe of þe freke and fele of þe guttes

2784 ffoloes his fole fotte, whene he furthe rydes!

Than rydes a renke to reschewe þat byerne,

Sir Raynald, the
renegade, proud-
ly presses in;
That was Raynalde of þe rodes, and rebelle to Criste,

Pervertede with Paynyms þat Cristene persewes;

2788 Presses in prowdly, as þe praye wendes,

ffore he hade in Prewsslande myche pryce wonnene;

ffor-thi in presence thare he profers so large!

but Sir Richer,
of the Round
Table,pierces him
with a spear.
Bot thane a renke syr Richere of þe rounde table,

2792 One a ryalle stede rydes hym aȝaynes;

Throwe a rownnde rede schelde he ruschede hym sone,

That the rosselde spere to his herte rynnes!

The renye relys abowte and rusches to þe erthe,

2796 Roris fulle ruydlye, bot rade he no more!

Sir Florent and
his five score
knights are sorely
pressed.
Now alle þat es fere and unfaye of þes fyve hundreth

ffalles on syr fflorent, a ffyve score knyghttes;

Be-twyx a plasche and a flode, appone a flate lawnde,

2800 Oure folke fongene theire felde, and fawghte theme

    agaynes.

The one side
shout "Lo-
Than was lowde appone lofte Lorrayne askryede,

Whene ledys with longe speris lasschene to-gedyrs,

And Arthure one oure syde, whene theyme oghte aylede.

raine," the other "Arthur."

2804 Than *syr* fflorent and Floridas in fewtyre þey caste,

ffruschene one alle þe ffrape, and biernes affrayede;

ffellis fyve at þe frounte thare they fyrste enteride,

And, or they ferke forthire, fele of þese oþere !

Sir Florent and Sir Floridas perform great deeds of valour.

2808 Brenyes browddene they briste, brittenede scheldes,

Bettes and beres downe the best þat þeme byddes,

Alle þat rewlyde in the rowte they rydene awaye,

So rewdly they rere theys ryalle knyghttes !

2812 When *syr* Priamous þat prince persayvede theire gamene,

He hade peté in herte þat he ne durst profire ;

He wente to *syr* Gawayne, and sais hym þese wordes,—

"Thi price mene fore thi praye putt are alle undyre,

Sir Priamus beseeches Gawaine that he may help Arthur's knights against the Saracens.

2816 They are with Sarazenes over-sette mo þane sevene

　　hundreth

Of þe Sowdanes knyghtes owt of sere londes ;

Walde þow suffire me, *syr*, for sake of thi Criste,

With a soppe of thi mene suppowelle theym ones."

2820 "I grouche not," *quod* Gawayne, "þe gree es þaire awene!

They mone hafe gwerddouns fulle grett graunt of my

　　lorde !

Bot the freke mene of Fraunce fraiste theme selfene,

ffrekes faughte noghte þeire fille this fyftene wyntter !

Sir Gawaine declares that they have only just enough to do to please them.

2824 I wille noghte stire with my stale half a stede lenghe,

Bot they be stedde with more stuffe thane one ȝone stede

　　hovys."

Thane *syr* Gawayne was warre with-owttyne þe wode

　　hemmes,

He sees the main body of the enemy approaching,

Wyes of þe Westfale appone wyght horsez,

2828 Walopande wodely, as þe waye forthes,

With alle þe wapyns i-wys that to þe werre longez ;

The erle Antele the olde the avawmwarde he buskes,

Aycrande one ayther hande heghte thosande knyghtez ;

headed by the Earl Antele, who leads 8,000 knights.

2832 He pelours and pavysers passede alle nombyre,

That ever any prynce lede purvayede in erthe !

Than þe duke of Lorrayne dresesse thare aftyre,
With dowbille of þe Duche-mene, þat doughtty ware
   holdene;

2836 Paynymes of Pruyslande, prekkers fulle noble,
Come prekkande be-fore with Priamous knyghttez.

Than saide the erle Antele to Algere his broþer,—
"Me angers ernestly at Arthures knyghtez!

2840 Thus enkerly one an oste awnters þeme selfene;
They wille be owttrayede anone, are undrone rynge,
Thus folily one a felde to fyghte with us alle!
Bot thay be fesede in faye, ferly me thynkes!

2844 Walde they purposse take, and passe one theire wayes,

Prike home to theire prynce, and theire pray leve,
They myghte lenghene theire lyefe, and lossene bott littille!
It wolde lyghte my herte, so helpe me oure Lorde!"

2848 "Sir," sais syr Algere, "thay hafe littille usede
To be owttrayede withe oste; me angers þe more!
The fayreste schalle be fulle feye, þat in oure floke ryddez,
Alls fewe as they bene, are they the felde leve!"

2852 Thane gud Gawayne, gracious and noble,

   Alle with glorious gle he gladdis his knyghtes;
"Gloppyns noghte, gud mene, for gleterand scheldes,
ȝofe ȝone gadlyngez be gaye one ȝone gret horsos!

2856 Banerettez of Bretayne, buskes up ȝour hertes!
Bees noghte baiste of ȝone boyes, ne of þaire bryghte wedis!
We salle blenke theire boste for alle theire bolde profire!
Als bouxome as birde es in bede to hir lorde,

2860 ȝeffe we feghte to daye, þe felde schalle be owrs!
The fekille faye salle faile, and fallssede be distroyede!
ȝone folk is one ffrountere, unfraistede theyme semes;
Thay make faythe and faye to þe fend selvene!

2864 We salle in this viage victoures be holdene,
And avauntede with voycez of valyant biernez;

Praysede with pryncez in presence of lordes,
And luffede with ladyes in dyverse londes!

2868 Aughte never siche honoure none of oure elders,

Unwyne ne Absolone, ne none of theis oþer!

Whene we are moste in destresse, Marie we mene,[1]

That es oure maisters seyne, þat he myche traistez ;

Let them put
their trust in
Mary.

2872 Melys of þat mylde qwene, that menskes us alle ;

Who so meles of þat mayde, myskaries he never !"

Be þese wordes ware saide, they ware noghte ferre behynde

The enemy come
upon them.

Bot the lenghe of a launde, and Lorayne askryes ;

2876 Was never siche a justynge at journo in erthe,

In the vale of Josephate, as gestes us telles,

Whene Julyus *and* Joatalle ware juggede to dy,

As was whene þe ryche mene of þe rownde table

Never was there
such a jousting.
Even that in the
valley of Jehosa-
phat was not
equal to it.

2880 Ruschede in-to þe rowte one ryalle stedes !

ffor so rathely þay rusche with roselde speris,

That the raskaille was rade, and rane to þe grefes,

And karede to þat courte as cowardes for ever !

The rascal rout
run, but the rich
men of the Round
Table fight
valiantly.

2884 "Peter!" sais syr Gawayne, "this gladdez myne herte !

That ȝone gedlynges are gone, that made gret nowmbre !

I hope that thees harlottez salle harme us bot littille,

ffore they wille hyde theme in haste with-in ȝone holte
enis !

Gawaine rejoices
at the flight of
the rabble.

2888 Thay are feware one felde þan þay were fyrste nombirde,

Be fourrty thousand in faythe, for alle theyre faire hostes."

Bot one Jolyan of Jene, a geante fulle howge,

Has jonede one *syr* Jerant a justis of Walis ;

A huge giant is
slain by a Justice
of Wales.

2892 Thorowe a jerownde schelde he jogges hym thorowe,

And a fyne gesserawnte of gentille mayles !

Joynter and gemows he jogges in sondyre !

One a jambe stede þis jurnee he makes ;

2896 Thus es þe geante for-juste, that errawnte Jewe,

And Gerarde es jocunde, and joyes hym þe more !

Than the genatours of Genne enjoynes att ones,

And frykis one þe frowntere welle a fyve hundreth ;

Sir Frederick at-
tacks the British
forayers.

2900 A freke highte *syr* ffederike, with fulle fele oþer,

fferkes one a frusche, and fresclyche askryes

To fyghte with oure fforreours, þat one felde hovis ;

[1] *nenene* erased, and *mene* written in margin.

And thane the ryalle renkkes of þe rownde table

The knights of
the Round Table
advance and fight
valiantly. 2904 Rade furthe fulle ernestly, and rydis theme agaynes,

Mellis with the medille warde, bot they ware ille machede;

Of siche a grett multytude was mervayle to here.

Seyne at þe assemble the Sarazenes discoveres

2908 The soveraynge of Sessoyne, that salvede was never;

Gyawntis for-justede with gentille knyghtes,

Thorowe gesserawntes of Jene jaggede to þe herte!

They hewe thorowe helmes hawtayne biernez,

2912 þat þe hiltede swerdes to þaire hertes rynnys!

Than þe renkes renownde of the rownd table

Ryffes and ruyssches downe renayede wreches;

And thus they drevene to þe dede dukes and erles,

2916 Alle þe dreghe of þe daye, with dredfulle werkes!

Sir Priamus and
his followers de-
sert to the side
of Arthur's men. Thane syr Priamous þe prynce, in presens of lordes,

Presez to his penowne, and pertly it hentes;

Revertede it redily, and a-waye rydys

2920 To þe ryalle rowte of þe rownde table;

And heyly his retenuz raykes hym aftyre,

ffor they his resone had rede on his schelde ryche.

Owte of þe scheltrone þey schede, as schepe of a folde,

2924 And steris furth to þe stowre, and stode be þeire lorde!

Seyne they sent to þe duke, and saide hym þise wordes,—

They upbraid the
Duke of Lorraine
for not having
paid them their
wages. " We hafe bene thy sowdeours this sex ȝere and more;

We forsake þe to daye be serte of owre lorde!

2928 We sewe to oure soveraynge in sere kynges londes;

Us defawtes oure feez of þis foure wynttres;

Thow art feble and false, and noghte bot faire wordes;

Oure wages are werede owte, and þi werre endide,

2932 We maye with oure wirchipe weend whethire us lykes!

I red þowe trette of a trewe, and trofle no lengere,

Or þow salle tyne of thi tale ten thosande or ovene."

The Duke an-
swers furiously. "ffy a debles!" saide þe duke, "the develle have ȝour bones!

2936 The dawngere of ȝon dogges drede schalle I never!

We salle dele this daye, be dedes of armes,

My dede and my ducherye, and my dere knyghtes!

Siche sowdeours as ȝe I sett bot att lyttille,

2940 That sodanly in defawte for-sakes theire lorde!"

The duke in his schelde and dreches no lengere,

Drawes him a dromedarie, with dredfulle knyghtez;

Graythes to *syr* Gawayne with fulle gret nowmbyre

2944 Of gomes of Gernaide, that grevous are holdene;

Thas fresche horsesede mene to þe frownt rydes,

ffelles of oure fforreours be fourtty at ones!

They hade foughttene before with a fyve hundrethe;

2948 It was no ferly in faythe, þofe they faynt waxene.

Thane *syr* Gawayne was grefede, and grypys his spere,

And gyrdez in agayne with galyarde knyghttez;

Metes þe maches of mees and melles hym thorowe,

2952 As man of þis medille erthe, þat moste hade grevede:

Bot on Chastelayne, a chylde of þe kynges chambyre,

Was warde to *syr* Wawayne of þe weste marches,

Cheses to *syr* Cheldride, a cheftayne noble,

2956 With a chasyng spere he chokkes hym thurghe!

This chekke hyme eschewede be chauncez of armes;

So þay chase þat childe, eschape may he never!

Bot one Swyane of Swecy, with a swerde egge,

2960 The swyers swyre-bane he swappes in sondyre!

He swounande diede, *and* on þe swarthe lengede,

Sweltes ewynne swiftly, and swanke he no more!

Than *syr* Gawayne gretes with his gray eghne;

2964 The guyte was a gude mane, begynnande of armes:

ffore the charry childe so his chere chawngide,

That the chillande watire one his chekes rynnyde!

"Woo es me," *quod* Gawayne, "that I ne wetene hade;

2968 I salle wage for that wye alle þat I welde,

Bot I be wrokene on that wye, that thus has hym won-
        dyde!"

He dresses hym drerily, and to þe duke rydes,

Bot one *syr* Dolphyne the derfe dyghte hym agaynes,

2972 And *syr* Gawayne hym gyrd with a grym launce,

That the groundene spere glade to his herte!

And egerly he hente owte, and hurte anoþer,

Then Hardolf,
happy in arms,
An haythene knyght, Hardolfe, happye in armes;

2976 Sleyghly in at the slotte slyttes hyme thorowe,

That the slydande spere of his hande sleppes!

Thare es slayne in þat slope, be elagere of his hondes,

and sixty more.
Sexty slongene in a slade of sleghe men of armes!

2980 Þofe syr Gawaynne ware wo, he wayttes hym by,

And was warre of þat wye that the childe wondyde,

He avenges the
Child,
And with a swerde swiftly he swappes him thorowe,

That he swyftly swelte, and on þe erthe swounes!

2984 And thane he raykes to þe rowte, and ruyschesone helmys;

and cuts his way
through the
enemy
Riche hawberkes he rente, and rasede schyldes;

Rydes one a rawndoune, and his rayke holdes;

Thorow owte þe rerewarde he holdes wayes,

2988 And thare raughte in the reyne this ryalle þe ryche,

And rydez in-to the rowte of þe rownde table.

The great deeds
of Arthur's chi-
valrous men se-
cure the victory.
Thane oure chevalrous men changene theire horsez,

    Chases and choppes downe cheftaynes noble!

2992 Hittes fulle hertely on helmes and scheldes,

Hurtes and hewes downe haythene knyghtez!

Ketelle hattes they cleve evene to þe scholdirs!

Was never siche a clamour of capitaynes in erthe!

2996 Thare was kynges sonnes kaughte, curtays and noble,

And knyghtes of þe contre, that knawene was ryche;

Lordes of Lorayne and Lumbardye bothene.

Laughe was and lede in with our lele knyghttez;

3000 Thas þat chasede that daye, their chaunce was bettire,

Swiche a cheke at a chace eschevede theyme never!

Sir Florent
presses on with
five score
knights.
When syr fflorent be fyghte had þe felde wonene,

    He fferkes ine before with fyve score knyghttez;

3004 Theire prayes and theire presoneres passes one aftyre,

With pylours, and pavysers, and pryse mene of armes.

Sir Gawaine fol-
lows with cau-
tion,
Thane gudly syr Gawayne gydes his knyghttez,

Gas in at þe gayneste, as gydes hym telles,

3008 ffore greffe of a garysone of fulle gret lordes

Sulde noghte gripe upe his gere, ne swyche grame wurche:

ffore-thy they stode at the straytez, and with his stale
    hovede,

Tille his prayes ware paste the pathe that he dredis;

3012 Whene they the cete myghte see that the kyng seggede,

Sothely the same daye was wit asawte wonnene.

An hawrawde hyes before, the beste of the lordes,

Hom at þe herbergage, owt of tha hyghe londes;

3016 Tornys tytte to þe tente, and to the kynge telles

Alle the tale sothely, and how they hade syede;—

"Alle thy forreours are fere, that forrayede with-owttyne,

Sir fflorent, and syr flloridas, and alle thy ferse knyghtez:

3020 Thay hafe forrayede and foghtene with fulle gret nowm-
    byre,

And fele of thy foo-mene has broghte owt of lyffe!

Oure wirchipfulle wardayne es wele eschevyde,

ffor he has wonne to-daye wirchipp for evere!

3024 He has Dolfyne slayne, and þe duke takyne!

Many dowghty es dede by dynt of his hondes!

He has presoners price, pryncez and erles,

Of þe richeste blode þat regnys in erthe!

3028 Alle thy chevallrous mene faire are eschewede,

Bot a childe Chasteleynne myschance es befallene."

"Hawtayne," sais þe king, "harawde be Criste!

Thow has helyd myne herte, I hete the for-sothe!

3032 I ȝife the in Hamptone a hundreth pownde large."

The kynge þan to assawte he sembles his knyghtez,
    With somercastelle and sowe appone sere halfes;

Skystis his skotiferis,, and skayles the wallis,

3036 And iche wache has his warde with wiese mene of armes.

Thane boldly þay buske, and bendes engynes,

Payses in pylotes and proves theire castes;

Mynsteris and masondewes they malle to þe erthe,

3040 Chirches and chapelles chalke whitte blawnchede.

Stone tepelles fulle styffe in þe strete ligges,

Chawmbyrs with chymnes, and many cheefe inns;

Paysede and pelid downe playsterede walles;

and sees the city which Arthur was besieging won on the same day,

for Arthur had been told of the victory of his knights by an herald,

and how Sir Gawaine had won mighty honour.

Then he rejoiced and gave a hundred pounds largess,

and, assembling his knights, assaults the city.

They carry all before them.

3044 The pyne of þe pople was pete for to here!
Thane þe duchez hire dyghte with damesels ryche,
The cowntas of Crasyne with hir clere madyns,
Knelis downe in the kyrnelles thare the kyng hovede,
3048 On a coverede horse comlyli arayede;
They knewe hym by contenaunce, and criede fulle lowde,—

The ladies sue for mercy.

"Kyng crownede of kynde, take kepe to þese wordes!
We be-seke ȝow, syr, as soveraynge and lorde,
3052 That ȝe safe us to daye, for sake of ȝoure Criste!
Sende us some socoure, and saughte with the pople,
Or þe cete be sodaynly with assawte wonnene!"
He weres his vesere with a vowt noble,
3056 With vesage verteuous, this valyant bierne;
Moles to hir mildly with fulle meke wordes,—

Arthur promises that no hurt shall befall them.

"Salle no mysse do ȝow, ma-dame, þat to me lenges;
I gyf ȝow chartire of pes, and ȝoure cheefe maydens,
3060 The childire and þe chaste mene, the chevalrous knyghtez;
The duke es in dawngere, dredis it bott lyttylle!
He salle I dene þe fulle wele, dout ȝow noghte elles."
Thane sent he one iche a syde to certayne lordez,

The city is surrendered.

3064 ffor to leve þe assawte, the cete was ȝoldene;
With þe erle eldeste sone he sent hym þe kayes,
And seside þe same dyghte, be sent of þe lordes:

The Duke is sent to Dover as a prisoner.

The duke to Dovere es nyghte, and alle his dere knyghtez,
3068 To duelle in dawngere and dole þe dayes of hys lyve;

Many of the in-habitants escape.

Thare fleede at the ferrere ȝate folke withowttynenombyre,
ffor ferde of syr fflorent and his fers knyghtez;
Voydes the cete and to the wode rȝnnys,
3072 With vetaile, and vesselle, and vestoure so ryche:
Thay buske upe a banere abowne þe brode ȝates
Of syr fflorent in ffay, so fayne was he never!

The knights see the sign of the capture of the city.

The knyghte hovys on a hylle, beholde to þe wallys,
3076 And saide, "I see be ȝone syngne the cete es oures!"
Sir Arthure enters anone with hostes arayede,

Arthur preserves strict discipline.

Evene at þe undrone etles to lenge;

In iche lev*er*e on lowde the kynge did crye,
3080 Of payne of lyf and lym and lesynge of londes,
That no lele ligemane that to hym lon*n*gede
Sulde lye be no ladysse, ne be no lele maydyns,
Ne be no burgesse wyffe, better ne werse ;
3084 Ne no bic*i*nez myse-bide, that to þe burghe longede.

Whene þe kyng Arthure hade lely conquerid,
        And the castell*e* cov*er*ede of þe kythe riche,
Alle þe crowell*e* and kene, be craftes of armes,
3088 Captayns and constables, knewe hym for lorde.
He devysede and delte to dyv*er*se lordez,
A dowere for þe duchez and hir dere childire ;
Wroghte wardaynes by wytte to welde all*e* þe londez,
3092 That he had wonnen*e* of werre, thorowe his weise knyghtez.
Thus in Lorayne he lenges as lord in his awen*e*,
Settez lawes in the lande, as hym leefe toghte ;
And one þe Lammese daye to Lucerne he wendez,
3096 Lengez thare at laysere with lykyng*e* i-nowe ;
Thare his galays ware graythede, a full*e* gret nombyre,
Alle glet*er*and as glase, undire grene hyllys,
With cabanes cov*er*ede for kynges anoyntede,
3100 With clothes of clere golde for knyghtez and oþer ;
Sone stowede theire stuffe, and stablede þeire horses,
Strekes streke ov*er* þe strem in-to þe strayte londez.
Now he moves his myghte w*it*h myrthes of herte,
3104 Overe mowntes so hye, þase m*er*vailou*s* wayes ;
Gosse in by Goddarde, the garett be wynnys,
Graythes the garnison*e* grisely wondes !
When*e* he was passede the heghte, than the kyng hovys
3108 With his hole bataylle, be-haldande abowte,
Lukande one Lumbarddye, and one lowde melys,—
" In ʒone lykand*e* londe, lorde be I thynke."
Thane they cayre to Combe, with kyngez anoyntede,
3112 That was kyde of þe coste, kay of all*e* oþer ·

Arthur provides for the government of Lorraine which he had conquered.

At Lammas he goes to Lucerne.

His fair galleys are assembled.

He leads his forces over the high mountains by marvellous ways ;

passes the St. Gothard after defeating the garrison ;

looks down on Lombardy, and advances to Como.

Sir fflorent and *syr* ffloridas þan fowndes before,
With ffreke mene of ffraunce welle a fyve hundreth ;
To þe cete unsene thay soghte at þe gayneste,

Sir Florent plants an ambush, 3116 And sett an embuschement, als þeme-selfe lykys;
Thane ischewis owt of þat cete fulle sone be þe morne,
Slale discoverours, skyftes theire horses ;
Than skyftes þes skoverours, and skippes one hyllis,

3120 Discoveres for skulkers that they no skathe lymppone;
Poveralle and pastorelles passede one aftyre,
With porkes to pasture at the price ʒates ;
Boyes in þe subarbis bourdene ffulle heghe,

3124 At a bare synglere that to þe bente rynnys.
Thane brekes oure buschement, and the brigge wynnes,
and captures the city. Brayedez in-to þe burghe wɩtʜ baners displayede,
Stekes and stablis thorowe that them aʒayne-stondes ;

3128 ffowre stretis, or þay stynte, they stroyene fore evere !
The city Combe is won. Nowes the conquerour in Combe, and his courte holdes
With-in the kyde castelle, with kynges enoynttede ;
Be consaillez the commons þat to þe kyth lengez,

3132 Comfourthes þe carefulle with knyghtly wordez ;
Made a captayne kene a knyghte of hys awene,
Bot alle the contré and he fulle sone ware accordide.
The Lord of Milan sends to offer submission and tribute. The syre of Melane herde saye þe cete was wonnene,

3136 And send to Arthure sertayne lordes,
Grete sommes of goldc, sexti horse chargegid,
Be-soghte hyme as soverayne to socoure þe pople,
And saide he wolde sothely be sugette for ever,

3140 And make hyme servece and suʒtte for his sere londes ;
ffor plesaunce of Pawnce, and of Pownte Tremble,
ffor Pyse, and for Pavy, he profers fulle large,
Bothe purpur, and palle, and precious stonys,

3144 Palfrayes for any prynce, and provede stedes ;
And ilke a ʒere for Melane a melione of goldc,
Mekely at Martynmesse to menske wɩtʜ his hordes ;
And ever withowttyne askynge he and his ayers

3148 Be homagers to Arthure, whilles his lyffe lastis.

The kynge be his concelle a condethe hym sendis,   He pays homage
to Arthur at
Como.
And he es comene to Combe, and knewe hym as lorde.

Into Tuskané he tournez, whene þus wele tymede,   Arthur enters
Tuscany,
3152   Takes townnes fulle tyte with towrres fulle heghe;
Walles he welte downe, wondyd knyghtez,
Towrres he turnes, and turmentez þe pople!
Wroghte wedewes fulle wlonke, wrotherayle synges,
3156 Ofte wery and wepe, and wryngene theire handis;
And alle he wastys with werre, thare he awaye rydez;   and ravages the
country.
Thaire welthes and theire wonnyges, wandrethe he
    wroghte!
Thus they spryngene and sprede, and sparis bot lyttille,
3160 Spoylles dispetouslye, and spillis theire vynes;
Spendis un-sparely, þat sparede was lange,
Spedis theme to Spolett with speris inewe!
ffro Spayne in-to Spruyslande the worde of hyme
    sprynges,
3164 And spekynnges of his spencis, disspite es fulle hugge!
Towarde Viterbe this valyant avires the reynes;
Avissely in þat vale he vetailles his biernez,   He pitches his
camp in the Vale
of Viterbo.
With vernage, and oþer wyne, and venysone bakene;
3168 And one the vicounte londes he visez to lenge.
Vertely the avawmwarde voydez theire horsez;
In the Vertennone vale, the vines imangez,
Thare suggeournes this souerayne, with solace in herte,
3172 To see whene the senatours sent any wordes;
Revelle with riche wyne, riotes hym selfene,
This roy with his ryalle mene of þe rownde table,   The king and his
knights make
great merriment.
With myrthis, and melodye, and many kyne gamnes;
3176 Was never meriere men made one this erthe!

Bot one a Saterdaye at none, a sevenyghte thare aftyre,
   The konyngeste cardynalle that to the courte lengede   The cunningest
Cardinal of Rome
Knelis to þe conquerour, and karpes thire wordes,—   is sent to him,
3180 Prayes hym for þe pes, and profyrs fulle large,
To hafe pete of þe Pope, þat put was at-undere;
Be-soghte hym of surrawns, for sake of oure Lorde,

Bot a sevenyghte daye to þay ware alle semblede,

And they schulde sekerlye hym see the Sonondaye
þeraftyre,

In the cete of Rome, as soveraynge and lorde;

And crowne hym kyndly with krysomede hondes,

With his ceptre, as soveraynge and lorde:

Of this undyrtakynge ostage are comyne,

Of ayers fulle avenaunt awughte score childrenne,

In toges of tarsse fulle richelye attyrde,

And betuke theme the kynge, and his clere knyghttes.

When they had tretide thiere trewe, with trowmpynge
þerafter

They tryne unto a tente, whare tables whare raysede;

The kynge hyme selfone es sette, and certayne lordes,

Undyre a sylure of sylke sawghte at the burdez:

Alle the senatours are sette sere be þame one,

Serfed solemply with selcouthe metes:

The kynge myghty of myrthe, with his milde wordes,

Rehetez the Romaynez at his riche table,

Comforthes the cardynalle so kynghtly hyme selvene;

And this roye ryalle, as romawns us tellis,

Reverence the Romayns in his riche table;

The tawghte mene and þe conynge, whene theme tyme
thoghte,

Tas theire lefe at þe kynge, and tornode agayne;

To þe cete þat nyghte thaye soughte at þe gayneste,

And thus the ostage of Rome with Arthure es levede.

Than this roy royalle rehersys theis wordes,—
"Now may we revelle and riste, fore Rome es
oure awene!

Make oure ostage at ese, þise avenaunt childyrene,

And luk ȝe hondene theme alle that in myne oste lengez;

The emperour of Almayne, and alle theis este marches,

We salle be overlynge of alle þat one the erthe lengez!

We wille by þe crosse dayes encroche þeis loydez,

And at þe Crystynmesse daye be crownned ther-aftyre;

Side notes:

and offers that the Pope shall crown him as Sovereign in Rome.

3184

Hostages are given for the truth of his words.

3188

3192

The Roman Senators are solemnly feasted

3196

3200

3204

Arthur glorifies himself for his great success.

3208

3212

He will be crowned at Christmas

Ryngne in my ryalltes, and holde my rownde table,

3216 Withe the rentes of Rome, as me beste lykes:

Syne graythe *over* þe grette see with gud men*e* of armes,

To revenge the renke that on*e* the rode dyede !"

Thane this comlyche knyge, as cronycles tellys,

3220 Bownnys brathely to bede with a blythe herte ;

Of he slynges with sleghte, and slakes gyrdill*e*,

And fore slewthe of slomowre on*e* a slepe fallis.

Bot be ane aftyre mydnyghte all*e* his mode changede ;

3224 He mett in the morne while full*e* m*er*vaylou*s* dremes !

And when*e* his dredefull*e* drem whas drefen*e* to þe ende,

The kynge dares for dowte dye as he scholde ;

Sendes aftyre phylosophers, and his affraye telles,—

3228 "Sen*e* I was formede in fayth, so ferde whas I nev*er* !

ffor-thy rawnsakes redyly, and rede me my swefen*n*ys,

And I sall*e* redily and ryghte rehersen*e* the sotho :

Me-thoughte I was in a wode willed myn*e* one,

3232 That I ne wiste no waye whedire þat I scholde,

ffore wolvez, and whild*e* swyn*n*e, and wykkyde bestez,

Walkede in that wastern*n*e, wathes to seche ;

Thare lyou*n*s full*e* lothely lykkyde þeire tuskes,

3236 All*e* fore lapynge of blude of my lele knyghtez !

Thurghe þat foreste I flede, thare floures whare heghe,

ffor to fele me for ferde of tha foule thyngez ;

Merkede to a medowe with montayngnes enclosyde,

3240 The meryeste of medill-erthe that men*e* myghte be-holde !

The close was in compas castyn*e* all*e* abowte,

With clav*er* and clereworte clede even*e* ov*er* ;

The vale was even*e* rownde with vynes of silv*er*,

3244 All*e* with grapis of golde, gretter ware nev*er* !

Enhorilde with arborye and alkyns trees,

Erberis full*e* honeste, and byrdez þere undyre ;

All*e* froytez foddenid was þat floreschede in erthe,

3248 ffaire frithed in frawnke appon*e* tha free bowes ;

Whas thare no downkynge of dewe that oghte dere

scholde,

in Rome, and hold his Round Table there.

He goes to bed and dreams.

He sends for his philosophers, and tells them the dream.

He was in a wood among wild beasts,

which were licking from their teeth the blood of his knights.

He flies to a beautiful meadow enclosed with mountains, and having vines of silver and grapes of gold.

With þe drowghte of þe daye alle drye ware þe flores!

Than discendis in the dale, downe fra þe clowddez,

3252   A duches dere-worthily dyghte in dyaperde wedis,

In a surcott of sylke fulle selkouthely hewede,

Alle with loyotour overlaide lowe to þe hemmes,

And with ladily lappes the lenghe of a ȝerde,

3256   And alle redily reversside with rebanes of golde,

Bruchez and besauntez, and oþer bryghte stonys,

With hir bake and hir breste was brochede alle over,

With kelle and with corenalle clenliche arrayede,

3260   And þat so comly of colour one knowene was never!

A-bowte cho whirllide a whele with hir whitte hondez,

Over-whelme alle qwayntely þe whele as cho scholde;

The rowelle whas rede golde with ryalle stonys,

3264   Raylide with reched and rubyes inewe;

The spekes was splentide alle with speltis of silver,

The space of a spere lenghe springande fulle faire;

There one was a chayere of chalke-whytte silver,

3268   And chekyrde with charebocle chawngynge of hewes;

Appone þe compas ther clewide kyngis one rawe,

With corowns of clere golde þat krakede in sondire :

Sex was of þat setille fulle sodaynliche fallene,

3272   Ilke a segge by hyme selfe, and saide theis wordez,—

'That ever I regnede one þir rog, me rewes it ever!

Was never roye so riche that regnede in erthe!

Whene I rode in my rowte, roughte I noghte elles,

3276   Bot revaye, and revelle, and rawnsone the pople!

And thus I drife forthe my dayes, whilles I dreghe
    myghte,

And there-fore derflyche I am dampnede for ever!'

The laste was a litylle mane that laide was be-nethe,

3280   His leskes laye alle lene and latheliche to schewe,

The lokkes lyarde and longe the lenghe of a ȝerde,

His lire and his lyghame lamede fulle sore ;

þe two eyne of the byeryne was brighttere þane silver,

3284   The toþer was ȝalowere thene the ȝolke of a naye,—

'I was lorde,' *quod* the lede, ' of londes i-newe,

And all*e* ledis me lowttede that lengede in erthe;

And nowe es lefte me no lappe my lygham to hele,

3288 Bot lightly now am I loste, leve iche mane the sothe!'

The secunde *syr* forsothe þat sewede them*e* aftyre,

Was sekerare to my sighte, and saddare in arm*e*s;

Ofte he syghede unsownde, and said theis wordes,—

3292 ' On ȝone see hafe I sitten*e*, as sov*e*rayne and lorde,

And ladys me lovede to lappe in theyre arm*e*s;

And nowe my lordchippes are loste, and laide for ev*e*r!'

The thirde thorowely was throo, and thikke in the

schuldyrs,

3296 A thra man to thrette of, there thretty ware gaderide;

His dyadem*e* was droppede down*e*, dubbyde wi*th* stonys,

Endente all*e* with diamawndis, and dighte for þe nonis;

'I was dredde in my dayes,' he said, ' in dyverse rewmes,

3300 And now dampnede to þe dede, and dole es the more!'

The fourte was a faire man*e*, and forsesy in arm*e*s,

þ*e* fayreste of fegure that fou*r*mede was ev*e*r!

' I was frekke in my faithe,' he said, ' whill*e*s I one

fowlde regnede,

3304 ffamows in fforre londis, and floure of all*e* kynges;

Now es my face defadide, and foule es me hapnede,

ffor I am fallen*e* fro ferre, and frendles by-levyde!'

The fifte was-a faire man*e* þan*e* fele of thies oþ*e*r,

3308 A fforsey man*e* and a ferse, with fomand lippis;

He fongede faste one þ*e* feleyghes, and fayled his arm*e*s,

Bot ȝit he failede and fell*e* a fyfty fote large;

Bot ȝit he sprange and sprente, and spradden*e* his arm*e*s,

3312 And one þe spere lenghe spekes, he spekes þire wordes—

' I was in Surrye a syr, and sett be myn*e* one,

As sov*e*rayne and seyngnou*r* of sere kynges londis;

Now of my solace I am full*e* sodanly fallen*e*,

3316 And forsake of my syn*e*, ȝone cete es me rewede!'

The sexte hade a sawtere semliche bowndn*e*e,

With a surepel of silke sewede full*e* faire,

He had been lord of many lands, but now was lost.

The second had been sovereign of the sea, and loved of ladies.

The third was stout and strong.

He had been mightily feared in his day.

The fourth was very fair, but foul mischance had now happened to him.

The fifth was very fierce and violent.

He had been sovereign in Syria, but was now fallen.

The sixth had a psalter well-bound, a harp, and a sling.

A harpe and a hande-slynge with harde flynte stones;

3320 What harmes he has hente he halowes fulle sone,—

'I was demede in my dayes,' he said, ' of dedis of armes

He had been held the doughtiest in his day, but had been marred by the maiden. One of the doughtyeste that duellede in erthe;

Bot I was merride one molde in my moste strenghethis,

3324 With this maydene so mylde, þat mofes us alle.'

Two kynges ware clymbande, and claverande one heghe,

Two kings are seen who challenge the chair hereafter, but fail to reach it. The creste of þe compas they covette fulle зerne;

'This chaire of charbokle,' they said, 'we chalange here aftyre,

3328 As two of þe cheffeste chosene in erthe!'

The childire ware chalke-whitte, chekys and oþer,

Bot the chayere abownne chevede they never:

The one was passing fair of feature, with a mighty forehead. 3332 The forthirmaste was freely with a frount large,

The faireste of fyssnanny þat fourmede was ever;

And he was buskede in a blee of a blewe noble,

With flourdelice of golde floreschede al over;

The other bore the cross as an ornament in token that he was a Christian. The toþer was cledde in a cote alle of clene silver,

3336 With a comliche crosse corvene of golde,

ffowre crosselettes krafty by þe crosse riftes,

And ther-by knewe I the kynge, þat crystnede hyme semyde.

Arthur accosts the Duchess, who welcomes him. 3340 Thane I went to þat wlonke, and wynly hire gretis,

And cho said, ' welcome i-wis! wele arte thow fowndene;

The aughte to wirchipe my wille, and thow wele cowthe,

Of alle the valyant men that ever was in erthe;

ffore alle thy wirchipe in werre by me has thow wonnene,

3344 I hafe bene frendely freke, and fremmede tille oþer;

That has þow fowndene in faithe, and fele of þi biernez,

ffore I fellid downe syr Frolle with frowarde knyghtes;

ffore-thi the fruytes of Fraunce are freely thynne awene.

He is chosen to achieve the chair, 3348 Thow salle þe chayere escheve, I chese þe my-selfene,

Be-fore alle þe cheftaynes chosene in this erthe.'

Scho lifte me up lightly with hir lene hondes,

and sit therein. And sette me softely in the see, þe septre me rechede;

3352 Craftely with a kambe cho kembede myne hevede,
That the krispane kroke to my crownne raughte;
Dressid one me a diademe, that dighte was fulle faire, *The kingly ornaments are given to him.*
And syne profres me a pome pighte fulle of faire stonys,

3356 Enamelde with azoure, the erth there-one depayntide,
Selkylde with the salte see appone sere halfes,
In sygne þat I sothely was soverayne in erthe:
Than broght cho me a brande with fulle bryghte hiltes, *A sword with bright hilt is brought for him.*

3360 And bade me brawndysche þe blade, 'þe brande es myne awene:
Many swayne with þe swynge has the swtte levede;
ffor whilles thow swanke with the sworde, it swykkede þe never.'
Than raykes cho with roo, and riste whene hir likede,

3364 To þe ryndes of þe wode, richere was never;
Was no pomarie so pighte of pryncez in erthe,
Ne nonne apparaylle so prowde, bot paradys one.
Scho bad þe bowes scholde bewe downe, and bryng to my hondes *He is taken to the wood, and the boughs are made to yield their fruit to him.*

3368 Of þe beste that they bare one brawnches so heghe;
Than they heldede to hir heste alle holly at ones,
The hegheste of iche a hirste, I hette ȝow forsothe:
Scho bade me fyrthe noghte þe fruyte, bot fonde whilles me likede, *He is bid take freely of the finest.*

3372 'ffonde of þe fyneste, thow freliche byerne,
And reche to the ripeste, and ryotte thy selvene!
Riste, thow ryalle roye, for Rome es thyne awene!
And I salle redily rolle the roo at þe gayneste,

3376 And reche the þe riche wyne in rynsede coupes.' *The lady draws wine for him out of the stream,*
Thane cho wente to the welle by þe wode enis,
That alle wellyde of wyne, and wonderliche rynnes;
Kaughte up a coppe-fulle, and coverde it faire;

3380 Scho bad me dereliche drawe, and drynke to hir selfene: *and bids him drink to her.*
And thus cho lede me abowte the lenghe of an owre,
With alle likynge and luffe, þat any lede scholde;
Bot at þe myddaye fulle ewyne all hir mode chaungede, *But at mid-day all was changed.*

3384 And mad myche manace with mervayllous wordez ;

Whene I cryede appone hire, cho kest downe hir browes,

She speaks to him fiercely, and tells him that he shall lose his life.

'Kyng, thow karpes for noghte, be Criste þat me made !

ffor thow salle lose this layke, and thi lyfe aftyre !

3388 Thow has lyffede in delytte and lordchippes inewe !'

She gives the wheel a whirl and sends him flying from the chair, bruised and injured.

Abowte scho whirles the whele, and whirles me undire,

Tille alle my qwarters þat whille whare qwaste al to peces !

And with that chayere my chyne was chopped in sondire !

3392 And I hafe cheveride for chele, sen me this chance

happenede.

Than wakkenyde I i-wys, alle wery for-dremyde,

And now wate thow my woo, worde as þe lykes."

The philosophers interpret the dream, and tell Arthur that his good fortune is passed.

"ffreke," sais the philosophre, " thy fortune es passede !

3396 ffor thow salle fynd hir thi foo, frayste whene the lykes !

Thow arte at þe hegheste, I hette the for-sothe !

Chalange nowe when thow wille, thow chevys no more !

Thow has schedde myche blode, and schalkes distroyede,

3400 Sakeles in sirquytrie, in sere kynges landis ;

He is to prepare for his end,

Schryfe the of thy schame, and schape for thyne ende !

Thow has a schewynge, syr kynge, take kepe ʒif the like !

ffor thow salle fersely falle with-in fyve wynters !

and to found Abbeys in France.

3404 ffownde abbayes in ffraunce, þe froytez are theyne awene,

ffore ffroille, and for fferawnt, and for thir ferse knyghttis,

That thow fremydly in ffraunce has faye belevede ;

He is bid take warning from the other kings who had tried the chair. The first was Alexander ; the second Hector ; the third Julius Cæsar ;

Take kepe ʒitte of oþer kynges, and kaste in thyne herte,

3408 That were conquerours kydde, and crownnede in erthe ;

The eldeste was Alexandere, þat alle þe erthe lowttede ;

The toþer Ector of Troye, the chevalrous gume ;

The thirde Julyus Cesare, þat geant was holdene,

3412 In iche jorne jentille, ajuggede with lordes ;

the fourth Sir Judas, the Maccabee ;

The ferthe was syr Judas, a justere fulle nobille,

The maysterfulle Makabee, the myghttyeste of strenghes ;

the fifth Joshua ;

The fyfte was Josue, þat joly mane of armes,

3416 That in Jerusalem oste fulle myche joye lymppede ;

the sixth was David, who slew great Goliath.

The sexte was David þe dere, demyd with kynges

One of þe doughtyeste þat dubbede was ever,

ffor he slewe with a slynge, be sleyghte of his handis,

3420 Golyas the grette gome, grymmeste in erthe ;

Syne endittede in his dayes alle the dere psalmes,

þat in þe sawtire ere sette with selcouthe wordes ;

The two clymbande kynges, I knawe it forsothe,

Of the two kings who were climbing, one should be called Carolus of France,

3424 Salle Karolus be callide, the kyng sone of Fraunce ;

He salle be crowelle and kene, and conquerour holdene,

Covere be conqueste contres ynewe ;

He salle encroche the crowne that Crist bare hym selfene,

3428 And þat lifeliche launce, that lepe to his herte,

When he was crucyfiede on crose, and alle þe kene naylis,

Knyghtly he salle conquere to Cristyne men hondes :

The toþer salle be Godfraye, that Gode schalle revenge

the other Godfrey of Lorraine, who should recover the true cross.

3432 One þe Gud Frydaye with galyarde knyghtes ;

He salle of Lorrayne be lorde, be leefe of his fadire,

And syne in Jerusalem myche joye happyne,

ffor he salle cover the crosse be craftes of armes,

3436 And synne be corownde kynge, with krysome enoynttede ;

Salle no duke in his dayes siche destanye happyne,

Ne siche myschefe dreghe, whene trowthe salle be tryede !

ffore-thy ffortune þe fetches to fulfille the nowmbyre,

Arthur is needed to make up the number of the nine noblest

3440 Alles nynne of þe nobileste namede in erthe ;

This salle in romance be redde with ryalle knyghttes,

Rekkenede and renownde with ryotous kynges,

And demyd one domesdaye, for dedis of armes,

He shall be celebrated for ever as the doughtiest on earth. Many clerks shall tell of his deeds.

3444 ffor þe doughtyeste þat ever was duelland in erthe :

So many clerkis and kynges salle karpe of ȝoure dedis,

And kepe ȝoure conquestez in cronycle for ever !

Bot the wolfes in the wode, and therwhilde bestes,

The wild beasts are wicked men that are worrying his people.

3448 Are some wikkyd mene that werrayes thy rewmes,

Es entirde in thyne absence to werraye thy pople,

And alyenys and ostes of uncouthe landis :

Thow getis tydandis I trowe, within tene dayes,

He will have some tidings within ten days.

3452 That some torfere es tydde, sene thow fro home turnede ;

I rede thow rekkyne and reherse un resonable dedis,

Ore the repenttes fulle rathe alle thi rewthe werkes !

He is bid to repent and amend.

Mane, amende thy mode, or thow myshappen*e*,

3456 And mekely aske mercy for mede of thy saule!"

The king rises and puts on his robes.

Thane rysez the riche kyng*e*, and rawghte on*e* his wedys,
    A reedde acton*e* of Rosse, the richeste of floures,

A pesane, and a paunson*e*, and a pris girdill*e*;

3460 And one he henttis a hode of scharlette full*e* riche,

A pavys pillion*e* hatt, þat pighte was full*e* faire

With perry of þe oryent, and pr*e*cyous stones;

His gloves gayliche gilte, and graven*e* by þe hem*m*ys,

3464 With graynes of rubyes full*e* gracious to schewe:

His hede grehownde, and his bronde, ande no byerne ell*e*s,

And bownnes ov*er* a brode mede, with breth at his herte;

ffurth he stalkis a stye by þa still*e* enys,

3468 Stotays at a hey strette, studyande hym*e* one;

He sees a man approaching in strange attire,

Att the surs of þe sonn*e*, he sees there com*m*ande,

Raykande to Romewarde the redyeste wayes,

A renke in a rownde cloke, with righte rowm*m*e clothes,

3472 With hatte, and w*it*h heyghe schene homely and rownde;

With flatte ferthynges the freke was floreschede all*e* ov*er*,

Many schredys and schragges at his skyrttes hynnges,

With scrippe, ande with slawyn*e*, and skalopis i-newe,

who appears like a pilgrim.

3476 Both pyke and palme, all*e*s pilgram hym scholde:

The gome graythely hym grette, and bade gode morwen*e*;

The kyng lordelye hymselfe, of langage of Rome,

Of Latyn*e* corroum*p*pede all*e*, full*e* lovely hym menys,—

He asks him whither he is going,

3480 "Whedire wilnez thowe, wye, walkande thyne onn*e*?

Qwhyll*e*s þis werlde es o werre, a wawhte I it holde!

Here es ane enmye w*it*h oste, undire ȝone vynes;

And they see the for-sothe, sorowe the be-tyddes;

3484 Bot ȝif thow hafe condethe of þe kynge selfen*e*,

and tells him the dangers of the way.

Knaves will*e* kill*e* the, and keppe at thow haves;

And if þou halde þe hey waye, they hente the also,

Bot if thow hastyly hafe helpe of his hende knyghttes "

3488 Thane karpes syr Cradoke to the kynge selfen*e*,

The stranger knight says that he fears no dangers.

    "I sall*e* for-gyffe hym my dede, so me Gode helpe!

Onye grome undire Gode, that one this grownde walkes!

Latte the keneste come, that to þe kyng langes,

3492 I salle encountire hyme as knyghte, so Criste hafe my
            sawle !

ffor thow may noghte reche me, ne areste thy selfene,

þoffe thou be richely arayede in fulle riche wedys ;

I wille noghte wonde for no werre, to wende whare me
            likes,

3496 Ne for no wy of this werlde, þat wroghte es one erthe !

Bot I wille passe in pilgremage þis pas unto Rome,   *He is bound in pilgrimage to Rome.*

To purchose me perdonne of the pape selfene ;

And of paynes of purgatorie be plenerly assoyllede ;

3500 Thane salle I seke sekirly my soverayne lorde,

Sir Arthure of Inglande, that avenaunt byerne!   *Then he has to find Arthur of England.*

ffor he es in this empire, as hathelle men me telles,

Ostayande in this oryente with awfulle knyghtes."

3504 "Fro qwyne come þou, kene mane," quod þe kynge
            thane,

"That knawes kynge Arthure, and his knyghttes also ?

Was þou ever in his courte, qwylles he in kyth lengede ?   *Arthur demands of the knight who he is.*

Thow karpes so kyndly, it comforthes myne herte !

3508 Well wele has þou wente, and wysely þou sechis,

ffor þou arte Bretowne bierne, as by thy brode speche."

"Me awghte to knowe þe kynge, he es my kydde lorde,   *He tells him that his name is Sir Cradok, a knight of Arthur's chamber, and keeper of Caerleon.*

And I calde in his courte a knyghte of his chambire ;

3512 Sir Craddoke was I callide, in his courte riche,

Kepare of Karlyone, undir the kynge selfene ;

Nowe am I cachede owtt of kyth, with kare at my herte,

And that castelle es cawghte with uncowthe ledys."

3516 Than the comliche kynge kaughte hym in armes,   *The king kisses and welcomes Sir Cradok.*

Keste of his ketille-hatte, and kyssede hyme fulle sone,

Saide, "welcome, syr Craddoke, so Criste mott me helpe !

Dere cosyne of kynde, thowe coldis myne herte !

3520 How faris it in Bretaynne, with alle my bolde berynes ?

Are they brettenede, or brynte, or broughte owte of lyve ?

Kene þou me kyndely whatte caase es be-fallene ;

I kepe no credens to crafe, I knawe the for trewe."

Sir Cradok tells him of the evil deeds of Modred.

3524 " Sir, thi wardane es wikkede, and wilde of his dedys;
ffor he wandreth has wroghte, sen þou awaye passede;
He has castelles encrochede, and corownde hym selvene,
Kaughte in alle þe rentis of þe rownde tabille;

3528 He devisede þe rewme, and delte as hym likes;
Dubbede of þe Danmarkes, dukes and erlles,
Dissevcride þeme sondirwise, and cites distroyede;

He has levied forces of paynims and infidels,

To Sarazenes and Sessoynes, appone sere halves,

3532 He has semblede a sorte of selcouthe berynes,
Soveraynes of Surgenale, and sowdeours many,
Of Peyghtes and Paynnyms, and provede knyghttes
Of Irelande and Orgaile, owtlawede berynes;

3536 Alle thaa laddes are knyghttes þat lange to þe mowntes,
And ledynge and lordechipe has alle, alles theme selfe
likes;
And there es *syr* Childrike a cheftayne holdyne,
That ilke chevalrous mane, he chargges thy pople;

who rob the religious and ravish the nuns.

3540 They robbe thy religeous, and ravichse thi nonnes,
And redy ryddis *with* his rowtte to rawnsone þe povere;
ffro Humbyre to Hawyke he haldys his awene,

He has seized the whole of England and all Arthur's castles.

And alle the cowntré of Kentt be covenawnte entayllide;

3544 The comliche castelles that to the corowne langede,
The holtes, and the hare wode, and the harde bankkes,
Alle þat Henguste and Hors hent in þeire tyme;

He has a fleet of seven score ships at Southampton.

Att Southamptone on the see es sevene skore chippes,

3548 ffraughte fulle of ferse folke, owt of ferre landes,
ffor to fyghte *with* thy ffrappe, whene þow theme assailles.

But, worst of all, he has taken Guinever, and lives with her as his wife!

Bot ȝitt a worde witterly, thowe watte noghte þe werste!
He has weddede Waynore, and hir his wieffe holdis,

3552 And wounnys in the wilde bowndis of þe weste marches,
And has wroghte hire with childe, as wittnesse telles!
Off alle þe wyes of þis worlde, woo motte hym worthe,
Alles wardayne unworthye womene to ȝeme!

3556 Thus has *syr* Modrede merrede us alle!
ffor-thy I merkede over thees mowntes, to mene þe the
sothe."

Than the burliche kynge, for brethe at his herte,
And for this botelesse bale alle his ble chaungide !

Arthur is over-
come by the
tidings, and vows
revenge.

3560 "By þe rode," sais þe roye, "I salle it revenge!
Hym salle repente fulle rathe alle his rewthe werkes !"
Alle wepande for woo he went to his tentis ;
Unwynly this wyesse kynge, he wakkenysse his berynes,

3564 Clepid in a clarioune kynges and othire,
Callys theme to concelle, and of þis cas tellys,—

He calls a Council
and tells them the
ill news.

"I am with tresone be-trayede, for alle my trewe dedis !
And alle my travayle es tynt, me tydis no bettire !

3568 Hym salle torfere betyde, þis tresone has wroghte,
And I may traistely hym take, as I am trew lorde !
This es Modrede, þe mane that I most traystede,
Has my castelles encrochede, and corownde hyme selvene,

3572 With renttes and reches of the rownde table ;
Has made alle hys retenewys of renayede wrechis,
And devysed my rewme to dyverse lordes,
To sowdeours and to Sarazenes owtte of sere londes !

3576 He has weddyde Waynore, and hyr to wyefe holdes,
And a childe es eschapede, the chaunce es no bettire !
They hafe semblede on the see sevene schore chippis,
ffulle of ferrome folke, to feghte with myne one !

3580 ffor-thy to Bretayne the brode buske us by-hovys,
ffor to brettyne the berynne that has this bale raysede !
Thare salle no freke men fare, bott alle one fresche horses,
That are fraistede in fyghte, and floure of my knyghttez :

They must pro-
ceed to Britain
at once with all
speed.

3584 Sir Howelle and syr Hardolfe here salle be leve,
To be lordes of the ledis that here to me lenges ;
Lokes in-to Lumbardye, that thare no lede chaunge,—
And tendirly to Tuskayne take tente alles I byde ;

Sir Howell and
Sir Hardolf are
left behind to
govern Rome and
Italy.

3588 Resaywe the rentis of Rome qwene þay are rekkenede ;
Take sesyne the same daye that laste waste assyguede,
Or elles alle þe ostage withowttyne þe wallys,
Be hynggyde hye appone hyghte alle holly at ones !"

3592 Nowe bownes the bolde kynge with beste knyghtes,
Gers trome and trusse and trynes forth aftyre ;

Arthur and his
best knights
journey rapidly
towards Britain.

Turnys thorowe Tuskayne, taries bot littille,

Lyghte noghte in Lumbarddye bot whene þe lyghte
    failede ;

3596 Merkes over the mowntaynes fulle mervaylous wayes,

Ayres thurghe Almaygne evyne at the gayneste ;

In Flanders his
fleet is assembled. fferkes evynne in-to fflawndresche with hys ferse
    knyghttes ;

Within fyftene dayes his flete es assembledo,

3600 And thane he schoupe hyme to chippe, and schownnes
    no lengere,

Scherys with a charpe wynde over þe schyre waters ;

By þe roche with ropes he rydes one ankkere,

He discovers the
fleet of the enemy
armed and pre-
pared for fight. Thare the false mene fletyde, and one flode lengede,

3604 With chefe chaynes of chare chokkode to gedyrs,

Charggede evyne cheke-fulle of chevalrous knyghtes ;

And in þe hynter one heghte, helmes and crestes,

Hatches with haythene mene hillyd ware thare undyre,

3608 Prowdliche prutrayede with payntede clothys,

Iche a pece by pece prykkyde tylle oþer,

Dubbyde with dagswaynnes dowblede they seme ;

And thus þe derfe Danamarkes had dyghte alle theyre
    chippys,

3612 That no dynte of no darte dere theme ne schoulde :.

Than the roye and þe renkes of the rownde table

Alle ryally in rede arrayes his chippis ;

Then he makes
ready his ships
for the battle, That daye ducheryes he delte, and doubbyde knyghttes,

3616 Dresses dromowndes and dragges, and drawene upe
    stonys ;

The toppe-castelles he stuffede with toyelys, as hyme
    lykyde,

Bendys bowes of vys brothly þare aftyre,

Tolowris tentyly takelle they ryghttene,

3620 Brasene hedys fulle brode buskede one flones,

Graythes for garnysones gomes arrayes ;

Gryme gaddes of stele, ghywes of iryne,

Stirttelys steryne one steryne with styffe mene of armes ;

3624 Mony lufliche launce appone lofte stoundys,
Ledys one leburde, lordys and oþer,
Pyghte payvese one porte, payntede scheldes,
One hyndire hurdace one highte helmede knyghtez.

3628 Thus they scheftene fore schotys one thas schire strandys,
Ilke schalke in his schrowde, fulle scheene ware þeire
  wedys.
The bolde kynge es in a barge and a-bowtte rowes,
Alle bare-hevvede for besye with beveryne lokkes;

and rows round the fleet to see that everything is prepared.

3632 And a beryne with his bronde, and ane helme betyne,
Mengede with a mawncelet of maylis of silver,
Compaste with a coronalle, and coverde fulle ryche;
Kayris to yche a cogge, to comfurthe his knyghttes:

He exhorts his knights to be of good courage,

3636 To Clegys and Cleremownde he cryes one lowde,—
"O Gawayne! O Galyrane! thies gud mens bodyes."
To Loth and to Lyonelle fulle lovefly he melys,
And to syr Lawncelot de Lake lordliche wordys,—

3640 "Lat es covere þe kyth, the coste es owre ownne;
And gere theme brotheliche blenke, alle þone blod-hondes!
Bryttyne them with-in bourde, and brynne theme þare
  aftyre!
Hewe downe hertly þone heythene tykes!

3644 They are harlotes halfe, I hette þow myne honnde!"
Than he coveres his cogge, and caches one ankere,
Kaughte his comliche helme with þe clere maylis;
Buskes baners one brode, betyne of gowles,

goes to his ship, and orders the anchor to be raised.

3648 With corowns of clere golde clenliche arraiede;
Bot þare was chosene in þe chefe a chalke-whitte maydene,
And a childe in hir arme, þat chefe es of hevynne:
Withowttene changynge in chace, thies ware þe cheefe
  armes

His device is a picture of our Lady and the Child.

3652 Of Arthure þe avenaunt, qwhylles he in erthe lengede.
Thane the marynerse mellys, and maysters of chippis,
Merily iche a mate menys tille oþer;
Of theire termys they talke, how þay ware tydd,

The sailors busy themselves to get the ships under weigh

3656 Towyne tresselle one trete, trussene upe sailes,

Bot bonettez one brede, bettrede hatches;

Brawndeste browne stele, braggede in trompes;

Standis styffe one the stamyne, steris one aftyre;

3660 Strekyne over þe streme, thare stryvynge be-gynnes.

ffro þe wagande wynde owte of þe weste rysses,

Brethly bessomes with byrre in berynes sailles;

With hir bryngges one burde burliche cogges,

3664 Qwhylles þe bilynge and þe beme brestys in sondyre;

So stowttly þe forsterne one þe stam hyttis,

þat stokkes of þe store-burde strykkys in peces!

Be thane cogge appone cogge, krayers and oþer,

3668 Castys crepers one crosse als to þe crafte langes:

Thane was hede-rapys hewene þat helde upe þe mastes;

Thare was conteke fulle kene, and crachynge of chippys!

Grett cogges of kampe crasseches in sondyre!

3672 Mony kabane clevede, cabilles destroyede!

Knyghtes and kene mene killide the braynes!

Kidd castelles were corvene with alle theire kene wapene,

Castelles fulle comliche, þat coloured ware faire!

3676 Upcynes eghelynge þay ochene þare aftyre,

With þe swynge of þe swerde sweys þe mastys;

Ovyre-fallys in þe firste frekis and othire,

ffrekke in þe forchipe fey es bylevefede!

3680 Than brothely they bekyne with boustouse tacle,

Bruschese boldlye one burde, brynyede knyghtes

Owt of botes one burde was buskede with stonys,

Bett downe of þe beste, brystis the hetches;

3684 Som gomys thourghe gyrde with gaddys of yryne,

Comys gayliche clede englaymous wapene!

Archers of Inglande fulle egerly schottes,

Hittis thourghe þe harde stele fulle hertly dynnttis!

3688 Sonne hotchene in holle the heþenne knyghtes,

Hurte thourghe þe harde stele, hele they never!

Than they falle to þe fyghte, ffoynes with sperys,

Alle the frekkeste one frownte þat to þe fyghte langes;

3692 And ilkone frechcly fraystez theire strenghes,

Were to fyghte in þe flete wiþ theire felle wapyne :

Thus they dalte þat daye thire dubbide knyghtes,

Tille alle þe Danes ware dede, and in þe depe throwene !
The Danes of Modred's fleet are all slain.

3696 Than Bretones brothely with brondis they hewene,

Lepys in up one lofte lordeliche berynes ;·

When ledys of owt londys leppyne in waters,

Alle oure lordes one lowde laughene at ones !
Arthur's lords laugh to see them leap into the water.

3700 Be thane speris whare spronngene, spalddyd chippys,

Spanyolis spedily sprentyde over burdez ;

Alle þe kene mene of kampe, knyghtes and oþer,

Killyd are colde dede, and castyne over burdez !
All Modred's keen men are killed.

3704 Theire swyers sweyftly has þe swete levyde,

Heþene hevande on hatche in þer hawe rysos,

Synkande in þe salte see sevene hundrethe at ones !

Thane syr Gawayne the gude he has þe gree wonnene,
Sir Gawaine distributes the ships among his knights.

3708 And alle þe cogges grete he gafe to his knyghtes,

Sir Geryne, and syr Grisswolde, and othir gret lordes ;

Garte Galuth a gud gome girde of þaire hedys !

Thus of þe false flete appone þe flode happenede,

3712 And thus þeis feryne folke fey are belevede !
But Modred the traitor has a land army of tried knights.

Ʒitt es þe traytour one londe with tryede knyghttes,

And alle trompede they trippe one trappede stedys ;

Schewes theme undir schilde one þe schire bankkes ;

3716 He ne schownttes for no schame, bot schewes fulle heghe !

Sir Arthure and Gawayne avyede theme bothene

To sexty thosandez of mene, þat in theire fyghte hovede ;

Be this the folke was fellyde, thane was þe flode passede ;

3720 Thane was it slyke a slowde in slakkes fulle hugge,

That let þe kyng for to lande, and the lawe watyre ;
Arthur's host wait for the tide to make before they land.

ffor-thy he lengede one laye for lesynng of horsesys,

To loke of his lege mene, and of his lele knyghtes,

3724 Ʒif any ware lamede or loste, life ʒife they scholde.

Thane syr Gawayne þe gude a galaye he takys,
Sir Gawaine wades ashore.

And glides up at a gole with gud mene of armes ;

Whene he growndide for grefe, he gyrdis in þe watere,

3728 That to þe girdylle he gos in alle his gylte wedys :

Schottis upe appone þe sonde in syghte of þe lordes,
Sengly with hys soppe, my sorowe es the more!
With baners of his bagys beste of his armes,

3732 He braydes up-on the banke in his bryghte wedys;

He byddys his baneoure, "buske þow belyfe
To ʒone brode batayle that one ʒone banke hoves;
And I ensure ʒow sothe I salle ʒowe sewe aftyre;

3736 Loke ʒe blenke for no bronde, ne for no bryghte wapyne,
Bot beris downe of þe beste and bryng theme o-dawe!
Bees noghte abayste of theire boste abyde one þe erthe;
ʒe have my baneres borne in batailles fulle hugge;

3740 We salle felle ʒone false, þe fende hafe theire saules!
Flightes faste with þe frape, þe felde salle be oures;
May I þat traytoure overtake, torfere hyme tyddes,
That this tresone has tymbyrde to my trewe lorde!

3744 Of siche a engendure fulle littylle joye happyns,
And þat salle in this journee be juggede fulle evene!"

Now they seke over þe sonde þis soppe at þe gayneste,
Sembles one þe sowdeours, and settys theire dyntys;

3748 Thourghe þe scheldys so schene schalkes þey towche,
With schaftes scheveride schorte of þas schene launces;
Derfe dynttys they dalte with daggande sperys;
One þe danke of þe dewe many dede lyggys,

3752 Dukes, and duszeperis, and dubbide knyghttys;
The doughttyeste of Danemarke undone are for ever!
Thus thas renkes in rewthe rittis theire brenyes,
And rechis of þe richeste unrekene dynttis;

3756 Thare they thronge in the thikke, and thristis to þe erthe
Of the thraeste mene thre hundrethe at ones!
Bot syr Gawayne for grefe myghte noghte agayne-stande,
Umbegrippys a spere, and to a gome rynnys,

3760 Þat bare of gowles fulle gaye, with gowces of sylvere;
He gyrdes hym in at þe gorge with his gryme[1] launce,
Þat þe growndene glayfe graythes in sondyre!

Side notes:
He bids his standard-bearer advance against Modred's host, and not fear their numbers.

He and his little band charge the whole army.

They slay three hundred of the bravest.

Sir Gawaine kills the king of Goth-land.

---

[1] *grown* erased from the text and *gryme* written in margin.

With þat boystous brayde he bownes hym to dye!

3764 The kynge of Gutlande it was, a gude mane of armes.

Thayre avawwarde than alle voydes þare aftyre,

Alles venqueste verrayely with valyant berynes;

Metis with medilwarde, that Modrede ledys!

The vanguard of the army flies.

3768 Oure mene merkes theme to, as theme myshappenede—

ffor hade syr Gawayne hade grace to halde þe grene hille,

He had wirchipe i-wys wonnene for ever!

Bot þane syr Gawayne i-wysse, he waytes hym wele

Gawaine rashly advances against the centre, where Modred is with the Montagus and other great lords.

3772 To wreke hyme on this werlaughe, þat þis werre movede;

And merkes to syr Modrede amonge alle his beryns,

With the Mownttagus, and oþer gret lordys.

þan syr Gawayne was grevede, and with a gret wylle

Gawaine puts a fresh spear in rest, and assails Modred with reproaches.

3776 ffewters a faire spere, and freschely askryes,—

"ffals fosterde foode, the fende have thy bonys!

ffy one the, felone, and thy false werkys!

Thow salle be dede and undone for thy derfe dedys,

3780 Or I salle dy this daye, ʒif destanye worthe!"

Thane his enmye, with oste of owtlawede berynes,

Alle enangylles abowte oure excellente knyghttez,

That the traytoure be tresone had tryede hym selvene;

The host of the enemy, numbering sixty thousand men, surround Gawaine and his little band.

3784 Dukes of Danemarke he dyghttes fulle sone,

And leders of Lettowe, with legyons inewe,

Umbylappyde oure mene with launcez fulle kene,

Sowdeours and Sarazenes owte of sere landys,

3788 Sexty thosande mene semlyly arrayede,

Sekerly assembles thare one sevenschore knyghtes,

Sodaynly in dischayte by tha salte strandes.

Thane syr Gawayne grette with his gray eghene,

Gawaine weeps and laments for the danger of his men.

3792 ffor grefe of his gud mene that he gyde schulde;

He wyste that thay wondyde ware, and wery for-
foughttene,

And what for wondire and woo, alle his witte faylede.

And thane syghande he saide, with sylande terys,—

3796 "We are with Sarazenes be-sett appone sere halfes!

I syghe noghte for myselfe, sa helpe oure Lorde;

Bot for to us supprysede, my sorowe es the more.

Bes dowghtty to-daye, ȝone dukes schalle be ȝoures!

3800 ffor dere Dryghttyne this daye dredys no wapyne.

He comforts them with promises of blessings in Heaven.

We salle ende this daye alles excellent knyghttes,

Ayere to endelesse joye with angelles unwemmyde.

Þofe we hafe unwittily wastede oure selfene,

3804 We salle wirke alle wele in þe wirchipe of Cryste.

We salle for ȝone Sarazenes, I sekire ȝow my trowhe,

Souppe with oure Saveoure solemply in hevene,

In presence of þat precious prynce of alle oþer

They shall sup with prophets, patriarchs, and apostles.

3808 With prophetes, and patriarkes, and apostlys fulle nobille,

Be-fore his freliche face that fourmede us alle!

Ȝondire to ȝone ȝaldsones, he þat ȝeldes hyme ever,

Perish the base slave that yields!

Qwhylles he es qwykke and in qwerte unquellyde with handis;

3812 Be he never mo savede, ne socourede with Cryste,

Bot Satanase his sawle mowe synke in-to helle!"

Then Gawaine grimly grips his weapon,

Than grymly syr Gawayne gryppis hys wapyne,

Agayne þat gret bataille he graythes hym sone;

3816 Radly of his riche swerde he reghttes þe cheynys,

In he schokkes his schelde, schountes he no lengare;

Bot alles unwyse wodewyse he wente at þe gayneste,

and rushes into the fray.

Wondis of thas werdirwyns with wrakfufle dynttys,

3820 Alle wellys fulle of blode, thare he awaye passes;

And þofe hym ware fulle woo, he wondys bot lyttille,

He performs mighty deeds of arms.

Bot wrekys at his wirchipe þe wrethe of hys lorde!

He stekys stedis in stoure, and sterenefulle knyghttes,

3824 That steryne mene in theire stcrapes stone dede þay lygge!

He rybys þe ranke stele, he rittes þe mayles;

Thare myghte no renke hym areste, his resone was passede!

He fights like a madman.

He felle in a fransye for fersenesse of herte,

3828 He feghttis and fellis downe þat hyme be-fore standis!

ffelle never fay mane siche fortune in erthe!

Into þe hale bataile hedlynge he rynnys,

And hurtes of þe hardieste þat one the erthe lenges!

3832 Letande alles a lyone, he lawnches theme thorowe,
     Lordes and ledars, that one the launde hoves!
     Ʒit syr Gawayne for wo wondis bot lyttille,
     Bot woundis of thas wedirwynes with wondirfulle dyntes,
3836 Alls he þat wold wilfully wastene hyme selfene;
     And for wondsome and wille alle his wit failede,
     That wode alles a wylde beste he wente at þe gayneste; *Like a wild beast he goes on wallowing in blood.*
     Alle walewede one blode, thare he awaye passede;
3840 Iche a wy may be-warre, be wreke of anoþer!
     Than he moves to syr Modrede amange alle his knyghttes,
         And mett hyme in þe myde schelde, and mallis hyme
             thorowe;
     Bot the schalke for the scharpe he schownttes a littille,
3844 He schare hyme one þe schorte rybbys a schaftmonde *He wounds Modred in the side.*
         large!
     The schafte schoderede and schotte in the schire beryne,
     Þat the schadande blode over his schanke rynnys,
     And schewede one his schynbawde, þat was schire burneste!
3848 And so they schyfte and schove, he schotte to þe erthe; *Modred falls to the earth.*
     With þe lussche of þe launce he lyghte one hys schuldyrs,
     Ane akere lenghe one a launde, fulle lothely wondide.
     Than Gawayne gyrde to þe gome, and one þe groffe fallis; *Gawaine strives to finish him with a dagger, but misses his blow.*
3852 Alles his grefe was graythede, his grace was no bettyre!
     He schokkes owtte a schorte knyfe schethede with silvere,
     And scholde have slottede hyme in, bot no slytte
         happenede:
     His hand sleppid and slode o-slante one þe mayles,
3856 And þe toþer slely slynges hym undire:
     With a trenchande knyfe the traytoure hym hyttes,
     Thorowe þe helme and þe hede, one heyghe one þe brayne: *Modred, with a sharp dagger, stabs Gawaine through the brain.*
     And thus syr Gawayne es gone, the gude man of armes,
3860 With-owttyne reschewe of renke, and rewghe es þe more!
     Thus syr Gawaynne es gone, that gyede many othire; *Gawaine, the good man of arms, is gone!*
     ffro Gowere to Gernesay, alle þe gret lordys
     Of Glamour, of Galys londe, þis galyarde knyghtes,
3864 ffor glent of gloppynyng glade be they never!

Kyng ffroderike offres fraythely þare aftyre,
  ffraynes at the false mane of owre ferse knyghte;

"Knew thow ever this knyghte in thi kithe ryche,

3868 Of whate kynde he was comene, be-knowe now þe sothe;
Qwat gome was he this with the gaye armes,
With þis gryffoune of golde, þat es one growffe fallyne;
He has grettly greffede us, sa me Gode helpe!

3872 Gyrde downe oure gude mene, and grevede us sore!
He was þe sterynneste in stoure that ever stele werryde,
ffore he has stonayede oure stale, and stroyede for ever!"

Than syr Mordrede with mouthe melis fulle faire;

3876 "He was makles one molde, mane be my trowhe;
This was syr Gawayne the gude, þe gladdeste of othire,
And the graciouseste gome that undire God lyffede,

Mane hardyeste of hande, happyeste in armes,

3880 And the hendeste in hawle undire hevene riche;
Þe lordelieste of ledynge qwhylles he lyffe myghte,
ffore he was lyone allossede in londes i-newe;
Had thow knawene hym, syr kynge in kythe thare he
  lengede,

3884 His konynge, his knyghthode, his kyndly werkes,
His doyng, his doughtynesse, his dedis of armes,
Thow wolde hafe dole for his dede þe dayes of thy life!"

Ʒit þat traytour alles tite teris lete he falle,

3888 Turnes hym furthe tite, and talkes no more,
Went wepand awaye and weries the stowndys,
Þat ever his werdes ware wroghte siche wandrethe to
  wyrke:
Whene he thoghte on þis thynge, it thirllede his herte;

3892 ffor sake of his sybb blode sygheande he rydys;
When þat renayede renke remembirde hym solvene,
Of reverence and ryotes of þe rownde table.

He rennyd and repent hyme of alle his rewthe werkes,

3896 Rode awaye with his rowte, ristys he no lengere,
ffor rade of oure riche kynge, ryve þat he scholde;
Thane kayres he to Cornewaile, carefulle in herte,

Because of his kynsemane that one the coste ligges :

goes into Cornwall,

3900 He taries tremlande ay, tydandis to herkene.

Than the traytoure treunted þe Tyseday þar-aftyre,

Trynnys in with a trayne tresone to wirke,

And by þe Tambire þat tide his tentis he reris,

and pitches his camp by the Tamar.

3904 And thane in a mette-while a messangere he sendes,

And wraite un-to Waynor how the werlde chaungede,

And what comliche coste the kyng was aryvede,

and from thence writes to Gunnever,

One floode foughtene with his fleete, and fellyd theme olyfe ;

3908 Bade hir ferkene so ferre, and fflee with hir childire,

Whills he myghte wile hyme awaye, and wyne to hir speche,

Ayere in-to Irelande, in-to þas owte mowntes,

bidding her fly into Ireland.

And wonne thare in wildernesse with-in tha wast landys ;

3912 Than cho ȝermys and ȝee at ȝorke in hir chambire,

Gronys fulle grysely with gretand teres,

Passes owte of þe palesse with alle hir price maydenys,

Towarde Chestyre in a charre thay chese hir þe wayes,

3918 Dighte hir ewyne for to dye with dule at hir herte ;

Scho kayres to Karelyone, and kawghte hir a vaile,

But she goes to Caerleon and takes the veil.

Askes thare þe habite in þe honoure of Criste,

And alle for falsede, and frawde, and fere of hir loverde !

3920 Bot whene oure wiese kynge wiste þat Gawayne was landede,

He al to-wrythes for woo, and wryngande his handes,

Arthur is grieved for Gawaine's rash landing, and follows him wading through the water.

Gers lawnche his botes appone a lawe watire,

Londis als a lyone with lordliche knyghtes,

3924 Slippes in in the sloppes o-slante to þe girdylle,

Swalters upe swyftly with his swerde drawene,

Bownnys his bataile and baners displayes,

Buskes over þe brode sandes with breth at his herte,

3928 fferkes frekkly one felde þare þe feye lygges ;

Of the traytours mene one trappede stedis,

He slays ten thousand men in his great wrath. Seven score of his knights are slain.

Ten thosandez ware tynte, þe trewghe to acownt,

And certane on owre syde sevene score knyghtes

3932 In soyte with theire sovcrayne unsownde are belcvede !

Arthur slays
dukes and earls,

The kynge comly over-kesté knyghtes and othire,
Erlles of Awfrike, and estriche berynes
Of Orgaile and Orekenay, þe Irosche kynges,

3936 The nobileste of Norwaye, nowmbirs fulle hugge,
Dukes of Danamarke, and dubbid knyghtes ;
And the enchedè kynge in the gay armes
Lys gronande one þe grownnde, and girde thorowe evene !

and makes his
way to where Ga-
waine's men are
surrounded,

3940 The riche kynge ransakes with rewthe at his herte,
And up rypes the renkes of alle þe rownde tabylle ;
Ses theme alle in a soppe in sowle by theme one,
With þe Sarazcnes unsownde enserchede abowte ;

3944 And syr Gawayne the gude in his gaye armes,
Umbegrippede the girse, and one grouffe fallene,

and sees Sir Ga-
waine lying dead.

His baners braydene downe, betyne of gowlles,
His brand and his brade sehelde al blody be-rovene ;

3948 Was never oure semliche kynge so sorowfulle in herte,
Ne þat sanke hyme so sade, bot þat sighte one.

With groans and
tears he kisses
the body

Than gliftis þe gud kynge, and glapyns in herte,
Gronys fulle grisely with gretande teris ;

3952 Knelis downe to the cors, and kaught it in armes,
Kastys upe his umbrere, and kysses hyme sone !
Lokes one his eye-liddis, þat lowkkide ware faire,
His lippis like to þe lede, and his lire falowede !

3956 þan the corownde kyng cryes fulle lowde,—

He bitterly la-
ments the good
knight.

" Dere kosyne o kynde, in kare am I levede !
ffor nowe my wirchipe es wente, and my were endide !
Here es þe hope of my hele, my happynge of armes !

3960 My herte and my hardynes hale one hym lengede !
My concelle, my comforthe, þat kepide myne herte !
Of alle knyghtes þe kynge þat undir Criste lifede !
þou was worthy to be kynge, thofe I þe corowne bare !

3964 My wele and my wirchipe of alle þis werlde riche

It was through
his wit that all
his conquests
were made.

Was wonnene thourghe syr Gawayne, and thourghe his
witte one !
Allas !" saide syr Arthure, " nowe ekys my sorowe !

I am uttirly undon*e* in myn*e* awen*e* landes!

3968 A dowttouse derfe dede, þou duellis to longe!

Why drawes þou so one dreghe, thow drownnes myn*e* herte!"

Than swetes the swete kyng*e* and in swoun*e* fallis,

Swafres up swiftely, and swetly hym kysses,

3972 Till*e* his burliche berd*e* was blody be-rown*e*,

Alls he had bestes britenede, and broghte owt of life;

Ne had *syr* Ewayne comen*e*, and othire gret*e* lordys,

His bolde herte had broustene for bale at þat stownde!

3976 "**B**lyve," sais thies bolde men*e*! "thow blondirs þi selfen*e*,

þis es botles bale, for bettir bees it nev*er*!

It es no wirchipe i-wysse to wryng thyn*e* hondes,

To wepe als a woman*e* it es no witt holden*e*!

3980 Be knyghtly of contena*u*nce, als a kyng scholde,

And lev*e* siche clamoure for Cristes luf*e* of heven*e*!"

"ffor blode," said the bolde kyng*e*, "blyn*e* sall*e* I nev*er*,

Or my brayne to-briste, or my breste oþ*er*!

3984 Was nev*er* sorowe so soft*e* that sanke to my herte!

Itt es full*e* sibb to myself*e*, my sorowe es the more!

Was nev*er* so sorowfull*e* a syght*e* seyn*e* with myn*e* eghen*e*!

He es sakles supprysede for syn*e* of myn*e* one!"

3988 Down*e* knelis þe kyng*e*, and kryes full*e* lowde;

With carefull*e* contena*u*nce he karpes thes wordes,—

"O rightwis riche Gode, this rewthe thow be-holde!

þis ryall*e* rede blode ryn*e* appon*e* erthe;

3992 It ware worthy to be schrede and schrynede in golde,

ffor it es sakles of syn*e*, sa helpe m*e* oure Lorde!"

Down*e* knelis þe kyng with kar*e* at his herte,

Kaughte it up*e* kyndly with his clen*e* handis,

3996 Kest*e* it in a ketill*e*-hatt*e*, and cov*er*de it faire,

And kayres furthe with þe cors in kyghte þar*e* he lenges.

"**H**er*e* I make myn avowe," *quod* the kyng*e* than*e*,

"To Messie, and to Marie, the myld*e* qwen*e* of heven*e*,

Arthur swoons for grief; then starts up and kisses the dead knight.

His beard is smeared in the blood of Gawaine.

Sir Ewaine and his knights reproach him.

He excuses himself on account of the greatness of the grief.

He collects Gawaine's blood in a helmet,

and carries away his body.

Then he makes a solemn vow that he will take no pleasure in the chase till Gawaine be avenged.

4000   I salle nev*er* ryvaye, ne racches un-cowpylle

At roo ne rayne dere, þat rynnes apponne erthe ;

Nev*er* grewhownde late glyde, ne gossehawke latt flye,

Ne never fowle see fellide, þat flieghes wi*th* wenge ;

4004   ffawkone ne formaylle appone fiste handille,

Ne ȝitt wi*th* gerefawcone rejoyse me in erthe ;

Ne regnne in my royaltez, ne halde my rownde table,

Tille thi dede, my dere, be dewly revengede !

4008   Bot ev*er* droupe and dare, qwylles my lyfe lastez,

Tille Drightene and derfe dede hafe done qwate theme

     likes !''

Than kaughte they upe þe cors wi*th* kare at theire hertes,

Karyed [it] one a coursere wi*th* þe kynge selfene ;

The body was sent straight to Winchester,

4012   The waye unto Wynchestre þay wente at the gayneste,

Wery and wandsomdly, wi*th* wondide knyghtes ;

Thare come þe pr*ior* of the plas, and professide monnkes,

and met by a procession of monks.

Apas in processione, and wi*th* the prynce metys ;

4016   And he be-tuke þame the cors of þe knyghte noble,—

Arthur gives orders that all honour should be paid to the dead.

"Lokis it be clenly kepyd," he said, " and in þe kirke

     holdene,

Done for derygese, as to þe ded fallys ;

Menskede wi*th* messes, for mede of þe saule :

4020   Loke it wante no waxe, ne no wirchipe ell*es*,

And at þe body be bawmede, and one erthe holdene.

Ȝiff thou kepe thi covent, encroche any wirchipe

At my comyng agayne, ȝif Crist will*e* it thole ;

4024   Abyde of þe beryenge tille they be broughte undire,

Þat has wroghte us this woo, and þis werre movede."

Sir Wycher advises that he should stay in Winchester and rally his forces.

Than sais *syr* Wychere þe wy, a wyese mane of armes,

     "I rede ȝe warely wende, and wirkes the beste ;

4028   Soiorne in this cete, and semble thi berynes,

And bidde wi*th* thi bolde mene in thi burghe riche :

Get owt knyghttez of contres, that castell*es* holdes,

And owt of garysons grete gude mene of armes,

4032   ffor we are faithely to fewe to feghte wi*th* them alle,

Þat we see in his sorte appon*e* þe see bankes."

With krewelle contenance thane the kyng karpis theis
wordes,—

"I praye the kare noghte, *syr* knyghte, ne caste þou no
dredis !

4036 Hadde I no segge bot myselfe one undir sone,

And I may hym see with sighte, or one hym sette hondis,

I salle evene amange his mene malle hym to dede,

Are I of þe stede styre halfe a stede lenghe !

Arthur declares
that he himself
alone is sufficient.

4040 I salle hym in his stowre, and stroye hyme for ever,

And þare-to make I myne avowe devottly to Cryste,

And to his modyre Marie, þe mylde qwene of hevene !

I salle never sojourne sounde, ne sawghte at myne herte,

4044 In ceté ne in subarbe sette appone erthe,

Ne ȝitt slomyre ne slepe with my slawe eyghne,

Tille he be slayne þat hym slowghe, ȝif any sleyghte
happene :

Bot ever pursue the Payganys þat my pople distroyede,

4048 Qwylles I may þare theme and pynne, in place þare me
likes."

He will never
sojourn in city
or town till Mo-
dred be slain.

Thare durste no renke hym areste of alle þe rownde table,

Ne none paye þat prynce with plesande wordes,

Ne none of his lige-mene luke hym in the eyghne,

4052 So lordely he lukes for losse of his knyghttes !

Thane drawes he to Dorsett, and dreches no langere,

Derefulle dredlesse with drowppande teris ;

Kayeris in-to Kornewayle with kare at his herte,

None dares to
oppose the fierce
words of Arthur.

4056 The trays of þe traytoure he trynys fulle evenne :

And turnys in be þe Treynte[1] þe traytoure to seche,

ffyndis hym in a foreste þe Frydaye there aftire ;

The kyng lyghttes one fott, and freschely askryes,

4060 And with his freliche folke he has þe folde nomene !

Arthur follows
Modred into
Cornwall and at-
tacks him.

Now isschewis his enmye undire þe wode eynys,

With ostes of alynes fulle horrebille to schewe !

Sir Mordrede the malebranche, with his myche pople,

4064 ffoundes owt of the foreste appone fele halfes,

A vast host of
aliens assault Ar-
thur's men.

[1] ? Tamar.

In sevene grett batailles semliche arrayede,
Sexty thowsande mene, the syghte was fulle hugge,
Alle fyghtande folke of þe ferre laundes,

There were sixty thousand against eighteen hundred.

4068 ffaire fettede one frownte be tha fresche strondes!
And alle Arthurs oste was amede with knyghtes
Bot awghtene hundrethe of alle, entrede in rolles;
This was a mache un-mete, bot myghttis of Criste,

4072 To melle with þat multitude in þase man londis.
Than the royalle roy of þe rownde table

Arthur on a charger arranges his men.

Rydes one a riche stedes, arrayes his beryns,
Buskes his avawmwarde, als hym beste likes;

4076 Syr Ewayne, and syr Errake, and othire gret lordes,
Demenys the medilwarde menskefully thare aftyre,
With Marrake and Menyduke, myghty of strenghes;
Idirous and Alymere, þire avenaunt childrene,

4080 Ayers with Arthure, with sevene score of knyghtes;
He rewlis þe rerewarde redyly thare aftyre,
The rekeneste redy mene of þe rownde table,
And thus he fittis his folke, and freschely askryes,

4084 And syene comforthes his mene with knyghtlyche
wordes—

He beseeches them to do well that day and not to fear.

"I beseke ȝow, sirs, for sake of oure Lorde,
That ȝe doo wele to daye, and dredis no wapene!
ffighttes fersely nowe, and fendis ȝoure selvene,

4088 ffellis downe ȝone feye folke, the felde salle be owrs!
They are Sarazenes ȝone sorte, un-sownde motte they
worthe!

If they are slain they will be taken straight up to Heaven.

Sett one theme sadlye, for sake of oure Lorde!
ȝif us be destaynede to dy to daye one this erthe,

4092 We salle be hewede un-to hevene, or we be halfe colde!
Loke ȝe lett for no lede lordly to wirche;
Layes ȝone laddes lowe be the layke ende!
Take no tente un-to me, ne tale of me rekke,

4096 Bes besy one my baners with ȝoure brighte wapyns,
That they be strenghely stuffede with steryne knyghtes,
And holdene lordly one lofte ledys to schewe;

ȝif any renke theme arase, reschowe theme sone.

4100 Wirkes now my wirchipe, to daye my werre endys!
ȝe wotte my wele and my wo, wirkkys as ȝow likys!
Crist comly with crowne comforthe ȝow alle,
ffor þe kyndeste creatours that ever kynge ledde!

4104 I gyffe ȝow alle my blyssyng with a blithe wille,
And alle Bretowns bolde, blythe mote ȝe worthe!"
They pype upe at pryme tyme approches theme nere,
Pris mene and priste proves their strenghes;

4108 Bremly the brethemen bragges in troumppes,
In cornettes comlyly, whene knyghttes assembles,
And thane jolyly enjoynys þeis jentylle knyghttes;
A jolyere journé a-juggede was never,

4112 Whene Bretones boldly embraces theire scheldes,
And cristyne encroyssede theme, and castis in fewtire!
Than syr Arthure oste his enmye askryes,
    And in they schokke theire scheldes, schontes no
        lengare;

4116 Schotte to þe schiltrones, and schowttes fulle heghe,
Thorowe scheldis fulle schene schalkes they touche!
Redily thas rydde mene of the rownde table
With ryalle raunke stele rittys theire mayles;

4120 Bryneys browddene they briste, and burneste helmys,
Hewes haythene mene downe, halses in sondre!
ffyghtande with fyne stele, þe feye blod rynnys
Of þe frekkeste of frounte, unfers ere be-levede.

4124 Ethyns of Argayle and Irische kynges
Enverounes oure avawmwarde with venymmos beryns;
Peghttes and paynymes with perilous wapyns,
With speres disspetousely disspoylles our knyghttes,

4128 And hewede downe tho hendeste with hertly dynttys!
Thorow the holle batayle they holdene theire wayes;
þus fersly they fyghte appone sere halfes,
That of þe bolde Bretones myche blode spillis!

4132 Thare durste non rescowe theme, for reches in erthe,
þe steryne ware þare so stedde, and stuffede wit othire:

To-day his war
ends!

He gives them
his parting bless-
ing.

The Britons fight
furiously.

The vanguard is
surrounded by
the enemy, and
many of them
slain.

He durste noghte stire a steppe, bot stodde for hyme
    selvene,

Tille thre stalis ware stroyede be strenghe of hyme one!

4136 "Idrous," *quod* Arthure, "ayre the byhoves!

I see *syr* Ewayne over-sette with Sarazenes kene!

Redy the for rescows, arraye thee sone!

Hye þe with hardy mene in helpe of thy ffadire!

4140 Sett in one the syde, and socoure ȝone lordes;

Bot they be socourrede and sownde, unsawghte be I
    never!"

Idrous hyme ansuers ernestly þare aftyre,—

"He es my fadire in faithe, for-sake salle I never!

4144 He has me fosterde and fedde, and my faire bretherene,

Bot I for-sake this gate, so me Gode helpe,

And sothely alle sybredyne bot thyselfe one;

I breke never his biddynge for beryne one lyfe,

4148 Bot ever bouxome as beste blethely to wyrke!

He commande me kyndly, with knyghtly wordes,

That I schulde lelely one þe lenge, and one noo lede elles;

I salle hys commandement holde, ȝif Criste wil me thole!

4152 He es eldare than I, and ende salle we bothene;

He salle ferkke be-fore, and I salle come aftyre:

ȝiffe hyme be destaynede to dy to daye one þis erthe,

Criste comly with crowne take kepe to hys saule!"

4156 Than remys the riche kynge with rewthe at his herte,

    Hewys hys handys on heghte, and to þe hevene lokes,—

"Qwythene had Dryghttyne destaynede at his dere wille,

þat he hade demyd me to daye to dy for ȝow alle,

4160 That had I lever than be lorde alle my lyfe tyme,

Off alle þat Alexandere aughte qwhilles he in erthe
    lengede."

Sir Ewayne and *syr* Errake, þes excellente beryns,

Enters in one þe oste, and egerly strykes;

4164 The ethenys of Orkkenaye and Irische kynges,

þay gobone of þe gretteste with growndone swerdes,

Hewes one þas hulkes with þeire harde wapyns,

Layed downe þas ledes with lothely dynttys;

4168 Schuldirs and scheldys þay schrede to þe hawnches,
And medilles thourghe maylcs, þay mcrkene in sondire!
Siche honoure never aughte none erthely kyng
At theire endyng daye, bot Arthure hyme sclvene!

4172 So þe droughte of þe daye dryede theire hertes,
That bothe drynkles they dye, dole was þe more!
Now mellys oure medille-warde, and mengene to-gedire.   <small>The centre of Arthur's army engages.</small>
Sir Mordrede þe Malebranche with his myche pople,

4176 He had hide hyme be-hynde with-in thas holte eynys,
With halle bataile one hethe, harme es þe more!   <small>Sir Modred had been watching the battle, and preparing to attack the king.</small>
He hade senc þe conteke al clene to þe ende,
How oure chevalrye chevyde be chaunces of armes!

4180 He wiste oure folke was for-foughttene, þat þare was
    feye levede;
To encowntere þe kynge he castes hyme sone,
Bot the churles chekyne hade chaungyde his armes;   <small>But first he changes his arms to conceal himself.</small>
He had sothely for-sakene þe sawturoure engrelede,

4184 And laughte upe thre lyons alle of whitte silvyre,
Passande in purpre of perrie fulle ryche,
ffor þe kynge sulde noghte knawe þe cawtelous wriche!
Becauso of his cowardys he keste of his atyre;

4188 Bot the comliche kyng knewe hym fulle swythe,   <small>ButArthurknows him at once, and points him out to Sir Cador.</small>
Karpis to syr Cadors þes kyndly wordez,—
"I see the traytoure come ȝondyr trynande fulle ȝerne;
ȝone ladde with þe lyones es like to hyme-selfene!

4192 Hym salle torfere betyde, may I touche ones,
ffor alle his tresone and trayne, alles I am trew lorde!
To day Clarente and Caliburne salle kythe theme to-gedirs,   <small>The two famous swords, Clarent and Caliburn, shall this day be tried one against the other.</small>
Whilke es kenere of kerse, or hardare of eghge!

4196 ffraiste salle we fyne stele appone fyne wedis:
Itt was my derlynge dayntevous, and fulle dere holdene,
Kepede fore encorownmentes of kynges enoynttede
One dayes when I dubbyde dukkes and erlles;

4200 It was burliche borne be þe bryghte hiltes;
I durste never dere it in dedis of armes,

Bot ever kepide clene, be-cause of myselvene;

Arthur recog-
nises his sword
which he had
left at Walling-
ford under the
care of the Queen.

ffor I see Clarent unclede, þat crowne es of swerdes:

4204 My wardrop of Walyngfordhe I wate es distroyede;

Wist no wy of wone bot Waynor hir-selvene,

Scho hade þe kepynge hirselfe of þat kydde wapyne,

Off cofres enclosede þat to þe crowne lengede,

4208 With rynges and relikkes, and þe regalc of ffraunce,

That was ffowndene one syr ffrolle, whene he was feye
levyde."

Than syr Marrike in malyncoly metys hyme sone,

Sir Merrick fights
with Modred
and is forced to
withdraw.

With a mellyd mace myghtyly hym strykes;

4212 The bordoure of his bacenett he bristes in sondire,

þat þe schire rede blode over his brene rynnys!

The beryne blenkes for bale, and alle his ble chaunges,

Bot ȝitt he byddys as a bore, and brymly he strykes!

4216 He braydes owte a brande bryghte als ever ony sylver,

þat was syr Arthure awene, and Utcre his fadirs,

In þe wardrop of Walyngfordhe was wonte to be kepede;

þare with þe derfe dogge syche dynttes he rechede,

4220 þe toþer with-drewe one-dreghe and durste do none oþer!

ffor syr Marrake was mane merrede in elde,

And syr Mordrede was myghty, and his moste strenghes;

Come none with-in the compas, knyghte ne none oþer,

4224 With-in þe swyng of swerde, þat ne he þe swete levyd:

þat persayfes oure prynce, and presses to faste,

Arthur forces his
way to Modred,

Strykes into þe stowre by strenghe of hys handis;

Metis with syr Mordrede, he melis unfaire,—

and upbraids
him.

4228 "Turne, traytoure untrewe, þe tydys no bettyre;

Be gret Gode thow salle dy with dynt of my handys!

The schalle rescowe no renke ne reches in erthe!"

Then he strikes
him with Cali-
burn and cuts
through his
shield and into
the shoulder.

The kyng with Calaburne knyghtly hym strykes,

4232 The cantelle of þe clere schelde he kerfes in sondyre,

In-to þe schuldyre of þe schalke a schaftmonde large,

þat þe schire rede blode schewede one þe maylys!

He schodirde and schrenkys, and schontes bott lyttile,

4236 Bott schokkes in scharpely in his schene wedys;

The ffelonne with þe ffyne swerde freschely he strykes,

The ffelettes of þe fferrere syde he flassches in sondyre,

Thorowe jopowne and jesserawnte of gentille mailes!

4240 The freke fichede in þe flesche an halfe fotte large,

That derfe dynt was his dede, and dole was þe more

That ever þat doughtty sulde dy, bot at Dryghttyns wylle!

Ʒitt with Calyburne his swerde, fulle knyghttly he strykes,

4244 Kastes in his clere schelde, and coveres hym fulle faire;

Swappes of þe swerde hande, als he by glenttis,

Ane inche fro þe elbowe, he ochede it in sondyre,

Þat he swounnes one þe swrathe, and one swym fallis;

4248 Thorowe brater of browne stele, and the bryghte mayles,

That the hilte and þe hande appone þe hethe ligges!

Thane frescheliche þe freke the ffente upe rererys,

Brochis hym in with the bronde to þe bryghte hiltys,

4252 And he brawles one the bronde, and bownes to dye.

"In faye," says þe feye kynge, "sore me for-thynkkes

That ever siche a false theefe so faire an end haves."

Qwene they had ffenyste þis feghte, thane was þe felde wonnene,

4256 And the false folke in þe felde feye are by-levede!

Tille a fforeste they fledde, and felle in the grevys,

And fers foghtande folke folowes theme aftyre;

Howntes and hewes downe the heythene tykes,

4260 Mourtherys in the mowntaygnes syr Mordrede knyghtes;

Thare chapyde never no childe, cheftayne ne oþer,

Bot choppes theme downe in the chace, it chargys bot littylle!

4264 Bot whene syr Arthure anone syr Ewayne he fyndys,

And Errake þe avenaunt, and oþer grett lordes,

He kawghte up syr Cador with care at his herte,

Sir Clegis, syr Cleremonde, þes clerc mene of armes,

Sir Lothe, and syr Lyonelle, syr Lawncelott and Lowes,

4268 Marrake and Meneduke, þat myghty ware ever;

(marginal notes)

Modred, though wounded, strikes Arthur and gives him a terrible wound in the side.

Arthur with Caliburn cuts off the sword-hand of Modred.

Modred dies.

Arthur declares that his end is too good for him.

Modred's men are defeated and pursued.

Arthur finds the dead bodies of his knights.

With langoure in the launde thare he layes theme to-
gedire,

Lokede one theyre lighames, and with a lowde stevene,

Alles lede þat liste noghte lyfe and loste had his myrthis;

4272 Than he stotays for made, and alle his strenghe faylez,

Lokes upe to þe lyfte, and alle his lyre chaunges!

Downne he sweys fulle swythe, and in a swoune fallys!

Upe he coveris one kneys, and kryes fulle oftene,—

4276 "Kyng comly with crowne, in care am I levyde!

Alle my lordchipe lawe in lande es layde undyre!

That me has gyfene gwerdones, be grace of hym selvene,

Mayntenyde my manhede be myghte of theire handes,

4280 Made me manly one molde, and mayster in erthe;

In a tenefulle tyme this torfere was rereryde,

That for a traytoure has tynte alle my trewe lordys!

Here rystys the riche blude of the rownde table,

4284 Rebukkede with a rebawde, and rewthe es the more!

I may helples one hethe house be myne one,

Alles a wafulle wedowe þat wanttes hir beryne!

I may werye and wepe, and wrynge myne handys,

4288 ffor my wytt and my wyrchipe awaye es for ever!

Off alle lordchips I take leve to myne ende!

Here es þe Bretones blode broughte owt of lyfe,

And nowe in þis journee alle my joy endys!"

4292 Thane relyes þe renkes of alle þe rownde table,

To þe ryalle roy thay ride þam alle;

Than assembles fulle sone sevene score knyghtes,

In sighte to þaire soverayne, þat was unsownde levede;

4296 Than knelis the crownede kynge, and kryes one lowde,—

"I thanke þe, Gode, of thy grace, with a gud wylle;

That gafe us vertue and witt to vencows þis beryns;

And us has grauntede þe gree of theis gret lordes!

4300 He sent us never no schame, ne schenchipe in erthe,

Bot ever ʒit þe overhande of alle oþer kynges:

We hafe no layscre now þese lordys to seke,

ffor ʒone laythely ladde me lamede so sore!

4304 Graythe us to Glaschenbery, us gaynes none oþer ;
    Thare we may ryste us with roo, and raunsake oure wondys
    Of þis dere day werke, þe Dryghttene belovede,
    That us has destaynede and demyd to dye in oure awene.''
4308 Thane they holde at his heste hally at ones,
    And graythes to Glasschenberye þe gate at þe gayneste ;
    Entres þe Ile of Aveloyne, and Arthure he lyghttes,
    Merkes to a manere there, for myghte he no forthire :
4312 A surgyne of Salerne enserches his wondes,
    The kyng sees be asaye þat sownde bese he never,
    And sone to his sekire mene he said theis wordes,—
    " Doo calle me a confessour, with Criste in his armes ;
4316 I wille be howselde in haste, whate happe so be-tyddys ;
    Constantyne my cosyne he salle the corowne bere,
    Alles be-commys hym of kynde, ȝife Criste wille hym thole !
    Beryne, fore my benysone, thowe berye ȝone lordys,
4320 That in baytaille with brondez are broghte owte of lyfe ;
    And sythene merke manly to Mordrede childrene,
    That they bee sleyghely slayne, and slongene in watyrs ;
    Latt no wykkyde wede waxe, ne wrythe one this erthe
4324 I warne fore thy wirchipe, wirke alles I bydde !
    I foregyffe alle greffe, for Cristez lufe of hevene !
    ȝife Waynor hafe wele wroghte, wele hir be-tydde !''
    He saide In manus with mayne one molde whare he ligges,
4328 And thus passes his speryt, and spekes he no more !
    The baronage of Bretayne thane, bechopes and othire,
    Graythes theme to Glaschenbery with gloppynnande
        hertes,
    To bery thare the bolde kynge, and brynge to the erthe,
4332 With alle wirchipe and welthe þat any wy scholde.
    Throly belles thay rynge, and Requiem syngys,
    Dosse messes and matyns with mournande notes :
    Relygeous reveste in theire riche copes,
4336 Pontyficalles and prelates in precyouse wedys,
    Dukes and dusszeperis in theire dule cotes,
    Cowntasses knelande and claspande theire handes,

Marginal notes:

He desires to be taken to Glastonbury.

He enters the Isle of Avelon and is taken to a manor there, for he could go no further. A surgeon is sent for,

but Arthur desires a Confessor.

He appoints Constantyne, his cousin, his heir.

Orders Modred's children to be slain.

To Guinever he wishes that "if she has well done she may fare well." Then he says "In Manus," and his spirit passes away.

The Barons of Britain bury Arthur at Glastonbury.

Great mourning was made at his funeral.

Ladys languessande and lowrande to schewe ;
4340 Alle was buskede in blake, birdes and othire,
That schewede at the sepulture, with sylande teris ;
Whas never so sorrowfulle a syghte seene in theire tyme !

This was the end
of Arthur of the
blood of Hector
and of Priamus
of Troy.

Thus endis kyng Arthure, as auctors alegges,
4344 That was of Ectores blude the kynge sone of Troye,
And of syr Pryamous the prynce praysede in erthe ;
ffro thythene broghte the Bretons alle his bolde eldyrs
In-to Bretayne the brode, as þe Bruytte tellys.
Etc. explicit.

Hic jacet Arthurus, rex quondam rexque futurus.

Here endes Morte Arthure, writene by Robert off Thorntone.

R. Thornton dictus qui scripsit sit benedictus.   Amen !

GLOSSARIAL INDEX.

Aleche, *adv.* alike, 194.

Alet, *s.* small plate of steel, 2565.

Alfyne, *s.* elfish creature, 1343.

Allblawsters, *s.* shooters with cross-bows, 2426

Ake, *s.* oak, 1096.

Allossede or alofede, *adj.* praised, famous, renowned, 2418. 3882

Alkyne, *adj.* all kinds of, 928.

Alowes, *v.* praises, 396; alowede, glorified.

Als, alls, or alles, *adv.* as, 845, etc.; als-swythe, immediately, 409. See Glossary to *Alliterative Poems.*

Amede, *v.* estimated, accounted, reckoned, 4069.

Anetis or anentis, *adv.* near, close to, 2568.

Anlace, *s.* dagger, 1143.

Apas, *adv.* walking in slow step, 4015.

Apperte (= a p*ar*ty, 212), separate or separately, apart, 688.

Arase or arace, *v.* tear away by force, 4099.

Aroumede, *v.* enlarged, 340.

Aryesede, *v.* summoned, 600.

Assaye, *v.* try, 2347.

Ascryeӡ, *v.* shouts, 1367.

At, *pron.* that, 1842.

Atheliste, *adj.* most noble, 1593.

Attamede, *v.* reached, 2175.

Auntyre, *v.* adventure, dare, 360.

Auntyre or awnter, *s.* adventure, 2007.

Avenaunt, *adj.* noble, becoming, 2627; 'Arthur the avenaunt,' 3652.

Aventaile, *s.* the vent, or moveable part of the helmet, 910.

Avires, *v.* directs, 3165.

Avyede, *v.* took the way, 3717.

Avyssely, *adv.* carefully, 2700.

Awke, *adj.* bold, 13.

Awkewarde, *adv.* badly, 2564; aside, 2247.

Ayele, *s.* grandfather, 2604.

Ayere, *v.* to go or be upon an expedition or business, 455, 617, 620, 1259.

Aythere, *adj.* either, each, 939.

Aӡayne-stonde, *v.* oppose, 3127.

Baite, *v.* feed, 2695, 2672.

Baiste, *adj.* abashed, frightened, 2857.

Baltyrde, *v.* capered, danced, 782.

Barehevydys, *s.* boars' heads, 177.

Barowes, *s.* porket-pigs, 191.

9

Bedgatt, bedfellow (?); byddeʒ, are (?), 1030.

Bekeʒ, *v.* warms, bakes, 1048.

Bekennyde or bekende, *v.* commended, entrusted, 482, 2340, 2355.

Bekyne, *s.* beacon, 564.

Bekyrs or bekers, *v.* skirmishes, attacks, 368, 2425, 2096.

Belde, *v.* rest in safety, 8.

Beneyde, *v.* brought, 2424.

Bente, *s.* plain or level ground, place, spot, 1054, 1067.

Bernake, *s.* wild goose, 189.

Bernes, biernes, byernes, berynes, *s.* men, knights, 255, etc.

Bes, bees, thou shalt be, 1688; *imp.* be, 2857.

Bessomes, *s.* tides (?), 3662.

Bestaile, *s.* beasts, 1050.

Besye, *s.* press of business, 3631.

Beteche, *v.* deliver up, 1611.

Betyne, *adj.* adorned; 'betyne of gowlles,' decked in red armour, 3647, 3946.

Beveryne, *adv.* flowing, wavy, loose, 3631.

Bewschers, *s.* buttocks, 1047.

Blasons, *s.* surcoats, 1860.

Ble or blee, *s.* colour, complexion, 2576, 3333, 3559.

Blemeste, *v.* blemished, wounded, 2578.

Blendez, *v.* blinds, or is blinded, 1799.

Blenke, *v.* wince, 3641; lessen, 2858.

Bleryde, *v.* mocked, insulted, 782.

Blonders, *v.* blunders, go along blindly, 3976.

Blonke, *s.* steed, horse, 453.

Blyne, *v.* stop, hesitate, cease, 1931, 2578.

Blysche, *v.* look, stare, 116. See Glossary of *Allit. Poems,* s.v. *blusch.*

Bonettez, *s.* small sails, 3657.

Bot, *adv.* except, unless, 356.

Botelesse or butelesse, *adj.* bootless, undefended, without remedy, 981, 1014.

Botures, *s.* butter-sauce (O.Fr.), 189.

Bownne or boun, *adv.* readily, 1633.

Bownes, *v.* hastens, 2697.

Bourdez, *v.* jokes, sports, 1170, 3123.

Bowes, *s.* limbs, legs, hams, 188.

Brankand, *v.* wounding, 1861.

Braggene, *v.* blow, sound, 1484.

Brater, *s.* vambrace, 4248.

Brathelle, *s.* brisket, 793.

Brathely, *adv.* quickly, 3220.

Braunchers, *s.* young hawks, 190.

Brayd, *v.* unsheath, draw out, 1172.

Brayde, *s.* stroke, 3763.

Brayedez, *v.* dash, rush quickly, 3126.

Brede, *adj.* broad, 1224.

Bredez, *s.* breads = meats, 1049.

Breklesse, *adj.* breekless, naked, 1048.

Bremly or brymly, *adv.* furiously, 117, 4108.

Brene or breny, *s.* cuirass, body armour, 1413, 1374, 1482, 1525, 1858.

Brenyede, *adj.* armed, 316.

Breth or broth, *s.* rage, anger, 107, 117, 214.

Brochede, *v.* spitted, 1050.

Brochez, *s.* spits, 1029.

Brochez, *v.* spurs, 918, 1449.

Brothely, brathely, or brethly, *adv.* angrily, fiercely, 1408, 3641, 1753.

Brothy, *adj.* shaggy, stiff, 1090.

Browdene, *adj.* broad, 1858.

Brustils, *s.* bristles, 1095.

Brynne, *v.* brain, dash out their brains, 3642.

Bryttyne or brittene, *v.* cut or tear in pieces, 106, 802, 963, 1067.

Bugande, *v.* reclining, lounging, 1045.

Bus, *v.* behoves, 1045.

Buscayle, *s.* copse, wood, 895, 1634.

Bustous, *adj.* boisterous, rough, strong, 615, 783.

Byggly, *adv.* proudly, grandly, 1376.

Byhowys, *adv.* to advantage, 1715.

Byrdez, *s.* ladies, 999.

Byrre, *s.* noise, rush, 3662.

Byswenkez, *v.* recovers himself, 1128

Caffe, *s.* chaff, refuse, 1064.

Cantelle, *s.* corner, 4232.

Caremane, *s.* carl-man, man, 957.

Carffes, *s.* cuts, 2714.

Carpe, *v.* speak, 143, 220, etc.

Chapes, *s.* fastenings, 2522.

Chare, *v.* turn, 1886.

Cheekke, *s.* invading force, 1986.

Chele, *s.* chill, cold, 3392.

Chese, *perf.* chis, *v.* choose, select, take the way, hence go, 1619.

Cheveride, *v.* shivered, 3392.

Chewyse, *v.* defend, 1750.

Chokefulle, quite full, 1552.

Chullede, *v.* chased, 1444.

Cleverande, *v.* scaling, climbing, 3325.

Clekes or clekys, *v.* clutches, 1164, 1865.

Clergyally, *adv.* skilfully, 200.

Clewes or cloughes, *s.* rocks, 941, 1639.

Clewide, *v.* fastened, 3269.

Close, *s.* defile, gorge, 1639.

Clowez, *s.* claws, talons, 783.

Cogge, *s.* boat, vessel, 476.

Comone, *v.* trade, chaffer, deal, 1580.

Condethes, *s.* conduits, 201.

Connyngez, *s.* rabbits, 197.

Corenalle, *s.* head-dress, 3259.

Corkes, *s.* bristles, 1091.

Corne-bote, *s.* retaliation, full recompense, 1786, 1837.

Corsaunt, *s.* saint, 1164.

Coseri, *s.* dealing, arrangement, 1582.

Cotte, *s.* coat, 1194.

Coutere, *s.* the piece of armour which protected the elbow, 2567.

Couthe (of), *adj.* famous for, 21.

Covaunde, *adj.* careful, 558.

Coverde, *v.* recovered, 28.

Cowle-fulle (*lit.* basket-full), brimful of, 1051.

Cowntere, *s.* clerk, man of words, 1672.

Cowpez, *v.* cuts, divides, 799.

Crayers, *s.* small ships, 738.

Cresmede, *adj.* christened, 1065.

Cretoyne, *s.* a sweet sauce, 197.

Cruel, *adj.* express, strong, clear, 'cruel wordes,' 88, etc.

Cundyde, *adj.* enamelled, 765.

Dagges, *v.* pierces, 2102, 3750.

Dagswaynes, *s.* rough coverlets, 3610.

Danke, *s.* moisture, 3751.

Dares, *v.* trembles, 3226, 4008.

Darielles or darioles, curries, 199. (*Lib. Cure Cocorum*, p. 38.)

Dawez, *s.* days; 'done of dawez,' taken from day, killed, 2056.

Deesse, *s.* dais, raised part of the hall, 218.

Deffuse, want, scarceness, 256.

Dere, *v.* hurt, injure, 2099, 3249.

Derfe, *adj.* strong, powerful, fierce, 312, 811, 2052, 2653.

Derflyche, *adv* dreadfully, strongly, 3278.

Derygese, *s.* dirges, 4018.

Dictour, *s.* guardian, 712.

Dischayte, *s.* ambush, 3790.

Disspite, *s.* anger, 3164.

Downkynge, *s.* moisture, 3249.

Drecchede, *v.* delayed, 754, abode, dwelt, 1264.

Dredleȝ, *adv.* certes, assuredly, 1504.

Dreghe, *s.* length, delay, 2916, 3277; 'one-dreghe,' behind.

Dreghe, *v.* suffer, 3438.

Dreghely, *adv.* carefully, cautiously, 2028.

Dromowndes, *s.* vessels of war, 3616.

Droupe, *v.* sorrow, 4008.

Drye, or dree, *v.* endure, suffer, 704, 1546.

Dryfande, *v.* driving, 761.

Drynchene or drenschene, *v.* destroy, 761, 816.

Dryssede, *v.* directed, ruled, 46.

Dule, *s.* sorrow, 256.

Duspere or duchpere, *s.* (douze-pairs), nobles, peers, 66.

Duttez, *s.* (probably an error for *duntez*, dints, blows) 787.

Dyspens, *s.* expense, 538.

Eghelynge, *adv.* edge-wise, 3676.

Ekkene, *v* eke, increase, 2009.

Elagere, *s.* strength, 2978.

Eldes, *s.* ages, times, 301.

Elfaydes, *s* elks? 'some kind of animal' (Halliwell), 2288.

Eme, *s.* uncle, 1347.

Enchede, *adj.* fallen, vanquished, 3938.

Encroche, *v.* obtain possession of, 3213.

Endordid, *v.* gilded, made to shine, 199.

"*Endore* it with yokes of eggs."
—(Lib. Cure Cocorum, p. 37).

Englaymez, *v.* makes slimy or slippery, 1131.

Englaymous, *adj.* covered with slime, sore, envenomed, 3685.

Engowschede, *adj.* swelled, puffed up, 2053.

Engyste, *v* constrain, 445.

Enkerly, *adv.* eagerly, 507.

Empayrede or enpayrede, *v.* impaired, diminished, 474.

Entamede, *adj* cut, torn, 1160.

Enveryde, *adj* inversed, 1694.

Erne, ears, 1086.

Escheffe, *v.* escape, 2301.

Ettelles, *v.* endeavours, claims, undertakes, 520, 554, 3078.

Ewyne or ewene, *adv.* even, 762, 774, 1122, 1293.

Eynes, *s.* thickets, 1283, 1760, 2516.

Fakene, *v.* fettle, set in order, 742.

Falterde, *adj.* hanging in folds, 1092.

Fande, *v.* try, endeavour, take care, 557, 656.

Fange or faunge, holds, seizes, 425, 1005, 1249.

Farlande, *s.* foreland, 880.

Fatthe, *s.* tribute, 425.

Fawcetez, *s.* cups, 205.

Fawe, *adj.* variegated, glancing, 747.

Fawntekyns, *s.* young children, 845.

Fax, *s.* hair, 1078.

Fay or fey, *adj.* dead; 'fay-levede,' left dead, killed, 394, 517, 978.

Felo, *adj.* many, 845, 2162.

Feletez, *s.* fillets, the flesh on the ribs, 1158, 2174.

Felle, *s.* skin, 1081.

Felschen, *v.* freshen, 1975.

Feraunt, *adj.* pleasant, good, 1811.

Fere, *adj.* whole, sound, unhurt, 2795, 3018.

Ferkes, *v.* hastens, goes, 933, 984, 1452.

Ferly, *s.* wonder, 2948.

Ferlyche, *adj.* wonderful, 925.

Fermysone, *s.* the closed time for hunting, also the enclosed and fatted deer as opposed to wild (?), 180.

Ferrers, *adj.* with iron hoops, 2715.

Ferrome, *adj.* foreign, strange, 3579; 'o ferrome,' afar, at a distance, 857.

Ferynne, *s.* far part, the other side, 1875.

Fette, *v.* fetch, 557

Fewle, *s.* foil, sword, 2071

Fowtyre, *s.* the rest which sup-

ported the spear, 1366, 'castys in fewtyre,' lays his spear in rest.

Feyed, *v.* mutilated, tore, 1114.

Feyne, *v.* relax, cease, 1147.

Fichene, *v.* pierce, 2098.

Filsuez, *v.* dwells, 881.

Filterde, *adj.* mixed, joined, 780; matted, 1078.

Firthe or frithe, *s.* wood, 1708.

Flay, *v.* terrify, 2441, 2780

Flayre, *s.* smell, odour, breath, 772.

Fleche, *s.* part, division, 2482.

Flecte, *v.* float, swim, 803.

Flemyde, *v.* burnt, consumed, 1155.

Fleryande, *adj.* grinning, 1088

Flcterede, *adj.* flitting, flying, 2097.

Flitt, *v.* strike, wound, 2097.

Flonez, *s.* arrows, 2097.

Floyne or floygene, *s.* a sort of ship, 743.

Fluke, *s.* flat-fish, 1088; floke-mouthed, 2780

Flyschande, *adj.* piercing, sharp, 2141, 2769

Foddenid, *v.* fed, produced, 3247.

Fome, *s.* foam, smoke, 1079.

Fonde, *adj.* foolish, mad, savage, 881.

Fonde or fonode, *v.* try, taste, 147, 366, 3371, 3372.

Fongede, *v.* took hold of, 3309.

Foode or fode, *s.* fellow, 3777.

Fore-lytenede, *v.* decreased, 254.

Fore-maglede, *v.* engaged, hardly pressed, 1534.

Fore thy, *adv.* wherefore, 225.

For-justede, *adj.* vanquished in fight, 2134, 2896.

Formaylle, *s.* the female hawk, 4004.

Forrayse, *v.* forays, lays waste, 1247.

Forsey, forsoey, or forsesy, *adj.* of great force, 3301, 3308.

For-wondsome, *adj.* very sorrowful, 3837.

Fosterde, *s.* foresters, 300.

Forthire, *adv.* forward, 300; 'the forthire,' the forward or, first part.

Foulde, *s.* earth, 1071.

Foundez, *v* goes, advances, 1228.

Fourtedele, *v.* fourth part, 946.

Foyle, *s.* box, 2705.

Fraisez, *v.* questions, examines, (perhaps) tortures, 1248.

Fraiste, *v.* try, prove, seek, 435, 1038, 3583.

Fraknede, *adj.* freckled, spotted, 681, 1081.

Frawnke, *s.* enclosure, 3248.

Frayne or fraine, *v.* ask, enquire, 337, 1441.

Fraythely, *adv.* suddenly, at once, 3865.

Freke, *s.* man, fellow, wretch, 557, 742, 973.

Frekke, *adj.* bold, eager, vigorous, 3303.

Frekkly, *adv.* boldly, rapidly, 556, 788.

Fremedly, *adv.* as a stranger, 1250, 3406.

Fremmede, *adj.* strange, unkind, 3344.

Fresone, *s.* Freisland horse, 1365.

Fretyne or fretene, *adj* consumed, 844; overlaid, 2142.

Frithed, *adj.* arranged in hedges, 3248.

Fromonde, *s.* forehead, 1112.

Froske, *s.* frog, 1081.

Froyt, *s.* fruit, 2708.

Frumentee, *s.* a dish of wheat, milk, plums, etc., 180 (v. *Lib. Cure Cocorum*, p. 7).

Frusche, *s.* sudden rush, 2901.

Fruschene, *v.* strife, rout, 2805.

Frythes, *v.* spare, 656, 1734.

Fulsomeste, *adj.* foulest, 1061.

Furthe, *s.* journey, course, 1525; path, roadway, 1897, 2144.

Fylede, *adj.* defiled, 978.

Gaddes, *s.* goads, spears, 3622.

Galede, *v.* screamed, chattered, 927.

Galte, *s.* pig, boar, 1101.

Gardwynes, *s.* rewards, 1729.

Garett, *s.* watch-tower, 562, 3105.

Gayneste, *adj.* nearest, 487.

Gayspande, *v.* gasping, 1462.

Gedlynges or gadlynges, *s.* useless fellows, wretches, 2885.

Geene, *s.* genies or spirits, 559.

Gerse, *s.* grasp, 3945.

Gersoms, *s* guerdons, rewards, 165.

Gerte (gers, gars, garte), *v.* caused, made, 1780, 3710.

Gettlesse, *adj.* empty, possessionless, 2728.

Ghywes, *s.* gyves, fetters, 3622.

Glapyns, *v.* is frightened, 3950.

Glaverande, *adj.* deceitful, treacherous, 2538.

Glayfe or glaive, *s.* the blade or steel part of the spear, 3762.

Gledys, *s.* sparks, 117.

Glent, *s.* glance, 3864.

Gliftes, *v.* looks, 3950.

Glopned, *v.* was astonished, frightened, 1074, 2580.

Glopynnyng, *s.* astonishment, 3864

Gloredc, *v.* glared, stared, 1074.

Gobbede or gabbede, *adj.* deceitful, 1346.

Gobelets, *s.* part of the armour for the legs, 913.

Gobone, ? govone, *v.* gave, 4165.

Gole, *s.* small creek, 3726.

Gome, *s.* man, 85, etc.

Gose, *imp.* of go; 'gose over,' recount, 1266.

Gowces, *s.* the pieces of armour to protect the arm-pits, 3760.

Gowke, *s.* cuckoo, 927.

Grame, *s.* anger, grief, 1077,3009.

Granes, *v.* groans, 2562.

Grape, *v.* feel, meditate, 2726.

Grassede, *v.* decked, furnished, 1091.

Graynes, *s.* red colour, 3464.

Graythide, *v.* gathered, arrayed, 373, 589, 602.

Grayvez, *s.* grieves, steel boots, 913, 2272.

Grees, *s* season allotted for sporting, 658.

Grette, *v.* greeted, 84.

Gretande, *v.* crying, weeping, 951.

Grevede, *v.* snarled, gnashed his teeth, 1075.

Grevez or grefes, *s.* groves, 927, 1874, 2282.

Groffe, *s.* face, 3851. In O.E. 'groveling,' face downwards.

Grucchande, *adj.* grumbling, 1076.

Grygynge, *s.* 2510..

Grylych or gryslyche, *adj.* horrible, 1101.

Grythgide, *v.* vexed, 2557.

Gumbaldes, *s.* dishes of pastry, 2964.

Gye, *v.* direct, walk aright, 4.

Halfes, *s.* parts, sides, 441; 'sere halfes,' several sides.

Hally, *adv.* wholly, 1085.

Halsez, *s.* necks, throats, and so heads, 1798.

Harlotte, *s.* common soldier, low fellow, 2446.

Harawnte, *v.* march, advance, 2449.

Harske, *adj.* rough, harsh, 1084.

Hathelle, *adj.* noble, great, 358, 988.

Haylede, *v.* dropped, 2077.

Hawe, *s.* awe, fear (?), 3705.

Heddys-mene, *s.* chief men, rulers, 281.

Hede-rapys, *s.* head-ropes, 3669.

Hedlynge, *adv.* headlong, 3830.

Hedoyne, *s.* a sauce, 184.

Heldede, *v.* inclined, obeyed, 3369.

Hele, *s.* health, comfort, 2631.

Hemmes, *s.* borders, hems, 1648.

Hende, *adv.* close at hand, 1283.

Hende, *adj.* gentle, 2631, 3880.

Houte, *s.* hold, 1842.

Hentez, *v.* seizes, holds, 1132, 2918.

Herbarjours, *s.* leaders, advanced guard, 2448.

Herbergage, *s.* lodging, encampment, 3015.

Herede, *adj.* covered with hair, 1083.

Herne-pane, *s.* brain-pan, skull, 2229.

Heslyne, *adj.* of hazel, 2504.

Hete or hette, *v.* promise, 2127, 2632.

Hethely, *adv.* contemptuously, 268.

Hethynge, *s.* scorn, 1842.

Hevede, *s.* head; 'appone-hevede,' head-foremost, 262.

Hewede, *v.* carried, 4092.

Lechyde, *adj.* cut in slices, 188; v.
 Lib. Cure Cocorum, pp. 13, 50.
Lede, *s.* lad, man, 138, etc.
Lemand, *adj.* glittering, gleaming, 2463, 2464.
Lendez, *s.* loins, 1047.
Lenge, *v.* lounge, delay, tarry, 72, 343.
Lesse, *v.* lose, 1599.
Lesse, *s.* lie, 159.
Letande, *v.* looking, 3832.
Letherly, *adv.* vilely, shamefully, 1268.
Leskes, *s.* flanks, 1097, 3280.
Leve, *v.* believe, 1099.
Levere, *s.* encampment, 3079.
Ligham, *s.* dead body, 3282, 4270.
Lire, *s.* flesh, face, 3282, 3955, 4273.
Lokerde, *adj.* distorted, 779.
Los or loosse, *s.* honour, praise, 254, 474.
Lothene, *adj.* hideous, 778.
Lowe, *s* flame, heat, glare, 194.
Lowrande, *adj.* sad, gloomy, 1446.
Lowttede, *v.* worshipped, bowed down to, 3286.
Loyotour, *s.* embroidery, 3254.
Lufe, *s.* the loof of a ship, 744, 750.
Luffly, *adv.* lovingly, 248.
Lugge or lygge, *v.* lodge, lie, stay, remain, 152.
Lussche, *s.* violence, force, 3849.
Lutterde, *adj.* crooked, twisted, 779.
Luyschede, *v.* lashed out, 2226.
Lyarde, *adj.* disordered, 3281.
Lygmane, *s.* liegeman, 420.
Lympyde, *v.* happened, befell, 292, 875.

Lyth, *v.* listen, 12.
"Thenne watz hit lif upon list to lythen the houndez."
  —(Sir Gawaine, 1719.)
Lythe, *adj.* gentle, smooth, 1517.
Lythe, *s.* land, property, kingdom, 994, 1653.
Lythyre, *s.* leader, ruler (?), 23.

Mangere, *s.* diet, keep of a prisoner, 1588.
Manrede, *s.* power, *lit.* homage, 127.
Masondewes, *s.* Maisons Dieu, hospitals, 3039.
Mele, *v.* speak, 382, 679.
Melle, *v.* mingle, communicate, 938.
Menske, *s.* honour, 126.
Menskes, *v.* deserves honour, 1303.
Merke, *v.* go, 427, etc.
Merkes, *s.* boundaries, 1147.
Mett, *v.* dreamed, 3224.
Mofes, *v.* overcomes, 3324.
Moles, *v.* 3057. See *Mele.*
Mone, *v.* shall (Prov.? *mun*), 813.
Mowe, *v.* may, 3813.
Mysese(? plural of *myx*) *s.* wretches, 667.
Mysse, *s.* evil, wrong, 1315.
Myx, *s.* wretch, 989.

Naye, *s.* (yolke of a nay, for ȝolke of an aye = egg) 3284.
Nedys, *s.* needs, demands, 85.
Neyvesome, *adj.* renowned, 523.
Notez, *v.* make use of, 1815.
Notte, *s.* business, affair, 1816.
Nomene, *v.* taken, 1437.
Nurree, *s.* adopted child, 689.

Oches, *v.* breaks, 2565, 3676.
O-dawe, *adv.* out of days, *i.e.* out of life (see *Dawez*), 3737.

On-dreghe, *adv.* at a distance, 786, 787.

Orfracez, *s.* embroideries, ornaments, 902, 2142.

Ostayande, *v.* sojourning, 3503

Overlynge, *s.* superior, ruler, 289, 520.

Ownd, *adj.* laced, slashed, 193.

Owte, *adj.* foreign, 30.

Palle, *s.* fine cloth, 1288, 2478.

Palyd, *v.* ornamented, 1287, 1375.

Pare, *v.* injure, 4048.

Pastorelles, *s.* shepherds, swineherds, 3121.

Paumes, *s.* hands, claws, 776.

Pavys, *s.* a shield, 3461, 3626.

Pavysers, *s.* soldiers armed with the pavys, 3005.

Payses, *v.* force, 3038, 3043.

Peghttes, *s.* Picts, 4126.

Pensels, *s.* small banners, 1289, 2411.

Perrye, *s.* jewellery, 2461, 3462.

Pertly, *adv.* apart, 2918.

Pertyes, *v.* parts, 1925.

Pillion (hat), *s.* priest's, or large hat.

Pilour, *s.* pilferer, robber, 2133.

Plasche, *s.* a marshy piece of ground, 2799.

Plattes, *s.* plankes for seats, 2478.

Plumpe, *s.* crowd, 2199.

Plyande, *v.* working, 777.

Pome, *s.* the kingly globe, 3355.

Pomelle, *s.* small globe at the head of a flag-staff, 1289.

Poveralle, *adj.* poor, labouring men, 3121.

Poyne, *v.* stitch with a bodkin, 2625.

Prys or pris, *adj.* precious, chief, 2, 569.

Pyghte, *adj.* decked, garnished, pitched, 212, 1300, 2478.

Pykes, *s.* points, 777.

Pyne, *s.* lamentation, 3044.

Pynne, *v.* pine, annoy, trouble, 4048.

Qwarelles, *s.* short arrows for cross bow, 2103.

Querte—'in querte,' equivalent to being in life; querte, joy, activity, life, 3811.

Qwarte, *v.* quashed, smashed, 3390

Qwyke, *adj.* alive, 1736.

Qwyne, *adv.* whence, 3504.

Raas, *v.* tear, snatch, 362.

Racches, *s.* scenting hounds, 4000.

Rade, *adj.* afraid, 2882

Radly, *adv.* swiftly, 1529.

Radness, *s* fear, 120.

Raike or rayke, *s* path, 1525, 2986.

Ramby or jambe, *adj.* prancing, spirited, 373, 2895

Ranez, *s.* rushes, 923

Raply, *adv* quickly, 1763.

Rared, *v.* roared, 784

Rasches, *v.* rush, go rashly, 2107.

Rathe, rathely, or raythely, *adv.* quickly, soon, 237, 1275.

Raw (on), *s.* in rotation, 633.

Rawnsakes (*imp.*) *v.* search, 3229, 3740; probe, 4305.

Raykede, *v.* rushed, flowed, ran, · 237, 1057, 2984.

Raylide, *v.* arrayed, ornamented, 3264.

Raymede, *v.* roamed, made incursion, 100.

Reched, *s.* jewels, 3264.

Reddour, *s.* violence, eagerness, succour, 109, 485, 1418.

Rede, *v.* advise, 550.

Redyne, *v.* disposed of, 52

Refede, *v.* deprived, 960.

Rehetede, *v.* received, entertained, cheered, 221, 411, 3199.

Reke, *s.* path, 1041.

Relevis, *v.* rally, 2278.

Remmes or remys, *v.* cries, laments, 2197, 4156.

Renayede, *adj.* renegade, 2914, 3573.

Renye, *s.* renegade, 2795.

Rependez, *v.* hasten, 2107.

Revaye, *v.* rejoice, 3276.

Revare, *s.* river, 62.

Rewe, *v.* have pity, 866.

Rewfulle, *adj.* sorrowful, 1049.

Reynes, *s.* journey, course, 3165.

Rigg, *s.* back, 800.

Rittes, *v.* rends, dashes in pieces, 2138, 3754, 3825.

Rog, *s.* assembly, people? 3273.

Roggede, *v.* rocked? 784.

Romede, *v.* growl, roar, groan, 424, 784, 888.

Roo, *s.* misfortune, evil, 1751.

Roo, *s.* wheel, 3363, 3375.

Roo, *s.* roe-deer, 922.

Rosers, *s.* thickets, 923.

Rosselde, *adj.* sharpened, 2881.

Rowme or rowmme, *adj.* wide, loose, roomy, 432, 1454, 3471.

Rusche, *v.* destroy, overthrow, 1339.

Rusclede, *adj.* russet-clad, 1096.

Ruyde, ruydly, or ruydlyche, *adj.* and *adv.* rude, rudely, fiercely, impetuously, 1049, 785, 1877.

Rybys, *v.* rips, tears, 3825.

Ryfez, *v.* thrusts, rives, tears, 1474, 2914.

Ryghttez, *v.* See *Rittes.*

Ryndez, *s.* thickets, 921, 1884, 3364.

Rype, *v.* search, 3941.

Ryste *adj.* rusty, rough, 1428.

Ryvaye, *v.* hunt, 4000.

Saghetylle, *v.* be satisfied or reconciled, 330.

Sakeles, *adj.* innocent, without blame, 3400, 3987, 3994.

Sale, *s.* hall, court, 82.

Sandismene, *s.* messengers, 266, 1429.

Saughte, *s.* peace, 1548, 3053.

Saynned, *adj.* blessed, cared for, 966, 969.

Schafte, *s.* spear, 2169.

Schaftmonde, *s.* spear length, 2546.

Schake, *v.* hasten, move, advance.

Schalkes, *s.* men-at-arms, soldiers, 1857, 2211, 2333, 2456, 3748.

Schalyde, *adj.* enclosed, 766.

Schathe, scaith, or skaithe, *s.* harm, mischief, 292.

Schawes or shawes, *s.* glades, 1723, 1760, 1765.

Schede, *v.* pour, 2923.

Schenchipe, *s.* disgrace, 4300.

Scherde, *v.* cut, wounded, destroyed, 1856, 2435.

Schiltrounis, *s.* bands, 1765, 1813, 1856.

Schire, *adj.* scanty, 1760; clear, bright, 3845, 3846, 3601.

Schoderide, *v.* shuddered, 2106.

Schone, *v.* shrink, retreat, 314, 1717.

Schowande, *adj.* bending (*lit.* shoving), 1099.

Schrowde, *s.* dress, 3629.

Schreede, *v.* shred, sprinkled, 767.

Schrympe, *s.* monster, dragon, 767.

Schuntes or schountes, *v.* hesitates, delays, 1055.

Seche, *v.* seek, 3234.

Sektour, *s.* successor, follower, 665.

Segge, *s.* servant, man, follower, 134, 1420, 1422.

Selcouth, *adj.* wonderful, curious, 75, 1308, 3197.

Semblant, *s.* pomp, 75.

Semble, *v.* cope with, meet, 967.

Sendelle, *s.* a sort of silken stuff, 2299.

Serfed, *v.* deserved, 1068.

Sere, *adj.* several, 192, 607.

Serte, *s.* decree, 2927

Sesyne or scizin, *s.* possession, 3589.

Sewand, *v.* following, 81.

Sewes, *s.* stews, made dishes, 192.

" Poure on the *sewe* and serve it."
(Lib. Cure Cocorum, p 21.)

Seyne (should be read *sebne*?), then, afterwards, 192, 464, 939.

Seyne, *s.* saint, 2871.

Seyne, *v.* boiled, cooked, 188.

" In hir own blood *seyn*."
—(Lib. Cure Cocorum, p. 21.)

Sirquytrie, *s.* pride, 3400.

Sittande, *adj.* fitting, becoming, 953.

Sittandly, *adv.* suitably, 159.

Skathelle or scathylle, *adj.* dangerous, 32, 1642.

Skathlye, *adj.* (should be read *skatheles*) without injury, 1562.

Skayres, *v.* frightens, 2468.

Skewe, *v.* rescue, 1562.

Skottefers, *s.* shooters.

Skowtte-waches, *s.* watchmen, 2468.

Skroggez, *s.* stunted bushes, scrub, 1642.

Skyst (should be read *skyft*?), shift, manage, arrange, 32, 1653.

Slakkes, *s.* pools, marshes, 3720.

Slale (should be read *skale*?), crafty, 3118.

Slawyne or slaveine, *s.* a pilgrim's mantle, 3475.

Sleghte, *s.* craft, sleight, 3419.

Slewthe, *s.* sloth, 3222.

Sleygly, *adj.* slyly, cunningly, 2976.

Slomowre, *s.* slumber, 3222.

Slope, *s.* valley, 2978.

Slote or slotte, *s.* pit of the stomach, 2254, 2976. See *Sir Gawaine* and *Glossary*.

Slottcde, *v.* stabbed, 3856.

Slowde, *s.* mud, slush, 3720.

Slyke, *adj.* such; 'then was it slyke,' then was there such, 3720.

Snelle, *adj.* quick, swift, 57.

Sope, *s.* a sup or hasty repast, 1890.

Soppe, *s.* company, body, 1493, 3730, 3746.

Spakely, *adv.* quickly, 2063.

Spalddyd, *adj.* shivered, 3700.

Spayre, *s.* spare-rib, 2060.

Spekes, *s.* spokes, 3264.

Speltis, *s.* splinters, stripes, 3265.

Spencis, *s.* consumption, wasting, 3164.

Sprente, *v.* spurted, leapt, 2062, 3701.

Sproutez, *v.* sprawls, 2063.

Stale, *s.* company, band (*lit.* seat), 377, 1355.

Stamyne, *s.* deck, 3659.

Stereborde, *s* starboard, 745.

Steryne, *adj.* stern, brave, 157, 377.

Sterys, steers, guides, 917.

Stirttelys (should be read *stightelys*?, arrays), 3623.

Stokes, *v.* strike, stab, 2554.

Stotais, *v.* abide, delay, 1435.

Stoundys, *v.* are placed, stand, 3624.

Stowndys, *s.* times, 3889.

Stour, *s* war, fight, 377.

Stowuntyng, *s.* stunting, stopping, 491.

Strates, *s.* streets, paths, 561.

Strekez, *v.* stretches, 1229, 3102.

Streke, *adv.* quickly, 3102.

Strenge, *s.* strong place, entrenchment, 1926.

Struye, *v.* destroy, 561.

Stuffe, *v.* treat, provision, 1932, 2369.

Stye, *s.* path, 3467.

Styghtylle or stightill, *v.* arrange, dispose of, 157.

Sulayne, *adj.* sole, alone, 2593.

Summes, *s.* assemblies, hosts, 606.

Surepel, *s.* cover, case, 3318.

Surrawns, *s.* assurance, treaty, 3182.

Surs, *s.* rising, 1978, 2511.

Suters, *s.* stalls, 501.

Swafres or swayfres, *v.* starts, 3971.

Swange, *s* loins, groin, 1129.

Swanke (*pret.* of swinke), *v.* toil, labour, hence strike with sword, 2962, 3362.

Swape, *s.* stroke, blow, 314.

Swarthe, *s.* sward, 1126.

Swayne, *s.* swain, man, 3361.

Swefennys, *s.* dreams, 3229.

Swefnyng, *s.* sleep, dreaming, 759, 812.

Sweperly, *adv.* swiftly, 1128, 1465.

Swelte, *v.* faint, die, 813, 2962, 2983, 1465, 1466.

Sweys, *v.* descends, falls, 57, 1467.

Swier, *s.* squire, 2960, 3704.

Swoghe, *s.* sound, 759.

Swowynge, *s.* sound of running water, 931.

Swtte, swete or swett, life, 2145, 3361. See Glossary to *Alliterative Poems.*

Swykede, *v.* deceived, failed, 1795, 3362.

Swym, *s.* swoon, 4247.

Swynge, *s.* blow, 3361.

Swyngene, *v.* overthrow, hurled down, 1466.

Swyre-bane, *s.* neck-bone, 2960.

Swythe, *adj.* quick, 409, 813, 1128.

Sybbe, *adj.* near of kin, 645, 681.

Sybredyne, *s.* kindred, 691, 4146.

Sydlynges or syddynges, *adv.* sideways, sidelong, 1039, 1243.

Sylande, *v.* gliding, 1297, 3795.

Syte or sytte, *s.* grief, sorrow, shame, 1060, 1305.

Sythyne or sithen, *adv.* afterwards, then, 56, 159, 169, 184.

Tachemente3, *s.* appurtenances, belongings, 1568.

Tachesesede, *v.* attached, 821.

Taghte, *adj.* courteous, well-trained, 178.

Takelle, *s.* tackle? 3619.

Talmes, *v.* is disheartened (*lit.* benumb, deaden), 2581.

Targe, *s.* document, paper, 89.

Temez, *v.* pours, empties, 1801.

Tempest, *v.* act violently, 2408.

Tene, *v.* grieve, 264.

Tene, *s.* sorrow, 1956.

Thee, *s.* thigh, 1846.

Thirllede, *v.* pierced, 1858.

Thole, *v.* suffer, endure, permit, 676.

Thraa or throo, *adj.* bold, 249, 3295, 3296.

Thrawe, *s.* agony, struggle, 1150.

Threppede, *v.* rushed, forced his way, 2216.

Throly, *adv.* fiercely, severely, 2217.

Thrynges, *v.* grips, 1150; struggles, fights, 2217.

Thrystez, *v.* thrusts, 1151.

Thursse, *s.* giant, 1100. (Still used in E. Ang. counties.)

Tide, *s.* season, fitness, right, 275.

Togers, *s.* coats, 178, 3190.

Tolowris, *s.* tiller of a boat (?), 3619.

To-rattys, *v.* tear, rend, scatter, 2235.

Torfere, *s.* torture, trouble, punishment, 1956.

To-stonayede, *adj.* confounded, astonished, 1436.

Towyne, *v.* tow, draw, 3656.

Towne, *adj.* well trained, 178. (Still exists in wan-*ton.*)

Toyelys, *s.* tools, furniture, weapons, 732, 3617.

Traise, *v.* go, 1629.

Traylede, *v.* dragged, drawn, 250.

Trayne, *s.* stratagem, turn, 1630.

Trayste, *v.* trusts, 1987.

Traystely, *adv.* safely, trustily, 1976.

Trete, *s.* row, 3656.

Trett, *v.* treat, 249, 250, 263.

Treunt, *v.* march, hasten, 1976, 2017, 3901.

Trewe, *s.* truce, 3192.

Tristly, *adv.* safely, 731.

Trofelande, *adj.* trifling, 1683.

Trome, *v.* array in order of battle, 3593.

Troufflyng, *s.* idle words, 114.

Trufles, *s.* lies, 89.

Trussez, *v.* pack up, load, 731, 1976, 3593.

Tryede *v.* (read *trynede*), went, 3592.

Tryne or trine (pret. *tron*), *v.* to go in procession or order, 1757, 3193, 3593.

Tydd, *v.* befallen, fared, 3655.

Tykes, *s.* dogs (applied to men), 3643.

Tymbyrde, *v.* contrived, fashioned, 3743.

Tyne, *v.* lose, 2934, 1954.

Tynt (pret. of *tyne*), lost, killed, 272, 770.

Tyte, *adv.* quickly, 737.

Umbeclappes, *v.* embraces, clasps, surrounds, 1779, 1819.

Umbrere, *s.* visor, 943.

Undroune, *s.* nine o'clock a.m. 463.

Unfaire, *adv.* badly, horribly, 1045.

Unfawghte (read *unsaughte*, q.v.).

Unfaye, *adj.* unwounded, alive, 2797.

Unfers, *adj.* weak, feeble, 4123.

Unfoundyde, *adj.* untried, unstable, 2485.

Unfraystede, *adj.* untried, inexperienced, 2737.

Unfrely, *adj.* vilely, 780.

Unsaughte, *adj.* at strife, 1306, 1457.

Unsaughtely, *adv.* unfriendly, 1501.

Unslely (for *unselely*), miserably, 979.

Unsownde, *adj.* dead, slain, wounded, 3932, 3943, 4295.

Unwemmyde, *adj.* spotless, 3802.

Unwynly, *adv.* sorrowfully, 955.

Upcynes, *s.* pinnacles, turrets? 3676.

Utters, *v.* ushers, conducts, 418.

Vernacle, *s.* the holy picture of Christ supposed to be miraculously emprinted on a handkerchief, 297, 309, 348.

Verrede, *v.* covered, 2573.

Vertly, *adv.* secretly? 3169.

Viage, *s.* journey, march, 2037.

Voute, *s.* mien, expression, 137.

Vyse, *s.* aim, 2612, 2424.

Wache, *v.* watch, 547, 613.

Wage, *v.* engage, hire, 547.

Wagge, *v.* move, lead, 333, 1615.

Wale, *adj.* beautiful, noble, choice, 182? 741, 2148.

Wale, *s.* gun-*wale*, side of ship, 740.

Walkyne, *s.* welkin, sky, 787.

Walopande, *adj.* swift, galloping, 2828.

Walowes, *v.* rolls, 1142.

Wandrethe, *s.* trouble, grief, 323, 384, 2370, 3158.

Wandsomdly, *adv.* sorrowfully, 4013.

Waresche, *v.* recover, be healed, 2186.

Warlow or werlaugge, *s.* warlock, unnatural wretch, traitor, 1140, 3772.

Warne, *v.* deny, forbid, refuse, 700.

Wasterne, *s.* desert, 3234.

Wathe or wawhte, injury, danger, 2669, 3234, 3481.

Wathely, *adv.* dangerously, 2090.

Watte, *v.* I watte = wot, believe, 2224.

Wayfe, *v.* wander, stray, 960.

Waykly, *adj.* weakly, sorrowfully, 697.

Wekyrly, *adv.* badly, 2104.

Welters, *v.* rolls, 890, 1140.

Wenez, *v.* thinkest, 963.

Weredes or werdes, *s.* destinies, fate, 385, 3890.

Werkande, *adj.* aching, sore, 2148.

Werkkes, *v.* aches, 2690.

Werraye, *v.* make war, 546.

Werpe or warpe, *v.* throw out, utter, 9, 150.

Wery, *v.* curse, 699, 959.

Wiet, *v.* know, 420.

Wightenez, *s.* valour, 1806.

Wille, *adj.* lonely, 3837.

Willed, *adj.* astray, 3231.

Wlonke, *adj.* fair, 3155, 3339.

Wodely, *adv.* madly, 2828.

Wodewyse, *s.* madman, 3818.

Wolfe-hevede, *s.* outlaw, 1093.

Wone, *s.* abode, dwelling, 1300, 2472.

Woonde or wonde, *v.* delay, stop, 1615.

Worthe, *v.* be; 'mote ȝe werthe,' may ye be, 4089, 4105.

Wraythe, *v.* thrust, twisted, 1093.

Wrethe, *s.* anger, wrath, 2225.

Wrokyne, *v.* avenged, 2225.
Wrothely, *adv.* fiercely, 1141.
Wrotherayle, *s.* ill-fate, 3155.
Wrythyne, *v.* struggle, 1141.
Wyderwyne, *s.* enemy, 2045.
Wyes or wyese (sing. *wy* or *wye*), men, 56, 533.
Wyghte, *adj.* quick, 1615.
Wyghte, *s.* man, 959.
Wyghtly, *adv.* quickly, 70.
Wyghtnesse, *s.* quickness, vigor, boldness, 258.
Wylnez, *v.* desires, wishes, 962.
Wynche, *v.* flinch, 2104.
Wynly, *adv.* pleasantly, 3339.

Wynlyche, *adj.* handsome, pleasant, 181.

Ythez, *s.* waves, 741, 747.

ȝapely, *adv.* quickly, 1502.
ȝernez, *v.* holds, keeps, 1938.
ȝermys, *v.* screams, cries, 3912.
ȝernez, *v.* desirest, 1502.
ȝitt, *adv.* yet, 1424, 1435.
ȝoldene, *v.* yielded, 2482.
ȝole, *s.* Yule, Christmas, 1629.
ȝomane, *s.* yeoman, 2629.
ȝorke (read *ȝoske*), cry, sob, 3912.

STEPHEN AUSTIN, PRINTER, HERTFORD.

Printed in the USA
CPSIA information can be obtained
at www.ICGtesting.com
LVHW052107020324
773392LV00003B/20